Improve your Copywriting

Improve your Copywriting
j. jonathan gabay

For UK order enquiries: please contact
Bookpoint Ltd, 130 Milton Park, Abingdon, Oxon OX14 4SB.
Telephone: +44 (0) 1235 827720. Fax: +44 (0) 1235 400454.
Lines are open 09.00–17.00, Monday to Saturday, with a 24-hour
message answering service. Details about our titles and how to
order are available at www.teachyourself.com

Long renowned as the authoritative source for self-guided learning –
with more than 50 million copies sold worldwide – the **Teach Yourself**
series includes over 500 titles in the fields of languages, crafts, hobbies,
business, computing and education.

British Library Cataloguing in Publication Data:
a catalogue record for this title is available from the British Library.

This edition published 2010.

Previously published as *Teach Yourself Copywriting*

The **Teach Yourself** name is a registered trade mark of
Hodder Headline.

Typeset by MPS Limited, A Macmillan Company.

Printed in Great Britain for Hodder Education, an Hachette UK
Company, 338 Euston Road, London NW1 3BH, by CPI Cox &
Wyman, Reading, Berkshire RG1 8EX.

The publisher has used its best endeavours to ensure that the URLs
for external websites referred to in this book are correct and active
at the time of going to press. However, the publisher and the
author have no responsibility for the websites and can make no
guarantee that a site will remain live or that the content will remain
relevant, decent or appropriate.

Hachette UK's policy is to use papers that are natural, renewable
and recyclable products and made from wood grown in sustainable
forests. The logging and manufacturing processes are expected to
conform to the environmental regulations of the country of origin.

Impression number   10 9 8 7 6 5 4 3 2 1

Year   2014 2013 2012 2011 2010

For all the students I have taught and those from whom I have yet to learn.

This third edition is dedicated to my mum.

Acknowledgements

With special thanks to Alison Frecknall, Antonia Maxwell, David Thorpe, Pat Mani, and all at the Chartered Institute of Marketing.

Contents

Meet the author

Hi my name is Jonathan. I am really looking forward to helping you teach yourself copywriting.

Working with some of the most prestigious coaching organizations in their fields, including the world's biggest marketing training body, I have addressed and mentored literally thousands of marketers. I am particularly proud that many students have carved out successful careers with globally admired and respected brands.

During three decades in advertising and marketing I have held several creative directorships as well as Head of Copy positions at renown advertising agencies.

My company, Brand Forensics, develops brands, explains core messages and so encourages employees, partners and markets to feel connected with propositions.

As a journalist I deliver insights behind brand-related headlines for some of the world's most trusted news organizations, including CNN, BLOOMBERG TV, ITN, BBC, SKY, Five News and many others.

Major educational establishments and academic bodies feature my books on business, marketing and copywriting. Other Hodder published titles include, *Make a Difference with Your Marketing* and the sister companion to this book: *Gabay's Copywriters' Compendium*.

So if you are ready to have fun whilst learning how to succeed in one of the most exciting areas of marketing communications, read on and let's explore your full copywriting potential.

How to use this book

Since the second edition of this book was published I have been inundated with requests to publish an updated version, taking into account the needs of the twenty-first-century copywriter and to be read in conjunction with *Make a Difference with Your Marketing and Gabay's Copywriters' Compendium*. Whether you are looking for some creative ideas for SOHO (Small Office Home Office) or social network marketing, working for a charity or even at an advertising agency, and want to dip in for extra hints and tips, this book is right up your street.

Throughout you'll find quick tips summarizing what you have read and exercises for you to do. If you want to brush up on all aspects of copywriting, then you should find something of interest in each section. If on the other hand you prefer to concentrate on one particular subject, simply look it up in the contents list or the index. At the end of the book, you'll find a practical glossary of terms. If you want direct feedback on your own copywriting or further copywriting training check out www.brandforensics.co.uk

Introducing ScotsdaleNorth.com and PenPal

Now it is time for you to become acquainted with two fictitious companies. They typify organizations of their size and type. Throughout this book, we'll be looking at how each uses copywriting to enhance their development plans.

SCOTSDALENORTH

This large multi-national food company supplies a vast range of fast-moving consumer goods (FMCG) via the web. FMCG refers to goods that usually move off supermarket shelves quickly. Examples include tinned foodstuffs, toothpaste, ready-made meals and soft drinks. Stores need to keep fresh stocks of FMCGs to replace those that are sold.

ScotsdaleNorth is a traditional retailer, established for 100 years. To celebrate its centenary, ScotsdaleNorth is planning an extensive publicity and advertising campaign. This will also steer its e-marketing drive.

ScotsdaleNorth intends to launch several new products exclusively available on the web, reinforce its corporate awareness advertising as well as open a nationwide internet-café chain.

PENPAL

PenPal is a small business. As yet, it hasn't been formally launched on to the market. PenPal has two key company directors. One invented the PenPal. The other is the sales director.

So what is PenPal? It is a pen encased in light-weight steel used in a recent space mission to Mars. PenPal is guaranteed to write underwater – without leaking – as well as at any angle. PenPal's nib can be easily changed from a fountain-pen style to a ballpoint style and even a marker pen.

As in the case of ScotsdaleNorth, this is going to be a crucial year for PenPal. Much of the company's success will depend on effective advertising.

So, now we have all been introduced, please join me as we embark on our journey to the world of copywriting. Your route is a tried and tested one that I have developed through teaching literally thousands of talented people like you. It is designed to help you grow to be your own best teacher.

Only got a minute?

Hello, I am a copywriter. Care to join me?

Thank you for buying this book. Over the next 320 pages or so, I hope to reveal and review the key aspects of copywriting.

Hmmm. How does that opening paragraph sound to you? Well, it starts off with a positive statement – 'Thank you'. Next, it is relevant to this product and, finally, it is enticing. Could you do a better job? Perhaps you would redirect the approach? Instead of thanking the reader up front for buying this book (which, I suppose, may appear a little insincere), you could proceed directly to the benefits derived from reading it. Then, of course, you have to consider the type of person buying this book.

We haven't met face to face but I can make a few assumptions about you. Firstly, the obvious ones. Copywriting interests you. Next, you probably believe that, given the right guidance, you could pursue a career in advertising or creative marketing. Perhaps you already work in the industry, which means you may be interested in picking up some tips to make your job more involving, rewarding and (let's face it) fun.

A great copywriter needs to possess more than just an understanding of grammar. Effective copywriting requires insights into areas such as psychology, the technicalities of awareness advertising, public relations, writing for the web, sales promotions, viral marketing, podcasts and blogging, branding and much more besides ...

5 Only got five minutes?

Why advertise?

**More to the point, why spend and devote so much time and
energy in getting the right mix of words and pictures to convey a
message? Clearly to sell. That is indisputable.** However, there is a
much more pertinent answer. Advertising provides the consumer
(both business-to-business as well as general consumer) with the
relevant information needed to make a purchasing choice.

The problem with this is that today, with so many brand names
vying for a cut of an increasingly shrinking 'piece of cake', you
could argue that there is too much choice. For example, according
to the UK's Channel 4 television channel, during a lifetime the
average Briton will have nibbled 10,534 chocolate bars, munched
5272 apples and drunk 74,802 cups of tea. It is clear that retaining,
let alone gaining, their attention is never going to be easy.

The word 'advertising' derives from the Latin *advertere*, meaning
'to turn towards'. Today people are constantly being asked to 'turn
towards' one message or another to such an extent that for many,
rather than 'turn towards' they 'turn away'.

This is where thoroughly planned copywriting comes into the
picture. Today's consumer is like a mollusc on a beach. Presented
with so many advertised messages offering such great choice, the
consumer only opens their guard (shell) to welcome marketing
messages when those are entirely pertinent to specific needs.

Explicit copywriting – supported by evocative images – explains
the benefits of a product or service to an individual and then
allows that person to make a considered decision based on facts,
aspirations and associations.

From a professional viewpoint, the natural home of copywriters is the advertising agency. It has been so since 1809 when the first recorded freelance copywriter, the essayist Charles Lamb, worked on a lottery account for the James White agency. Incidentally, the Thomas Smith agency in London was the first – in 1889 – to employ full-time 'ad writers'.

The recession of 2009 closed the doors to many people who would have otherwise made advertising or PR agencies their natural career habitat. As more companies demanded greater output from employees at lower costs, marketing functions like copywriting were increasingly kept 'in-house'. That added pressure on a lot of marketing professionals who would have otherwise handed copywriting assignments on to agencies. In turn new opportunities arose for independent copywritiers as well as in-house marketers to make their mark through understanding the craft of copywriting for themselves.

1

What it takes to be a copywriter

In this chapter you will learn:
* *about the roots of copywriting*
* *how to write with conviction*
* *how to understand motives.*

Have you got the write stuff?

Excuse the pun – also known as a 'homophone' (see page 73).

A copywriter is first and foremost a communicator. Copywriting is not simply about words. It is about words and images. Together they deliver a clear and/or intriguing message that encourages people to take action. Great copywriters are creative strategists who use intellect to integrate the marketing and sales principles of a specific sector with a literary style that may be informative, persuasive, subliminal or a combination of all three. Through all this, a copywriter communicates product or service benefits.

Did you know?
In June 2009 the millionth word was added to the English language. While the French have around 100,000 words in common use, the British have over 200,000. There are around 2000 words with different English/American meanings.
Each year around 5000 new words enter the language.
Over 800 million people around the world speak English.
It is the international language of airlines and the language of choice for the web.

Top languages spoken in the world

1	Chinese (Mandarin)	1.2B
2	Spanish	329M
3	English	328M
4	Hindi	260M
5	Arabic	221M
6	Portuguese	203M
7	Bengali	193M
8	Russian	144M
9	Japanese	122M
10	German	90M

Source: Ethnologue, 16th Edition

Top languages spoken on the Internet

1	English	452M
2	Chinese	321M
3	Spanish	129M
4	Japanese	94M
5	French	73M
6	Portuguese	73M
7	German	65M
8	Arabic	41M
9	Russian	38M
10	Korean	37M

Source: Internet World Stats

The tools of the trade

I have met scores of copywriters and even more would-be copywriters. The good ones share a remarkable ability to pinpoint, in words and pictures, key benefits of a particular product or service. A copywriter interprets those benefits convincingly, concisely and with originality.

TRAITS OF A GREAT COPYWRITER

- *Unstoppable curiosity about how things work.*
- *Fascination with images suggested by words.*
- *Enjoyment of every aspect of the media – not an elitist.*
- *Recognition of both ends of an argument.*
- *Natural leader – either passive or dominant.*
- *Totally interested in people and what makes them tick.*
- *Empathy for people's needs.*
- *Vivid imagination.*
- *Logical, lateral approach to technical matters.*
- *Good sense of humour – especially when, having worked all day long to craft a great piece of writing, someone returns their emailed copy with a green line through their favourite paragraphs!*

Did you know?

If you want a job in copywriting, a first-class degree in English certainly will not be a disadvantage. Neither will attending a course on the subject at somewhere like the Chartered Institute of Marketing (www.cim.co.uk) or visiting www.gabaynet.com. A respectable qualification in commerce and marketing is also useful, as is a fair knowledge of history and social psychology. However, even if you are not academically inclined you can still become a brilliant writer – as this book proves.

Rather than thinking of copywriting as just creative writing, use it as a selling skill. This applies even if you don't specifically sell something but want to encourage your audience to take the next step – such as donate some money to a charity.

Successful salespeople think laterally. Original thinking is essential to assimilate various pieces of information into a finely tuned message.

Make your product or service AIDCA:

> **Attractive**
> **Interesting**
> **Desirable**
> **Convincing**
> **Actionable.**

I used to teach that copy had to slavishly follow the classic AIDA formula – namely the same as AIDCA, minus the 'C'.

The idea of AIDA is that:

- ▶ *Attention leads to*   > *Interest in the product or service*
- ▶ *Interest leads to*   > *Desire to get hold of the offer*
- ▶ *Desire leads to*   > *Action either to make a purchase or follow an instruction to take the next step, for example surf a website.*

However, that formula is tired and, in most cases, redundant. AIDCA offers you the chance to *convince* your reader of a proposition through reasoning (which is why it is sometimes referred to as AIDRA). After all, without reasoning and substantiation why should anyone pay serious attention to you?

Did you know?

To remind students to add the 'C' I like to suggest they remember – of all things – the Daleks from the popular sci-fi television series *Dr Who*. These arch enemies of the Doctor always threatened to 'exterminate!' However, imagine that there is a special Dalek ... a copywriting Dalek! Instead of saying, 'Exterminate!' it says, 'Substantiate!' Keep on substantiating everything you write – or else – you guessed it, 'Exterminate!' the copy and start again.

FEATURES INTO ADVANTAGES, APPLICATIONS AND BENEFITS (FAAB)

Attend a standard sales training course and you will doubtlessly be told to turn your features into benefits. However, with copywriting you can be more profound.

Find three distinctive features related to the product or service that you are writing about. For each, list its specific 'Feature', followed by the practical 'Applications' of using that feature. Then the associated 'Advantages' to the specific reader (user of the service or product). Finally, summarize all your 'FAAs' into one 'Benefits' statement comprising no more than 16 words. Now you are beginning to focus your copy – and think like a professional copywriter.

COPYWRITING AND SUBJECTIVITY

It is often thought that copywriters must write for a particular audience in mind. This is true – but not completely true. If you only ever wrote for one specific audience your copy would end up sounding as if a politician wrote it; offering whatever the electorate (readership) required at that moment.

To address this, write TO your audience, THROUGH your company and with a degree of INDIVIDUALITY in mind:

▶ *TO your audience: cover the issues that appertain to THEM*
▶ *THROUGH your company: keep your corporate tone of voice and values in mind. (This delivers a sense of consistency throughout your message.)*

▶ *INDIVIDUALITY: remember that you are writing to people, not just prospects. Ensure that your copy is read like a printed conversation.*

FROM SONG WRITER TO COPYWRITER

Your very early creative writing and learning experiences may have already prepared you for a copywriting career. From pre-school age, words accompanied by provocative images conjure powerful feelings and attitudes towards yourself and the world.

For example, placed in a historical context, nursery rhymes may not really mean that much to toddlers. Their immediate attractiveness lies in their essential rhythm. However, once their basic sentiments can be understood – even at the most fundamental level – their influence on children becomes tremendously powerful, specifically by drawing them into group play. That involvement enables a toddler to explore activities such as holding hands with others and then falling down to the ground on a key phrase (as in 'Ring-a-Ring-o'-Roses'), encouraging them to further explore the world through words. In this way what may appear everyday sentences to you and me are potentially great adventures of discovery for the pre-school child.

DIRECTION THROUGH WORDS

The influence of creative words through media such as books, videos, the Internet and so on is that, providing those words have meaning to the beholder, it trickle-feeds into our subconscious. Take as an example tales from the Koran or the Bible. They are retold time and time again. Through listening to them, we are intended to gain some kind of moral direction and life purpose.

History has placed you in some sort of social chronology. As you grow in experience and knowledge you discover how, throughout time, people just like you have handled key decisions – the very same judgements that may also spur you to fight, negotiate, explore …. It's not surprising that the written word concerning historical, religious or fictional characters – and, more significantly, what they represent socially – impresses us deeply.

ROLE PLAYING AND LEADING

Throughout adolescence, song lyrics take on particular relevance and resonance in our lives. Love songs, for instance, can help us recover from a broken first love. Other songs or raps may even make us feel that through music and lyrics we hold the key to express feelings of rebellion against all the history that has preceded us and so declare our intention to redirect the course in a new, fresh direction.

Sometimes, the allure of songs and song writing is so compelling that we form hip-hop or rap, or pop etc. groups. For some, the creative lyric-writing process may turn what may be a boring English lesson into a voyage of self-awareness. For others, just listening to songs, or maybe reading gossip magazines about singers, provokes powerful images of empathy with the singer, whose words and performance often relates intimately to an adolescent's needs. For some this empathy develops to such an extent that the pop fan's centre of attraction turns away from themselves to the singer and all that they represent. So begins a form of hero-worshipping within which trends and ideals are set and followed.

Did you know?

I started to write songs when I was about 11 years old. The lyrics were meant only for me; unfortunately, I never had the chance or – if truth be told – the voice to become a pop hero! Others with creative instincts may turn to poetry, keep a diary or start a blog. All these forms of creative writing are an ideal preparation for the future copywriter.

When copywriting, the emphasis of this style of personal writing, about you and your world, needs gradually to shift from what is personally motivating to what touches an audience. More often than not – as happens in the case of the singer who is followed by adoring fans – this can be the same thing. It's all a matter of how you project your message so that your audience is left with the perception that it is perfect for their needs – be those needs personal, social, business, cultural and so forth.

First steps in the copywriting thought process

There is an old adage that to understand someone, first walk a mile in their shoes. Put yourself in someone else's shoes – the kind worn by your reader. Then prioritize the pros and cons of your proposition.

Imagine yourself in the sneakers of a teenage pop group lead singer. You need a pair of 150-watt speakers for a gig which you eventually plan to offer as an MP3 clip on the web. You don't know where to find this piece of equipment and you are on a shoestring budget.

You pin up a notice on a local information board. It must be no larger than A4. What should you write? Here is your first attempt:

> **WANTED**
>
> A pair of 150-watt speakers with Dolby 'c' control and amps.
>
> Must be cheap and in good condition.
>
> Email JJ on reinvent@me.com

That certainly gets the message across. However, does it cover everything? You're pretty desperate to get your hands on this particular pair of speakers. The gig is on Friday night and your web engineer is all wired up to record. Ideally you need to have everything in place by Wednesday at the latest. What about that limited budget of yours? You only have £300 to spend; you can't be too choosy.

On the other hand, who would want to 'give away' a perfectly good pair of speakers below the going price? How about your request that the speakers should be 'in good condition'. Can you be a little more precise here? Finally, what about the 'call to action' (how people can get in touch with you) – is it convincing enough? ('Convince' as in the 'C' in AIDCA.) What about adding a phone number or maybe link to your Facebook or Twitter page?

At this point you would be forgiven for thinking that if you were to include every requirement, you would need a lot more space than an A4 sheet stuck on a notice board! Consider the main restriction on your advert. It cannot cover more than an A4 sheet. If you use too many words it will become cluttered and difficult to read. Could you pep it up a bit with some colour in the headline?

Next, think about the type of people who are going to read this advertisement. It is being pinned up on the local community board. The readers may know you and if not they may assume that you live nearby. (This is important if they are expected to deliver the speakers.) Naturally, those interested will want to get as high a price as possible for their speakers. A bargaining factor would be the condition of the equipment.

Consider how potential sellers will perceive you. Maybe they will assume you don't have much money. If you did, surely you would be advertising in a trade magazine?

Now, let's sort all of this information into sections:

Your needs	Ad space	Prospect's needs
150-watt speaker.	A4 size.	Sell a speaker.
Dolby 'c' control.	Colour available.	Good price.
Good condition.	Not too many words.	Not too many delivery hassles.

Now consider possible motives behind this sale:

You	Your prospect
To be heard!	Has no need for an extra set of speakers.
To be more creative.	Needs to raise cash – quickly.
To get more gigs.	Has given up on music – band disbanded.
To gain experience.	Wants new, higher spec speakers.
To have fun playing as part of a band.	Needs more space.

Finally, imagine the speakers as a catalyst for emotions. In terms of feelings and tone of voice, how do they affect each interested party?

You	Your prospect
Happiness – as you can team up with your mates.	Nostalgia – for when they played in a band.
Confidence – as you can express your feelings creatively.	Happiness recollecting good times.
Pride – considering what you and the band have.	Sadness – when they had to give up music.
Concern – what will happen to the band?	Remorse for never having made the band a success.
Optimism that your band will be a success.	Pride recollecting their past achievements.

Now you have identified all your elements, revise the advert. A good copywriter gets to the heart of a proposition, drawing out a convincing set of motives for a prospect to discover more about a product or service. In this example, amongst the possible creative solutions you could try:

▶ *Pampering to your prospect's nostalgia values.*
▶ *Addressing the practicalities of disposing of a cumbersome and bulky piece of equipment.*
▶ *Combining approaches.*

Your tone of voice could be:

▶ Serious
▶ Humorous
▶ Begging
▶ Challenging

▶ Irreverent
▶ Formal
▶ Casual
▶ 'Cool' and trendy

What do you honestly think your prospect would want to hear?

One way of targeting your message is to match mutual key motives.

You	Your prospect
Happiness	Happiness
Confidence	Confidence
Pride	Pride
Sadness	Sadness

I wouldn't think that this particular advert calls for an all-out negative approach. Creative propositions rarely do, except in notable areas such as charity and some aspects of general public information. For example:

> DON'T DRINK AND DRIVE
> OR YOU COULD END
> UP IN A DEAD END STREET.

So, ditch the negative motive. What's left?

You	Your prospect
Happiness	Happiness
Confidence	Confidence
Pride	Pride

Review what you have written. Can you find a word connecting you and your prospect? How about, 'nostalgia'? The word 'nostalgia' derives from the Greek word *nostos,* meaning 'a return home'. Copywriting directing itself at a subject's home truths is copywriting at its best. Many brands use nostalgia in their campaigns to suggest brands that have authenticity, reliability and trust. Mainstream marketers know that for something to be perceived as being nostalgic, it has to be at least 25 years old. That's just long enough to start fading from memory and so able to be manipulated as being more valuable and esteemed than it originally was.

If you rewrote the advert using nostalgia as a creative catalyst, you could incorporate all the powerful evocative feelings associated with an up-and-coming band:

- ▶ *Challenging – like the motives behind the lyrics.*
- ▶ *Casual/easy going – like the key band members.*
- ▶ *Ambitious – as you are and as the then-younger prospect would probably have been when they originally purchased the speakers.*
- ▶ *Witty – like the band.*
- ▶ *Direct – like all youth.*
- ▶ *Intimate – like your songs.*

Let's give the advert another shot. Why not connect your practical and emotional needs with those of your prospect …

CAN YOU HEAR US AT THE BACK?

They could with your help!

We need a pair of 150-watt speakers (incl. Dolby 'c' and amps).

We offer £100 ono + the chance to see our band playing live.

Please don't turn a deaf ear on us.

Call JJ on 0218 900 1234 ASAP – we're live this Friday!

Notice that the advert is led by a strong proposition and closes on an emphatic instruction – 'call!'

This follows the classic copy structure found on page 94, namely:

- *Proposition (headline).*
- *Lead-in paragraph or sentence that connects to the proposition.*
- *Main body section, detailing who, what, why, where, when and how.*
- *Lead-out section, usually incorporating a call to action (informally known as CTA).*

OVER TO YOU

▶ *Based on the speakers advert in this chapter, write an advert adopting the following approaches:*
  ▷ *serious*
  ▷ *practical*

▶ *Write another advert, this time from a person wishing to sell, rather than buy, speakers.*

▶ *Think about the nursery rhyme 'Humpty Dumpty'.*

> **Humpty Dumpty sat on a wall,**
> **Humpty Dumpty had a great fall.**
> **All the King's horses**
> **And all the King's men**
> **Couldn't put Humpty together again.**

  ▷ *List four of the reasons Humpty Dumpty needs to be put together again.*
  ▷ *List three practical problems the King's men may have in putting Humpty Dumpty together again.*
  ▷ *Assuming Humpty Dumpty is the heir apparent to the throne and a father of two children, list three of his prime motives to be put together again.*
  ▷ *List three of the King's men's motives to put Humpty Dumpty together again.*
  ▷ *Finally, list the three main shared motives that Humpty Dumpty and the King's men have to put him together again.*

2

....

The big idea

In this chapter teach yourself:
- *to unlock your creativity*
- *to adapt classic copywriting formulae*
- *to brainstorm effectively*
- *to cross-examine a creative need*
- *to understand brands*
- *to conduct a SWOT analysis.*

Here's an idea

How many times have you sat in front of the television and admired the clever combination of words and visuals in an advertisement? I've done just that many times. Often I ask myself, 'How and from where did they get such a good idea?'

The philosopher Plato (427–347 BCE) believed that the mind and body were made up of different things. Each followed separate sets of rules. He taught that the mind was the most important of the two and that the so-called 'body' (things you could see, touch and so on) formed the foundations for reality. 'Platonic ideas' came about through a process of reasoning, by drawing a general conclusion about something mainly based on experience or through experimenting with the facts available.

Plato maintained that ideas represented the genuine basis for reality. In his opinion, once you had an idea about something, that idea was subjectively real. For example: You are walking by a coliseum. You think, 'Wouldn't it be great if the coliseum had a roof to protect everyone from the sun?' As far as your perception of the world is concerned, you have the ability to visualize the coliseum with a roof, and the roof might as well be there.

As a copywriter it is your job to become an 'idea transplant surgeon'. That means taking an idea out of your head and transplanting it into the mind of your reader. The tools to achieve this are meaningful words. Meaning takes its cue from interpretation. In turn, interpretation takes its cue from experience – the experience of your reader.

Here is an example: Think of an elephant. Now think of a mouse. Next, envision the mouse squashing the elephant. How would that be possible? Would the mouse be a cartoon? Would the elephant be tiny and the mouse gigantic? Would the mouse roll a bolder from a cliff top onto the unsuspecting elephant alone?

Which of these examples do you think most people could imagine as possible? Over the years, the cartoon example is the one that I have found to be most pertinent to most people. Once you understand what would make readers 'see' themselves using your products or services, then all you have to do is deliver your message through words and pictures that together provide meaning and understanding to your audience.

Unlocking your creative potential

John Locke (1635–1704) suggested that ideas are based solely on experience. According to Locke, a newly born baby can be likened to a blank sheet of paper. As the child develops, the sheet is filled with information acquired through experience. The adult, according to Locke, experiences two kinds of ideas:

▶ *Ideas of sensation (seeing, hearing, smell, sight, taste) – which he called simple ideas.*
▶ *Ideas of reflection (deliberation, construction) – which he defined as complex ideas.*

Simple ideas are based on experience, while complex ideas combine those experiences to create abstract concepts.

In copywriting, ideas have to be driven by powerful propositions. There are only two kinds of proposition that you can make. Either one based on logic, or one based on experience which gives context to make it logical. The hardest proposition is the one based on logic if that logic is difficult to understand through a reader's lack of direct experience in the subject. So if a distinguished scientist claimed that there were people living on Pluto – because his formulae suggest that they do – unless a reader can actually be shown Plutonians, such a proposition remains little more than a scientific theory, albeit one from an eminent scientist. On the other hand if you put forward a proposition that draws on your reader's experiences, that proposal becomes more accessible as well as acceptable.

Did you know?

Agoraphobia – fear of public spaces – can also be interpreted as fear of the public marketplace. Words are your bridge to reach that market fearlessly.

THE BASIC STEPS TOWARDS A NEW IDEA

How do we achieve a new idea? The seven basic steps are:

1 *Specific experience.*
2 *Thought about that experience.*
3 *Other experiences – material facts (perhaps not directly related).*
4 *Consolidation of all the experiences.*
5 *Fresh opinion or insight relating to the original experience.*
6 *The formulation of a plan to implement a completely new experience.*
7 *The materialization of that plan – a completely new experience or material fact.*

WHAT IF NOTHING BRILLIANT COMES TO MIND?

Most people have heard of the expression 'writer's block'. It refers to that frustrating point in a creative writing project when great ideas become spaghetti thoughts – all the strands are disconnected from the writing assignment itself. Every experienced writer faces this sometimes. There you sit, staring at the blank piece of paper, and there it (the sheet of paper) rests lifeless.

So you make a token effort and start to concentrate on the project. Then you become distracted by something like whether you should have chips or baked potatoes with your dinner. Perhaps (if you are particularly distracted) you turn to considering how long it would take to type out every number from one to a million. (The answer is five years and 2473 sheets of US A4 size paper – with normal line spacing.)

Let's address the problem of the roving mind.

Take a break

Writer's block may sometimes be your subconscious saying, 'This is tiring. Let's have forty winks and see if we can think of something else.' So relax, allow yourself to daydream for a while. Often that leads to a thought which is so different from your original line of thinking that it stimulates the innovative idea that you were looking for in the first place. (This is the basis of Edward de Bono's practical books on lateral thinking.)

Don't instinctively reach for the obvious approach to a copy assignment. One effect of the global recession of 2009 was that people became especially cynical and tired of advertising and marketing that looked the same as every other piece of advertising and marketing. Opting for the obvious 'standard' look or feel for a piece of creative work, designers found that their ideas were being ignored. People wanted copy that was different yet deeply empathetic with the needs of readers rather than appearing to be something that was written according to transparently obvious old techniques. Copy that follows the rules of your competitor (apart from regulations affecting legal, medical or financial issues) usually turns out to be copy that is based on work produced by another competitor. So everyone copies everyone else and the reader becomes either bored or blasé about everything.

No one can be brilliant everyday, so if the ideas don't come to you simply go back to your original brief (written requirements for a piece of creative work), ensure that your copy is structured (using the proposition – lead-in – main body and lead-out plan, see page 13) and most importantly, remember Gabay's Golden Rule for eliminating writer's block: *Write – then get it right.*

If you don't write the first word, the second will never follow, however earnestly you dream about it. Don't fret about writing gobbledegook – you won't – you have a brief. Believe in yourself and start making creative connections with your reader.

Copywriting and its influence on the mind

I once attended a course in problem solving (now I teach the subject!). The tutor drew a box containing six crosses in two rows. He asked the class to connect six of the crosses by drawing no more than three strokes through them, without taking the pen off the paper. The class found this quite simple.

Then he drew a square box containing nine crosses. We were asked to draw through all the crosses in just four strokes, without lifting the pencil off the paper or retracing any line in any direction. The class started to scribble various lines. Most either retraced a line or drew more than the permissible four lines.

The solution was to *think outside the box*. Human nature being what it is, most people assumed that the box containing the crosses also held the parameters to work within for the solution. However, the tutor never actually said that the class should be restrained in this way.

The solution was to think laterally – to go beyond the predictable ways of looking at things and use creative initiative:

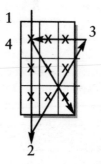

After this, the tutor asked the class to cross out sixteen squares within a square box using just six lines, without taking the pen from the paper. Eventually we arrived at the solution:

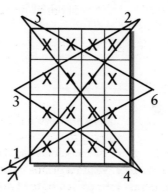

Again, the principle of *thinking outside the box* applied. While many people in business are aimed-led thinkers, and many in the creative services industry are lateral-based thinkers, in addition to taking the broad view you also need to balance the two extremes.

CONVERGENT AND DIVERGENT THINKERS

Are you an aimed-led (convergent) or lateral-based (divergent) copywriter?

Left thumb on top of right thumb – divergent.   Right thumb on top of left thumb – convergent.

Divergent thinkers	Convergent thinkers
Look at detail from multiple perspectives.	Identify the most important data.
Lots of possible statements.	Select specific problem statements.
Produce lots of ideas.	ID rich options
Develop criteria for evaluation of options.	Choose and apply criteria.
Evaluate possible actions.	Formulate a plan for action.

BRAIN TRAINING

Ever since experiments in California during the late 1960s and early 1970s, neurologists have believed that each side of the human brain specializes in certain regions of consciousness. The brain consists of two hemispheres housed within a pleated casing some 2.5 mm thick, called the cerebral cortex. Each of the two hemispheres has lots of cavities called ventricles. Prior to modern scientific understanding, people thought that these ventricles cupped the human spirit. Both hemispheres are connected by an intricate collection of nerve fibres called the *corpus callosum*. The left side of the brain deals with practical issues and controls the right-hand side of the body. The right side of the brain deals with creative and symbolic issues as well as controlling the left-hand side of the body.

Marketing researchers have developed these findings into an area of knowledge called 'braintyping':

▶ *A typical left-brain thinking person is very good at organizing things and appreciates order and structure.*
▶ *The typical right-brain thinking person is very creative and emotionally led.*

As advertising relies heavily on images and emotive issues, a great deal of it is processed within the right brain. Strategic marketers often claim that a typical left-brain thinking person is good at understanding order and structure. (This side is particularly apt at language skills.)

Ideally, at your most creative, you will make best use of both spheres. In fact your copy should be full of 'trigger-words'. They appeal to either the LEFT or RIGHT side of the mind. This is particularly effective as people often do things for logical reasons as well as emotive ones. Often for both. This reminds me of a very old advertisement for cream cakes. The advert featured a picture of scrumptious cake being eaten surreptitiously by a lady. The headline read: 'Naughty but nice!'

By addressing both logical as well as emotive aspects of a product or service people tend to appreciate all sides of your argument. The difficulty is avoiding being too biased to either logic alone or emotions. Generally, the more business related your product or service is, the more you lean towards the logical aspect of a proposition. However, you still have to remember that your reader is human. Once you understand this dual thinking, you can appreciate why copywriting has to do more than inform; it must address basic human traits.

Copywriting should be one or more of the following: intriguing, involving, charming, surprising, understanding, caring and, above all, rewarding.

Ascertaining whether or not a proposition is going to be rewarding is all down to an almond-shaped part of the brain called the 'amygdala'. You can find it as a cluster embedded within the temporal lobe of the brain. It helps with the formation and storage of memories associated with emotional events. As such it gives readers a 'gut-feeling' about a message. If your message has no emotional meaning, then even if, from a factual point of view, it is brilliantly written, it simply won't connect to your audience. They will have to force themselves to read and understand it, in the same way a student approaches a particularly boring subject.

Did you know?

A great way to grab attention is to select appropriate verbs and adjectives. Consider this sentence:

The copywriter wrote the brochure.

Now 'feel' as well as see what happens when you add an adjective:

The copywriter wrote the elegant brochure.

In 1971 Charles J. Fillmore, an American linguist and an Emeritus Professor of Linguistics at the University of California, Berkeley, asked students to watch a film of car crashes shot by a local safety council. He asked the students to estimate the speed at which the cars had crashed. The students' estimates varied according to Fillmore's chosen verb used to describe the crash impact.

Verb	Mean speed estimate (mph)
smashed	40.8
collided	39.3
bumped	38.1
hit	34.0
contacted	31.8

So it is that when you write copy, it is important to choose every word carefully and with consideration for its impact on gaining your reader's attention.

Once you have 'tickled' the amygdala, the reader becomes more inclined to read your copy. Much of the processing of 'hard' facts in your copy is handled within a part of the brain called the 'visual cortex'. Getting a reader's attention is one thing; you also have to offer value. For example, you may need to write an advertisement urging readers to save in a bank account. Emotionally the trigger of having savings to fall back on in the event of a 'rainy day' may be extremely strong. However, the reality of having to cut back on a daily budget to finance that rainy day may not be as alluring. This is where another part of the brain steps in: the 'posterior cingulate cortex' . This part of the brain is associated with measures of value. Once people recognize the value of something to themselves, they become even more inclined to take action.

The relationship between the amygdala and posterior cingulate cortex really starts to gel when writing copy for social network sites, such as Twitter. Initially deciding whether to follow or not to follow someone on Twitter is mostly based on emotional factors. To prove this, neuropsychologists invented fictional Twitter profiles of people, together with a picture. Reading the profiles, volunteer Twitterers asked themselves if individuals made them feel good (addressed in the amygdala). If so, they went on to check if a profile Twitterer's messages offered personal value. In this way, in terms of writing on Twitter at least, readers sought emotional triggers in online profiles rather than facts alone.

SHOULD YOU FOLLOW THE FORMULAE CROWD?

Nowadays it seems that just about every industry sector likes to produce its own pet formulae for instant and guaranteed success. In their favour, formulae help to impose a level of discipline. Think of them as reference points on a map. They suggest routes towards a destination. However, you should adapt these suggestions to help you reach your specific goal.

As mentioned earlier (see page 4), AIDA has always been touted by professional marketers as being the core communications formula. It was created during the roaring 1920s and was derived from another formula that advocated the following:

All advertising must be SRBRA:

Seen Read Believed Remembered Acted upon

The trouble with the original formula is that it is not that well defined. For instance, it lists 'remembered'. How detailed should your memory be? Does 'read' mean that you should study every single word at length? Besides, in all honesty, how do you pronounce SRBRA? (Answers on a postcard, please.)

Because it was inadequate, SRBRA begat AIDA and an entire lexicon of copywriting theories was born.

Once the word about formulae got around, just about everyone began to devise them.

Some classic formulae
BOB STONE'S MAIL FORMULA
Bob's formula is often quoted, notably in Successful Direct Marketing Methods. It is:

1 *Promise the most important benefit.*
2 *Enlarge on it.*
3 *Specify the order in full.*

4 *Provide proof and endorsements.*
5 *Say what you might 'lose'.*
6 *Rephrase benefits.*
7 *Incite immediate action.*

SAWYER'S SEVEN DEADLY SINS
The following list is based on Howard 'Scotty' Sawyer's checklist:

1 *Never be a braggart. A lot of industrial advertising insists that one man is better than the next. Claiming superiority in itself is not necessarily wrong; it is wrong if little or nothing is done to substantiate the claim in a friendly, persuasive and convincing manner.*
2 *Stop talking to yourself. Direct your remarks towards the interest of the readers, not the company doing the talking.*
3 *Don't preach. Never look down upon the reader from way up high. Instead, invite the reader to do something.*
4 *Don't blow your bugle. You don't have to make a big noise to get readers to stand to attention.*
5 *Stop making a mess. Nobody likes anyone who is untidy. Equally, people don't like inconsiderate advertising.*
6 *Quit being cute. Deliver your story in as straightforward a manner as possible.*
7 *Ditch dullness – the worst sin of all. Instead feature crisp presentation of visual elements and some fast-moving copy. It's the least you can do.*

Not wishing to be left out I have devised two core copywriting formulae, first a longer one:

GABAY'S COPY CHECK
1 *Before you reach for the mouse:*
  ▷ *Make sure you have an appropriate brief. If not, ask for one.*
  ▷ *Do you understand what is required of you?*
  ▷ *Do you have a convincing offer?*

- ▷ *Prioritize your benefits.*
- ▷ *Dismiss irrelevant ideas.*
- ▷ *Set the tone of your message.*

2 *Start as you mean to go on:*
  - ▷ *Think about your three biggest features – choose appropriate words to reflect those ideals.*
  - ▷ *Include the word 'you' in the first paragraph of your message (for direct marketing).*
  - ▷ *Make sure your introductory paragraph has some creative connection to your headline (proposition).*
  - ▷ *Be empathetic to your audience.*

3 *In the body text:*
  - ▷ *Ensure your copy is appropriately structured.*
  - ▷ *Keep the copy moving and your reader's interest alert.*
  - ▷ *Use link terms: 'like', 'therefore', 'so', 'however'.*
  - ▷ *Halfway through writing, ask yourself if you would honestly want to read further. (If not, there is barely any chance that your reader will feel inclined to read further.)*
  - ▷ *Have you covered every angle as detailed in your brief?*
  - ▷ *Can you provide proof and endorsements?*
  - ▷ *Have you reiterated your main benefits?*

4 *Close the deal:*
  - ▷ *Know where and why you want the copy to end.*
  - ▷ *Get there – either sell or invite an alternative response such as visiting a website.*
  - ▷ *If you are selling off the page, make sure you include all relevant details, including when the reader can expect delivery.*
  - ▷ *Review your presentation and content.*

ABCD
Gain:

- ▶ **Attention** in your headline and/or image. (This is your proposition.)
- ▶ **Build** interest in your first paragraph or sentence. The first sentence of your copy should immediately take up proposition as set out in your **Attention** section.

- ▶ Convince your reader through offering substantiation of claims throughout your copy. This involves providing all your reader needs to help them make an informed choice: who, what, why, where, when and how.
- ▶ Deal – what do you want them to do? Offer a clear call to action (CTA) and if possible, link your Deal with your opening proposition.

For example:

- ▶ Attention (Proposition)

Why you should treat yourself to our cakes?

- ▶ Build interest

Should you or shouldn't you take a nibble? Go on, you know you want to ...

- ▶ Convince

At only 90p for a delicious slice of heaven filled with fresh cream and a choice of seven scrummy fruit toppings to choose from, there's something special for every day of the week.

- ▶ Deal

So go on – treat yourself today at a Baker Inc. store near you.

THE HUMAN MOTIVATION MODEL

Arguably, one of the twentieth century's greatest psychologists was a man called Abraham Maslow. He devised a model of human motivation that many creative marketing experts refer to when assessing the motivation factors that influence a typical buyer.

Maslow's pyramid is constructed from five 'need' levels. Like every construction, its overall strength relies on the integrity of its foundation. Once your creative message satisfies one need level, it should naturally lead on to address the next.

Interestingly, nobody ever reaches the pinnacle. This is great news for copywriters. Just as a market is satisfied that it has the best possible deal, you are able to offer a more attractive option.

When promoting our fictitious company PenPal, for example, you could develop the model in the following way:

1 *Physiological needs.*
   Is it portable?
2 *Safety needs.*
   Will it leak?
3 *Social needs.*
   Does it match my business or leisure requirements?
4 *Esteem needs.*
   Will people admire my writing instrument and will it help me to produce well-presented work?
5 *Fulfilment needs.*
   Can I rely on it to adapt to any future requirements?
   Will it enable me to write down essential pieces of information at any given time?

In the case of a charity, the model may work like this:

1 *Physiological needs.*
   Will donating make me feel better about myself?
2 *Safety needs.*
   Will my donation help save lives?
3 *Social needs.*
   Will I feel that I have gone some way towards contributing towards a better society?
4 *Esteem needs.*
   Will I gain satisfaction from knowing that I have been able to help a good cause?
5 *Fulfilment needs.*
   Does this charity make me feel good?

How brainstorming drives the creative process

You can't sit behind an office desk and just wait to get creative. I encourage writers to do their own thing to get inspired – even go to the movies. As long as the work gets done to time and budget and is fresh in its concept, I am delighted!

One way to come up with original ideas is to arrange for a meeting of the minds. Brainstorming is so called because it involves a downpouring of spontaneous ideas – however practical or impractical they may be. The ideas can be generated by anyone, irrespective of the person's position within a company. If you are running a very small business, you could even consider asking friends to come over for a brainstorming afternoon. Serve drinks and you could call it a 'brainstorm in a coffee cup' meeting!

Whoever is present and wherever you attend a brainstorm meeting, remove all forms of creative inhibitions. This can be more difficult than it first appears. At almost every brainstorming group that I have attended, at least two types of people have attended:

▶ *The first is 'Eddy the Extrovert', who refuses to believe that a personal idea is unattainable.*

▶ *The other is 'Ingrid the Introvert', who at best refuses to believe she is capable of having any good ideas; at worst she is simply too shy to co-operate in the meeting.*

A professional facilitator – an independent person controlling the meeting – ensures that everyone gets a fair chance to speak and express their ideas, original or otherwise. A good facilitator will avoid introducing brainstormers to a project too early.

Now let's look at some brainstorming techniques.

FOOD FOR THOUGHT

Any professional dietician will tell you that the worst way to slim is to stop eating. This deprives the body of essential nutrients which burn to produce energy and which in turn burn the calories. Don't deprive your brainstormers of essential nutrients. Encourage them to exercise their minds and pig-out on a creative feast of ideas – even if initially such ideas may sound farfetched.

VIRTUAL BRAINSTORMING

Since the first edition of *Teach Yourself Copywriting* was published I have developed a particularly effective mode of brainstorming designed for the twenty-first century. It is called Virtual Brainstorming™.

Led by a trained market researcher with psychological marketing skills, brainstormers who make up a synectics-led focus group (originally developed at Harvard) are invited to step into a surreal world appropriate to the subject being brainstormed. Then they are led through a highly structured method of rationalizing their thoughts.

Because it is held in a chimerical environment, a Virtual Brainstorming™ session can be conducted anywhere your imagination can conceive – from a jungle to the top of a mountain – provided the location enhances imaginative thought and group-dynamic energy.

Synectics sessions

Synectics sessions were originally developed at Harvard. A research director leads the thinking and a senior member of the team suggests possible directions to pursue. At a synectics session people who are unconnected to the product, service or even company are invited to pitch in their ideas. All ideas are jotted down on a flip chart and made available for everyone to review. Invariably fresh ideas from a mass of off-the-wall thinking emerge at the end of the session.

Did you know?

What with PDAs buzzing and people interrupting all day, it can be difficult to find a quiet space to be creative. If the creative project is substantial, consider holding your brainstorming session away from the office. An away day frees you and your colleagues from possible interruptions and allows you to relax in a different atmosphere, such as a hotel.

IDEAS FLOURISH FROM FACTS

Let's return to the idea process. If you accept Plato's theories, innovative ideas come about through either the direct or indirect connection of one set of facts with another ('mind' and 'body' in unison). The process is a bit like being a detective searching for all the available clues, examining the facts, drawing conclusions and piecing together a picture of the truth. Similarly, a great deal of the business of creative copywriting requires pure detective work. Like a detective, you need to identify all the material facts. Then you have to find ways to link these pieces of information together.

From blank page to powerful sales message

Assimilate your facts and you can style copy that complements your presentation. Imagine that individual facts formed a kind of Identi-kit generalized description of a product or service. Consider each fact to be a 'suspect'. Any suspect – either individually, or working as part of a team – could be the main culprit who wants to make the buyer an offer they simply cannot refuse.

This 'offer' is known as the Unique Sales Proposition, or USP. Your job is to narrow down the guilty suspect(s). The way to do this is to set up an identification parade. You shouldn't enter into the exercise with preconceived prejudices about any of your suspects. For example, let's say you are asked to write about nuts and bolts. As a copywriter, it's your professional job to introduce them to the products. If you are the supplier of a product or service, be prepared to accept that the consumer may base their purchasing decision on reasons other than those first assumed by you. In many cases, those reasons can enhance your sales pitch.

You have to balance each party's indisputable facts with their subjective views – including your own. So keep an open mind and an attentive attitude. Somewhere in the middle of what you assume, the product claims and what the target audience actually needs is the creative Holy Grail. Go find that big idea!

The six-stage cross-examination
Take a good, long, hard look at your apparent facts or 'suspects'. Flick on the spotlight and uncover the truth.

1   **What are we doing here?** *It may sound obvious, or even the sort of question to put to a philosopher, but why exactly do you or your client want to advertise in the first place? To make money? Is that all? Maybe there is a hidden agenda? It could be to inform, educate, compete, launch, announce ... Once you know what it is that you are really trying to achieve, you can approach the business of fact interrogation appropriately.*
2   **Face the facts.** *What do the facts inform you about the product or service?*
3   **Who or what is the missing link?** *Are there any missing bits of information that would help you complete the picture?*
4   **Where will you uncover the clues?** *Who has the answers to technical or distribution issues and so forth concerning your product?*

5 Do you believe the facts? *Even if the answers are readily forthcoming, will they make practical sense to your readers?*

6 Clamp down on any unsubstantiated claims. *A fact is not a fact until it is substantiated (see the section on Features into Advantages, Applications and Benefits (FAAB) on page 5).*

Research

All forms of research should be undertaken with one clearly defined aim – to understand:

▶ *Why and how a client wants to sell the product.*
▶ *Why the buyer wants to buy the product.*

Specific ways in which research can help identify a target audience are discussed in full in *Teach Yourself Marketing* and to some extent in Chapter 6, which deals with direct response advertising (mailings). You use research to reinforce facts and give you a basis for a sound strategy, thus enabling you to define clearly a creative and coherent message that stimulates fresh ideas.

So-called desk research makes use of a wide variety of sources. These include:

▶ *published work available, such as company reports*
▶ *clippings from trade magazines*
▶ *information on the Internet*
▶ *specialist online subscription-based services (available via a computer link).*

Your project may be so innovative that there isn't any directly relevant and useful information available. If so, instead look at the closest possible service or product to the one that you intend to promote. Find out if there would be a demand for your product or service and if so why and potentially how great that demand is.

The services of a market research specialist may be just what you need in these circumstances.

Market research companies can provide an entire portfolio of research techniques, ranging from group discussions to regional surveys and questionnaires by post or telephone. Bear in mind that – particularly in the case of the small business carrying out its own copywriting – another important reason for conducting research is to check out the competition.

GET A COPY RESEARCH KIT

As of tomorrow – or, even better, today – I want you to buy a box file and give it the title, 'My Copy Research Kit'. In it assemble the following:

- ▶ *Examples of previous letters/promotions.*
- ▶ *Notes on which ones worked.*
- ▶ *A record of who replied (lists).*
- ▶ *Samples of competitors' material (How can it be improved? You should try to rewrite an example of your main competitor's material at least once a year. You'll be amazed how it helps you brush up your own copywriting techniques.)*
- ▶ *Customers' comments*
- ▶ *Sales results.*

Did you know?

The world's first known agency was based in London in 1786. It booked advertisements in the provincial press, charging a handling fee of 6d or 1s. The first international agency was Gordon & Gotch, which opened for business in Melbourne in 1855 and had its first overseas branch in London in 1867.

Creativity's role in the competitive commercial world

It is a common misunderstanding that companies primarily carry out research on competitors to uncover inside trade information. The true main objective for studying competitors is to find out at least as much as your customers know about:

- ▶ *What is available?*
- ▶ *Where?*
- ▶ *At what cost?*

Once you have uncovered these facts, you can begin to compare your (or your client's) products against that of your competitors as regards price, quality and distribution. Most important of all, you can begin to understand what I call the Elvis factor.

The Elvis factor

There have been many contenders to the throne left vacant by the last century's King of Rock and Roll – Elvis Aaron Presley. Even during his reign, the likes of Cliff Richard, Bill Haley and Jerry Lee Lewis hotly contested the crown worn by Elvis. However, although many talented contenders had personality and show-business appeal, none could match him in the market sector that he had carved uniquely for himself.

Ultimately, you or your client's company have to demonstrate at least one Point of Difference (POD) of a product or service that no other company can either match or beat. I like to refer to that element (or, if you are really fortunate, that list of aspects) as the Elvis factor.

Today, as technology spreads beyond helping one person do their job better towards enabling one person to do two people's jobs equally well, successful distinction between one company and another relies on a variation of the 80–20 rule.

The greatest proportion of a company's sales and profits may derive from a relatively small proportion of its customers and products. For instance, 20 per cent of the workforce may produce 80 per cent of the product or service.

Given that a growing number of companies are assuming dual roles – for example, many building societies have also become banks – you have to ask yourself to define the 20 per cent Elvis factor.

ScotsdaleNorth's Elvis factor may be that they are the country's favourite food and grocery retailer.

PenPal's Elvis factor may be that they are the first to incorporate Mars space technology into an interchangeable pen – everyone else can only imitate, never lead.

Get to know other companies' Elvis factors. They may include:

▶ *heritage*
▶ *size*
▶ *cost*
▶ *age appeal*
▶ *fashion*
▶ *quantity*
▶ *quality*
▶ *range*
▶ *taste*
▶ *scent, and so forth.*

The G spot

Having worked out your Elvis factor, you can then go on to identify the most important market segment of them all – what I like to call the G spot.

The G spot is the commercially sensual region that lies between
two Elvis factor areas that already capture loyal customers.
Initially, these customers would take far too much of your time,
effort and cash to woo away.

Once you have established a G spot of your own, you can
concentrate on enhancing your position. This is far easier than
defending it against a bigger competitor as well as simultaneously
finding creative ideas to sell the product or service.

Understanding the brand portfolio

Be specific about your G spot. For example, if you or your client's
company produces a vast range of products, that's fine. However,
if range is one of your main strengths, never fall into the trap of
always featuring every product range in the advertisements that
you offer. Instead, concentrate on one product at a time. In this
way you can start to build individual brands.

A well-positioned portfolio of brands can be likened to a
well-trained army. Use the G-spot methodology to address
creatively and so add value to every product or service in your
range, however great or small each may be. The result is an
invincible force that any competitor will find difficult to beat.

GIVE YOUR TROOPS BRAND NAMES

The British forces are regarded as one of the most effective
armed units in the world. Each of its divisions has a significantly

outstanding attribute. Tactically people often think of the British army in terms of regiments rather than an entire force. This diagram shows how it is organized.

Brands can be likened to such a structure. Each brand (division or regiment) has a core value.

TYPES OF BRAND

Family brands
Some companies are effectively families or groups with a wide range of products or activities. These include Cadbury, Lever, Heinz and so on.

Product line brands
Some companies have specifically created subsidiary brand names, like Teach Yourself, Homebase and Do It All.

Umbrella brands
Often the main family brand is used to endorse a specific sub-brand. Examples are Cadbury's Snack, Elite Instant Coffee, McVitie's Go Ahead and Heinz Big Soup.

Individual brands
In this group are specific brand names, like Rice Krispies, Cheerios and Persil. Keep in mind that individual products and services may come and go through the natural course of their product life cycle. The master brand, however, goes on and on.

Own label brands

Middlemen, or dealers, may also put their names to a brand – these are often referred to as private brands or wholesaler's brands. For instance, a major retailer may include its name on labels. These goods are often referred to as 'own label' brands. Examples are Better Buy's Baked Beans, Corner Shop Cola and so on. When groups of retailers market own labels, the brand is sometimes referred to as a distributor's brand.

Don't associate own label brands exclusively with consumers who simply want to save a few pennies on products. They may have different motives. It is known that dieters, for instance, may purchase own label brands instead of mainstream brands. This is because psychologically they want to feel deprived of enjoying 'the best'.

Own brands shouldn't be confused with discounting. A retailer not directly associated with a major brand sometimes sells it at a discounted price (a supermarket may sell branded jeans cheaply). In such instances, under a ruling by the European Court of Justice, the supermarket is allowed to advertise the branded goods as long as the advertisement doesn't 'seriously damage the reputation of the trade mark'.

Virtual brands

Sometimes the brand owner doesn't actually handle any part of the production process. Instead, that is conducted by an outside supplier. Richard Branson's Virgin Cola is one example.

Just because consumers go for a lesser-known cola, it doesn't necessarily follow that they will opt for other lesser-known brands as well. As pointed out in the section on research (see pages 34–5), human intellect is far more complicated than that.

Web brands

Web brands are rapidly developed through the Internet. Because the Internet is highly scalable, small and international companies compete equally on the web. Therefore, making your brand distinctive becomes even more important. This requires consistent promotion through all supporting media as well as the web. When writing for the web, ensure your content offers surfers a sense of community affiliation with a brand message. This could be achieved through anything from integrating social media into your site, to offering useful frequently asked question (FAQ) pages.

Measuring brand loyalty

Brand loyalty occurs when consumers return to a specific brand time after time. It relies on a core set of values that never change. These may include quality, service and care.

It is possible to measure a brand's popularity. Look at the following table. When you are writing copy, you will need to know how your brand measures up.

Brand extent	Brand magnitude	Brand sway	Brand affinity	Brand sensitivity
Development into new pastures as well as brand stretching into related product/ service areas without compromising the core potency of a brand's original set of values.	Supremacy in terms of esteem rather than purely a portion within a market sector.	The relative significance of personal association the brand attracts from various segments of the market, including the internal market (employees and shareholders).	The allegiance and admiration the brand attracts from existing as well as potential customers.	The level of feeling and emotions evoked by the brand.

Over time keen competitors will attempt to match your brand attributes. The classic reaction to this is to produce advertising known as sales promotions. This is often price or styling led. For example: buy one for the price of two, or buy a limited edition box set.

Sales promotion helps to fight off hostile armies of would-be G-spot owners. However, in the long term consumers tend to return to those brands whose core values remain sound. For example, cola brands may compete on price to such an extent that a price war overtakes the original reason for buying a cola – taste. At the end of the day, one cola may be cheaper than another or both may be equally priced. However, you can be certain that eventually the consumer will return to their favourite cola – one that has endured the test of time, money-off promotions and contenders to its Elvis factor. Ultimately, consumers pay for the quality and reassurance of a 'well-known' brand.

Thanks to globalization, many core brands have become mass-market, commodity-led products ('cheap and cheerful' clones). Typical product examples include executive pens, sportswear, wristwatches, mobile phones, and of course PMPs (Personal Music Players).

On the other hand, competition has also encouraged major brand names to enhance products by constantly adapting to change through restyling, repricing, re-enforcing service and re-creating a healthy and fresh image.

Did you know?

The first-ever gift coupon appeared in 1865. A New Yorker called Benjamin Talbert Babbit overprinted soap wrappers with the word 'coupon'. Ten coupons entitled the customer to claim a 'beautiful lithograph picture'.

When writing copy to reflect your brand remember to consider:

▶ *the brand's personality*
▶ *how it functions*

- *what it symbolizes*
- *its position*
- *its value to market (actual)*
- *its value to community (avidly interested partner) – perceived*
- *its proposition*
- *whether it is competitive*
- *its credibility*
- *its clarity of message*
- *its consistency of message.*

Typical product life cycles

One way to help you plan each stage of your creative message is to consider the typical life cycle of a new product.

1 *The introduction phase of the cycle usually features low sales. After all, no one has heard of the product as yet. Marketing costs are high and advertising is directed towards the key distributors such as retailers. In this phase, profit margins are low if not non-existent.*
2 *The next phase is growth. Sales slowly start to build. The price of converting enquiries into sales improves. If the product is good, competitors start to move towards your G spot. In terms of advertising and marketing, it is time to look at price, product variations and guarantees. Creatively, the message usually directs itself towards the broader market by building awareness and therefore interest.*
3 *The next phase is maturity. Sales reach their pinnacle. From here on, they either maintain their position or fall, becoming casualties of competition. Your costs are low and profits are high (assuming you have firm control of your G spot). Your first, more adventurous customers may have gone on to try other products. Your mainstream customers will be prime targets for loyalty-type creative messages. Competitors will either operate in parallel against you or drop out of the game. New product ranges are introduced, pricing is aimed against competitors and sales promotion campaigns are introduced to combat brand switching.*

(Incidentally, consumers who frequently practise brand switching are sometimes called spinners or rate-surfers because they have the tendency to 'spin' or 'surf' between one brand and another.) All of these initiatives require strong creative messages.

4 *The final phase is decline. Profits fall, sales fall. Even the mainstream consumers begin to move on to fresher ideas. Brand lines are rationalized, distribution is revisited. The bulk of your creative message is directed towards keeping the loyal customers.*

How the circle of life could affect PenPal

Introduction

PenPal launches onto the market. There is a big spend on marketing in order to announce the launch.

Growth

People hear about PenPal. They try it out at demonstrations. They like it. They tell their friends. Their friends see the advertising and sales grow. Unfortunately, all this good news about the exciting product also reaches the ears of competitors, who launch their own variations on PenPal.

Price variations and guarantees

With others encroaching into PenPal's G spot, it's time to consider strategic tactics to prevent sales from declining. The company tries offering specially priced pens and even brings out new accessories. Guarantees are made more attractive.

Maturity

It was a long, hard fight, but PenPal made it through – at least for a while. The consumers know that PenPal is first in the market, not just historically speaking but in terms of quality, innovation and reputation. PenPal must maintain its pole position – which requires a new kind of advertising strategy.

Position enforcement

A hard-hitting campaign is launched to reinforce PenPal's values and at the same time keep the competition from matching price and product range.

Decline

PenPal falls into the trap of becoming complacent about its position. It slows down the advertising and marketing process. This opens a gap for the competition. People get bored with PenPal. Spinners start to influence buying habits. The competition is much more fierce and new products are more useful. Farewell PenPal.

Product life-cycle phases vary in length and duration according to the individual product or service.

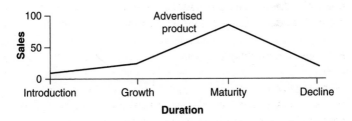

You can configure the strength and exposure of your creative message over a given period. The figure below is an example of this. By extending the message beyond the decline stage, the creative message may help restimulate product interest.

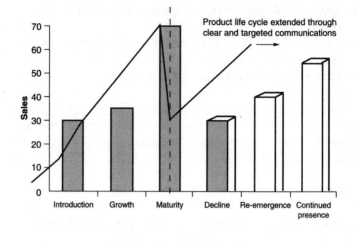

Researching competitors

It's time to be even more selective about competitive research.

▶ *Who is trying to move into you or your client's territory with similar services or products?*
▶ *How are they attempting to achieve their goal?*
▶ *To whom is their advertising directed?*
▶ *How often do they advertise?*
▶ *Is their creative tone friendly, professional, casual?*
▶ *Which advertising media do they use?*
▶ *What kind of creative messages do they use?*
▶ *If you are trying to compete, what will your creative message say?*

First steps in media selection:

I shall discuss specific media later in this book (see Chapter 5). As part of your plan of action, consider which media to use:

▶ *Which will be most effective: newspapers, TV, radio, the web …?*

- *Read the relevant papers to determine their style and content.*
- *Surf sites. What kind of advertiser advertises on them? Are banner ads flexible?*
- *How will an ad reproduce on paper?*

Download a 'media pack' – a fact kit that tells you about, for example, a newspaper's readership (the total number of people reached by a specific publication) and circulation (the officially audited number of subscribers to a publication).

UNDERSTANDING THE SWOT ANALYSIS TECHNIQUE

A useful way to summarize your findings is to use the SWOT analysis technique. SWOT helps you consider:

Strengths Weaknesses Opportunities Threats

S W O T

- *Strengths can relate to either your company's or your competitors' enhanced value to a customer. For instance, a supermarket may offer shorter queues at their checkouts. A manufacturer may have a particularly good distribution system, so you can purchase a specific product virtually anywhere in the country.*
- *Weaknesses could refer to a small advertising budget or an inefficient customer service department.*
- *Opportunities could relate to changing consumer habits, or to competitors who have become uncreative in their approach and in what they offer.*
- *Threats may arise from a competitor moving onto your G spot.*

The SWOT analysis is also useful for assessing media (see Chapter 5).

Now you have an idea of what to write about, pick up a pen or sit down in front of a word processor and start writing!

The big idea quick tips

▶ *Never settle for an obvious answer.*
▶ *Appeal to both sides of the brain.*
▶ *Balance your views with those of your client and its customers.*
▶ *Research a creative brief as fully as possible.*
▶ *Fight for and then defend your G spot.*
▶ *Adapt your creative message to suit the life cycle of the product or service.*
▶ *Turn a daydream into an idea-generation opportunity.*
▶ *Follow the AIDCA formula.*
▶ *If you are stuck for inspiration, try brainstorming.*
▶ *Never dismiss an idea instantly.*
▶ *Interrogate your client's product.*
▶ *Know your USPs and PODs as well as those of your competitors.*
▶ *Consider the different areas of branding and where your product or service sits in the branding hierarchy.*
▶ *Use a SWOT analysis on your company and its competitors.*

OVER TO YOU

▶ *Imagine you are the inventor of PenPal. Refer to the seven basic steps towards a new idea (see page 17). In seven steps, explain how you arrived at the idea of inventing a pen that had an interchangeable nib.*

▶ *You are the marketing director of ScotsdaleNorth.com. Refer to the AIDCA formula. Which of the following statements is the best to apply to an advertising message?*
  ▷ *We sell an extensive range of goods.*
  ▷ *We sell an extensive range of goods that are reduced in price until the end of the month.*
  ▷ *We sell an extensive range of goods that are competitively priced and available, and are all easily accessible via the web.*
  ▷ *We sell an extensive range of competitively priced goods.*

▶ *Now list the AIDCA points in the statement you selected.*

▶ *You are again in the hot seat at PenPal. This time, you are the managing director. You are meeting a particularly demanding client. She's anticipating a dull introduction to PenPal's product benefits. In two minutes list six 'one-line' ways in which you could praise PenPal's tremendous benefits.*

▶ *Jot down the most attractive idea of the six you have listed.*

▶ *In two minutes, list every secondary idea that your chosen six benefits suggest.*

▶ *First, take a break – have a short nap. Then think about promises that politicians make. In one minute, write down the first thirty things that come to mind.*

▶ *List other ideas that come to mind, thanks to your nap.*

▶ *Now list your choice of the top three ways to promote PenPal.*

3

How to structure your copy

In this chapter you will learn:
- *how to develop a brief*
- *how to develop your USP*
- *how to develop perceptions*
- *how to classify an audience.*

Great copywriting is an exercise in conducting an adult conversation. To do so, you have to plan what you are going to say, anticipate objections and then deliver your targeted message. To achieve this, you need a creative brief.

The creative brief

Without a good creative brief facts remain vague and unfocused. All too often you may find that your boss may not want to take the time to commit an instruction to paper. To address this:

▶ *Design a briefing form that is as easy to complete as it is to understand.*
▶ *Buy a digital pocket recorder and record the instructions, then write down those instructions as a brief.*
Make sure everything is signed off by all the parties concerned.

ESTABLISH A POSITIONING STATEMENT

Before you can write a formal brief, you need firm foundations upon which to construct a proposition.

To achieve that you should be able to answer two simple questions:

▶ *Who is your target audience?*
▶ *Why should they consider your company?*

In other words, you need to establish positioning:

▶ *for*
▶ *only*
▶ *it is*
▶ *because.*

My own company's positioning statement is:

For marketing professionals wishing to sustain a top of mind positioning in an already crowded market, www.brandforensics. co.uk provides value-added, imaginative and innovative through-the-line creative solutions. Because only Brandforensics' award-winning marketing writing, training, design and strategic brand insights are featured by industry, the media and public institutions alike. This is complemented by a mission to ensure that clients pay for expertise rather than overheads. (©www.brandforensics.co.uk).

EIGHT STEPS TOWARDS UNDERSTANDING A BRAND POSITION

1 *Pin-point the brand's meaning.*
2 *Identify the audience's:*
    a *behaviour*
    b *attitudes*
    c *demographics.*

3   *Establish the problem or need being addressed.*
4   *How does the competition address this?*
5   *Target the benefit.*
6   *How can that benefit be supported?*
7   *What is the brand personality?*
8   *Positioning statement.*

Did you know?

Plan what you are going to write, think about who your
reader is and why they would pay attention to your message,
anticipate objections then deliver that focused message.

Always follow a brief and ALWAYS get both the person who
is briefing and being briefed to sign-off the briefing form.
Think about your points of differences (PODs).

Types of brief

Briefs help you focus. Many argue that they are only useful
for external agencies. On the contrary! I believe that briefs
really come into their own for small businesses juggling with
lots of tasks.

Overall, briefs help separate personal opinion from facts. Here are
some of the best:

Briefing form for direct mail letter writing
THE FULL LETTER BRIEF
1   *Describe your audience (age, sector, job titles, etc.).*
2   *What's the key benefit making your offer distinctive: the
    Unique Selling Point?*
3   *Has the audience heard from you before? If so when and how
    often? (Provide examples.)*
4   *What is the featured offer, as opposed to the distinctive
    benefit? For example, are you offering price cuts, or tie-in
    discounts with partner companies?*

5 *Explain the product or services in terms of its strengths and
   weaknesses (see SWOT on page 47).*

6 *How do you want people to feel about your brand? Have you
   conducted any research to show how they currently feel?*

7 *List the top three most common customer descriptions that
   come to mind when people discuss dealing with your company.*

8 *Is your product or service essential – or does the concept need
   a detailed description?*

9 *Can you discuss your service/product's associated benefits?
   Rank them from sixth position to first place.*

10 *Name your top three competitors.*

11 *Provide recent examples of their work.*

12 *Are you testing elements of the letter? (This could include
   special offers, geographic distribution tests, response device
   tests or specific recipient type tests – e.g. job titles.)*

13 *What action (such as dial a telephone number) do you want
   the reader to take?*

14 *Are there any size/length restrictions?*

15 *When are you going to post your letter and to whom?*

16 *Are there any restrictions to take into consideration (such as
   legal requirements)?*

17 *When do you expect to see the letter copy?*

18 *Do you expect a first draft or completed letter?*

19 *Who will approve the final text?*

THE SHORTER LETTER BRIEF: GIVE ME FIVE!

1 *What's in it for the reader?*

2 *Why is this service /product so different than any other on the
   market?*

3 *How will it improve the reader's life/work/education/finances/
   health ...?*

4 *Why can't the competition match it?*

5 *What do you want the reader to do next?*

The straightforward copy brief

1 *What's the big message? (For example, you may be
   selling insurance, but the big message is: 'Gain peace of
   mind.')*

2   *What's needed (press advertisement, leaflet, brochure, etc.)?*
    Remember to describe dimensions and print restrictions.
3   *What's on sale? (For example, your big message may be*
    'a sense of independence' while you are selling a credit card.)
4   *What is the Unique Selling Point?*
5   *What's the Emotional Selling Point (the aspect which people*
    personally identify with)?
6   *Who wants it?*
7   *What do you want the readers to do?*
8   *What do they get out of it?*
9   *When and where will the communication appear?*
10 *How much can you spend on creativity?*
11 *What's the format?*
12 *What's the background?*
13 *What's next and when do you want it?*

Website copy brief

1   *For the front page (homepage), write a description of what*
    your website contains, what your company offers and who the
    website is aimed at (including why), that could be read in
    40 seconds (120 words).
2   *For individual sections of your site, divide your website*
    according to the types of surfers who will view each section.
    Then answer the following:
    This section of my website needs to:
    ▷ **Convince**
    ▷ **To**
    ▷ **Because**
    ▷ **Evidence**
    ▷ **Must include**

For example:

Convince	▷ *Dave, the student from Manchester*
To	▷ *surf onto my football site instead of footballfans.com*
Because	▷ *it's all the sports news and views – by students for students*
Evidence	▷ *editorial is direct from 150 colleges*
Must include	▷ *all latest football fixtures*

Then follow the same principles throughout the site.

Branding positioning copy brief
1 *Identify your audience*
- ▷ *Behaviour*
- ▷ *Attitudes*
- ▷ *Demographics*
- ▷ *Psychographics*

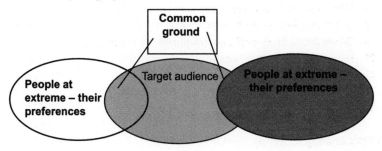

2 *What is the problem or need being addressed?*
3 *How does the competition address this?*
4 *Target benefits (ranked)*
- **1**
- **2**
- **3**
5 *How can those benefits be supported?*
6 *Describe your brand's personality?*
- ▷ *Warm and friendly*
- ▷ *Smart and modern*
- ▷ *Traditional and cautious*
- ▷ *Other*
7 *If the brand could be personified by a well-known celebrity, who would it be and why?*
8 *Positioning statement*
- ▷ *My brand is for these types of people* _____
- ▷ *Aiming to achieve* _____
- ▷ *Given a choice of competitors, my brand is outstanding because* _____
- ▷ *I can support this claim because* _____

Leaflet and brochure copy platform brief

1 *Purpose: what are my company's real motives? What is my reader's real motive?*
2 *Key issue: if the reader only remembers one thing, what will it be?*
3 *Audience: who is my primary reader?*
4 *What does my reader need to know about the subject?*
5 *What's in it for my reader?*
6 *What's the angle: technical? lifestyle …?*
7 *What's my reader's attitude towards the topic?*
8 *Last, but not least, remember the 'Six Journalist Friends', as inspired by Rudyard Kipling, who wrote:*

> *I keep six honest men,*
> *They taught me all I knew,*
> *Their names are;*
> *What and why,*
> *When and how*
> *And who.*

Immaculate concepts

Ask any journalist to list the key attributes of a successful business or compelling news story and the chances are that 'have a good angle' will be in a leading position. The 'angle' in question is the approach to a message that you adopt. This should not be confused with a product or service's POD (Point of Difference). The most valuable information to help you decide on the right angle is your understanding of the target audience.

Beyond the POD

So far I have told you to concentrate on a product or service's main USP or POD as a firm foundation for constructing an advertisement. In terms of a USP, a unique attribute may be fine for one segment of your target audience but totally inappropriate for another. For example, if you intend to concentrate on a lifestyle value-added statement, consider the ESP (Emotional Sales Proposition). Once you believe you have found the ideal USP, POD or ESP, how can you be certain that it is appropriate?

Think of them as seductive Arabian exotic dancers. Let's now take a look at the USP/TSP/ESP dance of the seven veils.

Imagine that ScotsdaleNorth.com wants to promote its range of baby foods. You have managed to target the POD as one of several possibilities:

▶ *Convenient, innovative packaging.*
▶ *Fresh ingredients (never more than 24 hours old before being canned).*
▶ *Tasty – recipes from award-winning chefs.*
▶ *Cost effective – usually 10 per cent cheaper than the leading brand.*
▶ *Healthy – winner of several healthy eating awards.*

Now, start peeling off each seductive veil of promise.

Convenient
▶ *For mum.*
▶ *For baby.*
▶ *For storage.*
▶ *No cooking.*
▶ *Self-contained in the package.*
▶ *No mess.*
▶ *Long shelf life.*

Next, go through the same process with each of your other four possibilities. In this example, this process will provide you with up to 35 possible USP/POD/ESPs. (If you really cannot find seven distinct features for each possibility, don't waste time searching for one just to make up the numbers – PODs should leap out at you.)

You can perform the same exercise in reverse, casting away each choice that is weak or too similar to another. Try to get down to two or fewer features per heading. In the case of the baby food, this leaves you with ten possibilities. Now once again consider, in terms of benefits, which PODs cross over and then discard them.

Your final list can be shown to someone or some group not directly involved with the project. Alternatively, if it's down to you to decide which USP/POD/ESP wins, think about who or what ultimately benefits from it.

For example, you may cut your baby food USP down to:

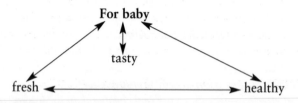

Of these, which is probably the most beneficial to the baby? My suggestion would be 'healthy'. (See also list on pages 63–66.)

Conceptions and perceptions

There are four key factors that influence a person's positive or negative attitude towards a group or individuals, namely:

1 *Cultural issues.*
2 *Situational (or interpersonal) issues.*
3 *Historical and economic concerns.*
4 *Individual experience.*

Let us look at these in turn.

1 CULTURAL ISSUES

Where people live and how people work influence the type of approach they make to everything, from purchasing

washing-up powder to investing in the stock market.
For instance:

Local area overcrowding affects how people relate to each other.

▶ *On the negative side it may lead to increased crime.*
▶ *On the positive side, it may lead to a greater integration of cultural backgrounds and a broader understanding of different cultural values. This in turn affects the street language and interpersonal relationships of the locals. It may lead to greater competition in the job market. It may also result in a wider acceptance of new technology. This results in a heightened need for products such as Webware (Internet software).*

2 SITUATIONAL (OR INTERPERSONAL) ISSUES

Following the crowd is a basic human instinct. Peer pressure is tremendously powerful throughout our lives (see 'From song writer to copywriter', page 6). People like to conform. Even nonconformists conform with nonconformists. The reward for conforming is peer group acceptance. For example, in the American deep south, restaurant owners used to display signs that read: 'I'M NOT PREJUDICED, BUT MY CUSTOMERS WOULDN'T LIKE IT.' This was meant to justify their refusal to allow blacks to eat at their premises.

Many house-cleansing material commercials are typical examples of how the advertisers try to be empathetic towards a particular social peer group (often a housewife or, to a lesser extent, a house husband). They discuss the possible repercussions in a family unit if the spouse and kids discover that their clothes are not as clean as they should be. Worse still,the possible scandal if poor domestic management by the house-keeper was discovered is hinted at. Be wary; don't overplay the scenario as it could end up as a farce – unless, of course, you want the social group to appear to be making fun of itself. A concept should be angled to cater for cliques without appearing to come across as a cliché.

3 *HISTORICAL AND ECONOMIC CONCERNS*

Often people's attitudes are social inheritances from a bygone age.

> **'We don't trust doctors because our parents didn't.'**
> **'We drink it because we've always done so.'**
> **'We only trust this brand of wholemeal bread – so we'll leave their white loaves on the shelf.'**

4 *INDIVIDUAL EXPERIENCE*

Just as people like to feel they socially fit, they also like to retain their individuality. Doing this may result in their learning some harsh lessons about life. When things go wrong with competitors, advertisers such as banks like to reassure customers that, thanks to the service they offer, the consumer need never be put in an uncomfortable or compromising position again.

These four factors identify the broad character types. The headings themselves contain many subheadings, each a refinement of each broad type. These often link with other traits. For every product there is an ideal advertising target identifiable by analysing character traits. This target would ideally be addressed through traditional one-to-one selling techniques. Alternatively, direct marketing can be used. (This is explained in Chapter 6.) For now, it is important to remember not to mis-interpret the categories by stereotyping. If you were to do that, your copy would be one-dimensional and have little substance – all sizzle and no steak.

Social categorization

'Socio-economic groups' or 'social grading' were first developed in the early part of the last century, in 1921. Social status is classified according to interests, social backgrounds and occupations. Each piece of data reflects the job of the head of the household. In the past, however, some systems of socio-economic classification graded people by their income.

Social grade	Social status	Occupation of head of household
A	Upper middle class	Higher managerial, professional
B	Middle class	Intermediate managerial
C1	Lower middle class	Clerical
C2	Skilled working class	Skilled manual worker
D	Working class	Unskilled manual worker
E	Lowest level	State pensioner, widow, casual worker, people dependent on social security

Source: JICNARS (Joint Industry Committee for National Readership Surveys)

Armed with this level of information, you can hone your target audience's lifestyle with great accuracy.

Did you know?

In the United States, there is no universal system to grade people socially. Instead, there is reliance on lifestyle data and neighbourhood data such as those used in UK direct marketing (see Chapter 6).

GET A LIFE

Psychographic or psychometric classification of targeted consumers by attitudes and other intellectual characteristics has led to various acronyms for and classifications of typical consumers.

One way of name-tagging groups of people into types is the values and lifestyles approach (VALS). This puts people into categories ranging from being totally unmotivated to having outstandingly balanced perceptions of society and their role in it.

Survivors	Extremely poor and despondent.
Sustainers	Poor but slightly optimistic about the future.
Belongers	Conventional, middle-of-the-road types who like to fit in.
Emulators	Aspiring, upwardly mobile and status conscious.
Achievers	Successful leaders.
I-am-me's	Young, self-aware and self-driven. Usually acting on the spur of the moment.
Experimentals	Sybarites ready to try a new experience.
Society conscious	Strive to wipe out social injustice.
Mature integrated	Socially balanced, inwardly confident.

At the beginning of the third millennium the UK government suggested the following customer group classifications. Despite its authorship, marketers rejected the idea outright.

Class 1	The Queen and owners of large companies.
Class 2	Company executives, managers of more than 25 people.
Class 3	Doctors, lawyers, scientists, teachers, librarians, insurance underwriters and computer engineers.
Class 4	Policemen, nurses, fire fighters and prison officers.
Class 5	Sales managers (small companies), farm managers and small hotel managers.
Class 6	Office supervisors, civil servants and lab technicians.
Class 7	Computer operators, professional athletes, nursery nurses, medical technicians, dental nurses, paramedics and secretaries.
Class 8	Businessmen employing under 25 people, newsagents, garage owners and publicans.
Class 9	Self-employed bricklayers, driving instructors, TV engineers.

Class 10	Factory foremen, shop supervisors, senior hairdressers.
Class 11	Craft and related workers, plumbers, motor mechanics, printers.
Class 12	Shop assistants, telephone operators, lorry drivers, traffic wardens and taxi drivers.
Class 13	Assembly line workers, cleaners and waiters.
Class 14	Low skill job-hoppers.
Class 15	Skilled unemployed.
Class 16	Unemployed – previously worked.
Class 17	Unemployed, no skills – never worked.

To segment lifestyles, many marketing companies develop acronyms even further. Here are a few popular psychographic terms, including acronyms, that may help you define your target audience.

Very young	Young/ dynamic	Married	Established	Retired
Baby Boomer Originally people who grew up after the 1960s baby boom. Also refers to people born at historical periods of population increase.	*Skotey* Spoiled kid of the 1980s. *Millennium Junkie* Early adopter who wants to change society. *Buppies* Black upwardly mobile professionals.	*Dinkies* Dual income, no kids, married couple. *Empty nesters* Couple, no kids. *Managing mums* Guilt-ridden mothers.	*Woopies* Well-off (over 55). Pre-retirement (aka Grey Panthers). *Glams* Greying, leisured, affluent middle-aged.	*Wrinklies* People in their 20s during World War II. *Crinklies* Same as Wrinklies. *Silver market* People aged 60+.

(Contd)

Very young	Young/dynamic	Married	Established	Retired
Baby Busters Born just after original Baby Boomers generation so, in the 1990s, had less need of housing and goods.	*Road Warriors* Well-travelled executives – usually sales-persons.	*Minks* Multiple income, no kids.	*Markas* Middle-aged re-nester, kids away.	*Internots* Anti-webs cyber phobes.
		Puppies Previous young upwardly mobile pro-fessionals.	*Jolies* Jet-setting 49–59, free of financial worries.	*Dippies* Dual income pensione[rs]
	Crusty Lifestyle: rough clothes, matted hair.			*Farte* Fearful of ageing or retiring too early.
Current Boomers – *45–55* Baby Boomers resist 'growing old'. They offer the imaginative marketer a great opportunity to produce youth-oriented campaigns far longer than the traditional young/dynamic.	*Yuppies* Young upwardly mobile professionals.	*Islington Person* Social left winger.	*Whannies* We have a nanny.	*Guppies* Breed guppy fish.
	Y-people Y-person, Yuppie.	*Foodie* Hobby is food.	*Holiday Junkies* 'Hooked' on holidays.	*Grey Panthers* *Cocoons* *Golden Oldies*
	NETizen Member of Net Heads community.	*Tik* Two incomes with kids.	*Methuselah market* Rich – five years pre-retirement.	*Coffin Dodgers*
	Cybernaut Surfer. *Bimboy* Male bimbo.	*Muppie* Middle-aged urban pro-fessional.	*Power Bimbo, Killer Bimbo* Careerist, previous airhead.	*Wrinklies with Attitude*

Very young	Young/dynamic	Married	Established	Retired
Hence Baby Boomers will often be open to accept youth culture language and concepts.	*Cyberkids NetGen Grumpies* Grim ruthless upwardly mobile professionals.	*Tins* Two incomes, no sex.	*Lombard* Lots of money but a real dickhead.	*Grannies with Readies*
Sandwich generation Cares for ageing parents and children.	*Nummpie* New upwardly mobile media person fascinated with New Media marketing (pronounced Nu Me Yah).		*Fluffy Feminine* Loving, understanding, faithfully yours – typified anti-feminist wives of the late 1990s.	
The Millennials The *Millennium Generation Generation 2000 Echo Boomers The Baby Boomlet The Baby Clickers* Brought up in an era of clicks rather than actual writing pen.	*Hoho* Happy, optimistic, home owner.			

(Contd)

Very young	Young/ dynamic	Married	Established	Retired
	Inbetweeners They don't fit neatly in pigeon holes. *Generation P* The Pokémon Generation. *Generation Why* Why not? *Generation Next* The next generation that social researchers can't understand. *Bridger Generation* Bridging the gap between Xers and Boomers. *Net Generation* *The Dreamcast Generation* *Generation Wired*			

Remember: Connect with your reader's sensibilities through incorporating emotional sales propositions (ESPs).

Remember the four key factors that influence a person's positive or negative attitude towards a group or individuals, namely:

1 *Cultural issues.*
2 *Situational (or interpersonal) issues.*
3 *Historical and economic concerns.*
4 *Individual experience.*

Consider your reader's social or economic grouping – never write 'up' to them or 'down' to them – understand their motives and write direct to them, with empathy.

OVER TO YOU

▶ Visit two local supermarkets near home. Which specific audiences are they appealing to and how does their advertising encourage those people to shop?

▶ Look at three different adverts for mobile phones. In each case, what is the featured offer, as opposed to the distinctive benefit? Compare the three phones' SWOTs

▶ Go on the web and search for two popular insurance brokers. Rank each broker's distinctive benefits from sixth position to first place.

▶ Save two pieces of direct mail that you receive at home. For each piece, ask yourself:
  ▷ What's in it for the reader?
  ▷ Why is this service /product so different than any other on the market?
  ▷ How will it improve the reader's life/work/education/finances/health?
  ▷ Why can't the competition match it?
  ▷ What do they want the reader to do next?

4

··

Getting to grips with your copy

In this chapter you will learn:
- *how to understand grammar*
- *how to use copy techniques such as clichés and colloquialisms*
- *how to use punctuation*
- *how to develop headlines*
- *how to build bodycopy*
- *how to construct subheads*
- *how to develop slogans*
- *how to measure readability.*

Grammar and copy

Knowing how much of a stickler my English teacher was for precise grammar, I think that he would have given up on my sentence construction as a copywriter. Often, copywritten sentences are a complete grammatical nightmare. For example, an advertisement headline for a competitively priced laptop disk drive:

Drive. A Hard bargain.

Breaking up sentences like this makes use of an emphatic full stop (a full stop between two thoughts). The verb is separated. As it stands, the headline is intriguing enough to make you take a second glance and so, hopefully, lead you into the bodycopy – main text of your advertisement.

SELL VERSUS TELL

Copywriting is very different from formal business writing. It is primarily concerned with selling, whilst, for example, journalism is all about 'telling'. In great journalism, called, 'reportage', only the facts are told, so that the story is unbiased. The job of writing an eye-catching news headline or caption rests with the sub-editor.

The copywriter, on the other hand, has to consider the advertisement from every creative angle:

- *headlines*
- *sub-headlines*
- *bodycopy*
- *design*
- *illustration*
- *size*
- *frequency of appearance*

A copywriter can be likened to a musical composer who is also a conductor. The advertising message (the copy) is the musical score. It is up to the copywriter to ensure that every note in it is harmonious and keeps tempo.

USING CLICHÉS

Unlike other forms of writing, copywriting tends to rely on one of the all-time big 'no-noes' of correct grammar – the use of clichés.

Providing they are not overused, clichés help to make advertisements immediate. They provide impact and can stimulate action. Copywriters like them because they help to convey a message quickly. Flick through most mainstream magazines or newspapers. Before long, you'll probably come across one of the following advertising clichés:

Buy now	Act now
Exclusive offer	Yours free
Limited offer	Open now
Order now	At last

Of these 'yours free' used to be a sure-fire way to gain attention. However, thanks to the overwhelming flood of spam these days, writing 'yours free' in a subject line of an email will probably get your e-shots (emailings) stopped by firewalls. That said, wherever possible, try to get 'you', 'you'll' or 'yours' in the first paragraph of your copy.

In addition to literal clichés, consider visual clichés – but remember the old proverb, 'everything in moderation and nothing in excess', so don't automatically reach for pictures from photo libraries (especially if on closer examination they are exactly the same choices made by your competitors).

Did you know?

During the late 1950s the British Conservative party planned to run a series of advertisements featuring a photograph of a bright-eyed, ready-for-anything person waking up. The headline read: 'Get up and go with the Conservatives.' Everyone thought it was a good advert. However, just as it was about to run in the papers, someone noticed the bedside alarm clock in the photograph – the time on it was 09.45. Not exactly very get up and go! The entire advert had to be scrapped.

The moral: it's true, photography may offer detail that can never be matched by illustration. However, unless you pay attention to everything during the shoot, those details could be your downfall.

COMPARISON COPY

In the Victorian age, people were petrified of being drowned in sewage, hence the expression, 'I'm in it up to here'. Here are some more comparison copy lines. Try adding to them.

▶ *Copy comparing health*
  ▷ *Our relationship is dead.*
  ▷ *This book makes me sick.*

▶ *Copy comparing food*
  ▷ *That's a half-baked idea.*
  ▷ *She looks very tasty.*
  ▷ *I can't swallow your argument.*
  ▷ *It leaves a bad taste in my mouth.*

FIGURATIVE LANGUAGE

There are lots of useful literary devices at your disposal:

Similes
The fundamental key to writing a powerful simile is to feature the words 'as' or 'with'. The real 'trick' however is to ensure that any comparisons are directly connected with either the product or service, visual, or target audience's needs or emotions.

The following is an example of a great simile:

> *Business without advertising is like winking at a girl in the dark; you know what you're doing, but nobody else does.*

This one allows the copywriter to demonstrate to the reader a real empathy about having a thumping headache:

> *Does your head feel like a bucket of wet sand?*

Whilst the following two examples are technically similes – they simply don't 'feel' right. Firstly they are tired and secondly they don't actually mean anything:

> *Are you as busy as ants at a picnic?*

> *Is your copywriting as dull as cold tea?*

So, when writing a simile, never forget to check the meaning, connection to the audience and of course subject, as well as ensuring that wherever possible it demonstrates a sense of originality.

Metonymy

In metonymy the name of one thing is applied to something with which it is closely associated. For example, 'the turf' stands for horse racing and 'the crown' stands for a monarch.

Metaphors

A metaphor signifies one kind of thing, quality or action applied to another without expressing a relationship between them. For example, 'She drank in every word'. In this way, metaphors draw resemblances such as:

▶ *a tiger = ferocious person*
▶ *a pussycat = gentle person*

Like similes, they paint pictures with words and so add vigour to your range.

Homophones

Homophones are words that sound the same (or similar) but are spelled differently. For example:

▶ *The finest Scottish whisky is kept under loch and quay.*
▶ *Hire cars at lower prices.*
▶ *Spend £10 at Virgin and get a Young Person's Rail Card for a tenor.*

Homonyms

Homonyms are two words with the same meaning. They first appeared within English language in the seventeenth century. For example:

▶ *Have you seen the light? (To advertise a new brand of torch.)*
▶ *Enjoy the lighter side of life. (To advertise a diet plan.)*

Alliteration

The repetition of letters, words or syllables, has the same kind of effect as one of those niggly tunes you can't seem to get out of your head. Eventually the message becomes deeply embedded. Every time your reader thinks of a particular type of product or service, thanks

to alliteration your slogan comes to mind. This technique is
even more effective if the slogan is written as a musical jingle.
For example:

> *You can't put a better bit of butter on your knife.*
> *(To advertise Countrylife butter.)*

Oxymorons and chiasmus

As a word, 'oxymoron' comes from the Greek word meaning
'keenly foolish' or 'sharply dull'. From this you can see that
an oxymoron is a figure of speech or expressed idea in which
apparently contradictory terms appear in conjunction. They are
useful for copy in speeches. Examples are 'plainly magnificent',
'horribly wonderful', 'simply ingenious', 'clearly confusing'.

A chiasmus is the reversal in the order of words in two otherwise
parallel phrases. For example:

▶ *Never let a fool kiss you or a kiss fool you.*
▶ *A statesman is a politician who places himself at the service of*
the nation. A politician is a statesman who places the nation at
his service.

Synecdoche

'Synecdoche' derives from a Greek expression meaning 'to receive
jointly'. It relates to when the name of a part of something is used
to refer to the whole thing. For example:

▶ *She's all hands. (In an advert for a hand cream.)*
▶ *You're all heart.*
▶ *She's got ten mouths to feed.*

INTRODUCING IDIOMS

Idioms are great for brochures, leaflets or direct mail letters and
envelopes. They encourage readers either to open the brochure,
read further into the leaflet or dip into an envelope – all so that
they can complete the meaning of a sentence. Idioms add realism to
a message and often, at the same time, humour. For example,

a poster for a trichologist showing a balding man has the following slogan: 'Keep your hair on mate!'

Idioms can be used in a corporate context. For example, you're producing an advert for ScotsdaleNorth.com. Your idiom could be used as a strapline (or sign-off line) that appears at the foot of every ScotsdaleNorth.com advertisement.

You could choose something like:

▶ *ScotsdaleNorth.com – for goodness sake.*
▶ *ScotsdaleNorth.com – the net catch of the day.*
▶ *You're WWWelcome, any day of the week.*

Perhaps you want to advertise the ScotsdaleNorth.com's cyber-café division:

▶ *Where you, coffee and the web clicks.*

Alternatively, you could extend the idiom:

▶ *Where you click with coffee, the web, friends ... an entire network of good times and great surfing ... at a price you can afford.*

The specific use of straplines will be dealt with later in this chapter (see page 120).

COLLOQUIALISMS

Another thorn in the side of grammarians is the use of colloquialisms. Generally, mass-media advertising that directs itself towards the ordinary person in the street adopts a lot of colloquial language. It enables the copywriter to communicate to people at an informal one-to-one level. Colloquial use of language subtly tones down the advertising sales pressure. See for yourself:

The company would like to invite you to participate in viewing our new website.

Or:

Surf our site.

A word of warning about the use of colloquialisms. Usually there is little to gain from poor sentence construction 'just coz you reckon your audience is downmarket'. Plus, just because your words are correct, without substance and credibility your message becomes laughable. As T.S. Eliot so aptly put it, 'If we spoke as we write, we should find no one to read.'

PROVERBS

These should be used only if they are relevant to a product or service. The best way to use them is to add a different angle to their meaning. If ScotsdaleNorth.com wanted to advertise two chickens for the price of one, they could adapt a proverb, like this:

A bird in the shopping basket is worth two at the checkout.

CREATIVE PERSUASION

Copywriters walk a very fine line between overtly pushing a product or service and gently persuading a person to buy it. The art of persuasion is far more subtle than ram-raiding the sales message. On occasion, you will have to think of various indirect ways of making sure a product name is seen, or a message is heard, time and time again. Here are some ways of doing that:

▶ *Use direct or indirect repetition in the headline.*
▶ *Repeat your point in the picture caption.*

- *Repeat it in the bodycopy.*
- *Repeat it in the coupon.*
- *Repeat it in the strapline.*
- *Repeat it in a jingle.*
- *Let them hear what you have to say, first time. Your aim is to lead them to a buying conclusion every time.*

A classic way to slip in repetition is to turn a product name into a noun. For example:

Add style to letters. PenPal them.

This cutting of a word into a sentence is sometimes called a 'diacope' or 'tmesis'.

Gabay's 'Copywriters' Guide to Grammar'

**Every name is called a NOUN,
Such as Coke and Apple, even Nike Town;
In place of noun the PRONOUN stands
As in he and she design their stands;
The ADJECTIVE describes a thing,
Such as magic ad and marketing scheme;
The VERB means action, something done –
To read, to write, to jump, to run;
How things are done, the ADVERBS tell,
As quickly, slowly, badly, well;
The PREPOSITION shows relation;
as in the meeting or at the station;
CONJUNCTIONS join in many ways,
Sentences, words, or phrase and phrase;
The INTERJECTION cries out, 'Hey!
I need this brochure done today!'
Copywriters now know how each
of these make up THE PARTS OF SPEECH.**

COMMON GRAMMAR CONFUSIONS

Whose

'Whose' is a possessive pronoun like 'his', 'her' and 'our'.

I haven't seen David, whose brother is nine, for a long time.

It also means 'of whom' (but not 'of which') in questions:

Whose camera is this?

Who's

Who's is an abbreviated form of 'who has' or 'who is':

Who's going to pay for the damage?

Who/Whom

To choose correctly among the forms of 'who', re-phrase the sentence, selecting between 'he' and 'him'. If you want 'him', write *whom*; if you want 'he', write *who*.

Who do you think is responsible? (Do you think he is responsible?)

Whom shall we ask to the party? (Shall we ask him to the party?)

Give the box to whomever you please. (Give the box to him.)

Give the box to whoever seems to want it most. (He seems to want it most.)

Whoever shows up first will win the prize. (He shows up first.)

That or this?

That – from a distance.

This – closer.

That often refers to the past or something previously mentioned.

Which/that
Both are used in a defining clause.

The school which/that they attend.

Use 'which' for incidental information

The course, which was delivered by Gabay, made me think.

Which can be used to relieve 'that'.

His Ford: He remembered that that was the car which [not that] had run out of petrol on that motorway.

That/which
'That' is used with restrictive phrases. (A restrictive clause *restricts* the identity of the subject in some way. Introduce a restrictive phrase with the word 'that' and no comma. (When the subject is or was a person, use 'who' to introduce the clause.) Correct restrictive use:

The silver box that was on the table was taken away to be cleaned.

'Which' is used with non-restrictive phrases. Non-restrictive phrases state incidental information. For a phrase to be considered non-restrictive it will still make general sense even if the incidental information (between two commas) is removed from the sentence. Correct non-restrictive use:

The silver box, which was on the glass table, was stolen.

(Removing the incidental information) *The silver box was stolen.*

Further examples:

The book that you lent me is in my bag.

The book, which has a black cover, is in my bag.

You can also combine restrictive and non-restrictive clauses. This provides both limiting and non-limiting information about a subject in your sentence.

The black table that was in the library, which was opened in 2010, was broken.

The restrictive clause beginning with 'that' tells the reader that there was only *one* black table in the library and that it was *broken*.

The non-restrictive clause beginning 'which' tells the reader that this particular library was *opened in 2010*. However there may be *other libraries* as well.

Which/who
A noun referring to a group of people takes 'which', not 'who'.

In/at
'At' is traditionally used to indicate the name of a small place (village, district). 'At' is a more specific location than 'in'.

Did you know?
According to the Campaign for Plain English:

- *You may start a sentence with 'and', 'but', 'because', 'so' or 'however'.*
- *You may split infinitives (the most famous TV example of the last century comes from the movie series, Star Trek : 'To boldly go where no man has gone before.').*
- *You may repeat the same word twice in a sentence if you can't find a better word.*

CHECK YOUR SPELLING

Always check your spelling by reading through your copy. Don't rely on your word processor's internal spell-checking program. This is particularly important for website copy.

I have a spell cite programme
Its part of my win doze
It plainly marks for my revue
Ear ors I did knot no
I've run this poem on it
Its letter purr fact you sea
Sew I don't have too worry
My pee see looks after me.
The tills are alive with the sound of copy

Browse around your local High Street. Read the slogans on the posters and the leaflets, take a look at the product packaging, and just about everywhere you will find musical advertising alliteration:

▶ *Beans Meanz Heinz*
▶ *You can't fit better than a Kwik-Fit fitter.*
▶ *Save a buck. Rent a Duck. (slogan for US car rental company)*
▶ *anytime, anyplace, anywhere*

The possibilities of creative alliteration are enormous. A theatre group could use the technique like this:

▶ *Centre stage, centre attraction.*
▶ *Life. Whatever your stage we stage it on ours.*
▶ *Local theatre. Once you've booked, you'll be hooked.*

A charity could use the technique like this:

▶ *Every penny means ever so much.*
▶ *Show you care about the air. (environmental charity)*
▶ *Making it better by getting together. (charity to find parents for children)*

Grammar quick tips

▶ *Never use two words if one is enough.*
▶ *Never opt for a long word if a short word will do.*

(Contd)

- ▶ *Be specific – talk, not communicate.*
- ▶ *Check your words – computer program, not computer programme.*
- ▶ *Don't use bureaucratic banality – not 'in due course, the management board will inform you of its decision'; instead, 'we'll let you know'.*
- ▶ *Always veer towards the positive thought rather than the negative – 'You've won second prize in our contest', not, 'You have not come first in our contest'.*
- ▶ *Heu, modo itera omnia quae mihi nunc narravisti, sed nunc, Anglice. (Oy! Repeat everything you just told me, but this time in plain English.) We speak English, not Latin. Caesar est mortuus!*

Did you know?

Powerful copy is straightforward and understandable. This said, not all words from people in power are either clear or clear-cut.

'I mean a child that doesn't have a parent to read to that child or that doesn't see that when the child is hurting to have a parent and help neither parent's there enough to pick up the kid and dust him off and send him back into the game at school or whatever, that kid has a disadvantage.'

Former US President, George W. Bush

Punctuation

Advertising copy needs to be arresting and beguiling. At the heart of copy construction is punctuation. Long sentences are rare. Yet in certain circumstances, length can contribute to a sales proposition, especially when it is important to squeeze in a lot of relevant detail that enhances the product sale, leaving the prospect gasping for breath. This is ideal if, for example, you are promoting a medical charity and wish to demonstrate what it feels like to be an asthma sufferer.

Often, sentences are short.
Taken out of context.
Like building blocks.
Individually intriguing.
Collectively inspiring.

The use of ellipses can reinforce the tempo. For example:

> Now ... forever ... flowers say it all.

Short, sharp headlines with an emphatic full stop can make a proposition particularly arresting. Here are some:

> cheat on your wife.
> (don't let her know that the meal came out of a packet.)
> get ahead. change your head.
> (could be used for the PenPal product.) get stuffed.
> (ScotsdaleNorth's range of chicken stuffing?)

Refer also to page 97. This type of headline could work as a complete advert without any supporting bodycopy.

Using punctuation is using an artist's brush. At a stroke, you can create a highly complex picture or a simple one. You can surprise people.

Sentences could start with a lower case letter for particular effect.

They could incorporate a dropped initial capital letter or even an entire dropped word. (This particular technique is at least as old as Magna Charta.)

KEY PUNCTUATION MARKS

Full stop (full point)
A full stop separates statements between which there is no continuity of thought. However, in some cases the full stop has been erased from the copybooks altogether, such as when lists are shown in columns, as well as in abbreviations. For example:

9 a.m./9 am
U.S./US

Commas
Commas are used for a variety of reasons:

BRACKETING (OR ISOLATING) COMMAS
A 'pair' of bracketing commas is used to mark off a 'weak interruption' in a sentence. *The singer, in a solemn tone, sang a tribute song.*

Remove the bracketing comma and still the sentence would make sense.

The singer sang a tribute song.

Occasionally a 'weak interruption' belongs at the beginning of a sentence.

Taking the results of the campaign into account, the creative team was satisfied with the outcome of the advertising.

Some 'weak interruptions' appear at the beginning or end of a sentence, such as: after, although, even though, because, before, if, since, when, whenever.

Although the Cleveland Cavaliers beat Atlanta Hawks, the crowd hissed at Cleveland's key player – LeBron James.

LISTING COMMAS
The listing comma is mostly used to separate items in a list, replacing the word 'and' or 'or'. Generally there is no comma after the penultimate item in a list. However, if a comma clarifies the meaning – as is often the case if the items in the list are clauses or phrases – place the comma.

All of these are correct:

You can travel to Birmingham by train, coach or car.

My all-time favourite sports celebrities are Beckham, Woods, and the Williams sisters.

A listing comma can also be used between words that modify the same object.

His long, black, glossy hair attracted her.

The comma is only necessary if two (or more) adjectives are of the same type. For example, the comma is not necessary here:

A broken stained-glass window

JOINING COMMAS
Only use a joining comma if it follows a suitable connecting word. Typical connecting words (conjunctions) are: and, or, but, while, yet. For example:

I fancy a pint, and you can pour it for me.

The comma is not necessary if the sentences to be joined are short and closely linked.

He arrived and she left.

He asked her to marry him but she declined.

The colon (:)
A colon shows that what follows is an explanation, elaboration, exemplification, restatement or interpretation of what came before. It is regularly preceded by a complete sentence, though what follows may not necessarily be a complete sentence. A colon can also replace 'as follows', 'namely' and 'that is'. A colon is not normally followed by a capital letter.

Asher was sure of one thing: he would never kiss such an ugly girl.

The semicolon (;)

A semicolon joins two complete sentences into a single sentence, providing that the two sentences are closely related and are of equal samples. For example:

I know this book like the back of my hand; I wrote it.

The semicolon must be preceded by a complete sentence and followed by a complete sentence.

David played his fiddle loudly; the audience walked out in protest.

A semicolon may be used instead of a comma preceding a conjunction, where the emphasis is on the first sentence.

Truth ennobles the man; and learning adorns him.

The apostrophe (')

There are several instances when you would use an apostrophe. First in contractions (shortened forms of words from which one or more letters have been left out). For example:

it's – it is or *it has*

we'll – we will or *we shall*

aren't – are not

won't – will not

can't – cannot

In each case, the apostrophe appears precisely in the position of the missing letters.

Some words are still written with apostrophes even though they are rarely used in their full form.

o'clock – of the clock

THE POSSESSIVE APOSTROPHE

To indicate possession add *'s* to the end of a noun.

my brother's sister, the boy's shirt, a month's work

Note this common mistake made on in-store promotional copy:

Baker's Special not *Bakers Special*

When a noun is plural, the second '*s*' is not required.

Three weeks' time

However, be careful with words that are plural but don't have an '*s*' at the end.

children's not *childrens'*

people's not *peoples'*

women's not *womens'*

DOUBLE POSSESSIVES

The double possessive can help to distinguish between *a picture of my son* (the boy in the picture) and *my son's picture*.

The en dash (–)
Don't get this confused with the hyphen, which is a shorter dash. Its purpose is to show an interruption to the flow of thought.

Team, if we get this copy finished – and I don't doubt we will – we will paint this town red!

The en dash has four other uses:

1 *To show a sudden turn away from the original thought of the sentence.*
   Here are my two gerbils, Geoff and Crispin – hey, Crispin is stuck on his treadmill!
2 *To show hesitation or missing letters.*
   Er – um – oooh – I'm lost!
3 *In place of the word* to *in ranges of numbers and dates (except if the word* from *precedes the first date).*
   2005–2006 (but from 2005 to 2006)
   Jan–Feb
   Friday–Monday
   (Note that there are no spaces either side of the dash here.)
4 *To replace* and *or* to *where words linked together are of equal status and can be reversed without altering the meaning.*
   a writer–editor relationship

The hyphen (-)
This links together words that cannot stand alone and/or cannot be swapped around without altering the meaning. For example:

mother-in-law

twenty-five

non-specific

For new words coined with the prefix *e* denoting electronic, you should only use the hyphen when you have a strained connection or when the expression hasn't already been established. For example:

e-art, e-book, e-tailer

Once the expression has been accepted in common usage, you can drop the hyphen and close up the space. That is why email evolved as follows:

electronic mail, e-mail, email.

A hyphen can also be used when a word has to split over two lines. It is important to hyphenate compound modifiers which act as adjectives.

MJ gave Josh a high-five.

Without the hyphen, this would mean: mum gave her baby a *good night* kiss.

Other common adjectival forms to watch out for:

common-sense approach

part-time job

short-term plan

Inverted commas: single ('...') and double ("...")
These enclose direct speech or quoted material.

I'm not sure what is meant when the contract refers to 'other persons'.

Mrs Jones of Smethwick was pleased with her Wash-o-matic: 'It has changed my life!'

Note that when quoting direct speech, the closing punctuation mark goes within the quotes. It's entirely up to you whether you use single quotes or double quotes: it may depend on your company brand style.

Inverted commas (single or double, according to whichever style is your preference) are used to indicate titles of short poems, articles, chapter titles, song titles, titles of TV and radio programmes, such as 'Britain's Got Talent'. Note that titles of books, films, magazines, periodicals, long poems, albums, plays and TV series should not be in quotes but should be italic, and titles of holy books, such as the Bible and the Koran, should be in plain Roman text.

Quotation marks (single or double) need to be placed around the direct word(s) of a quotation. Quotation marks separate the writer from a word or phrase and show that the copywriter is using that word or phrase with a different meaning.

Brackets

PARENTHESES (ROUND BRACKETS)

Round brackets enclose comments or explanations that are an aside from the main topic of the sentence. Their contents should be so secondary to the main statement that if you were to remove them you would be left with no gap in either sense or punctuation.

Parentheses must always be in pairs. If a pair of parentheses is embedded within a sentence there should be no capital letter and no closing punctuation (with the exception of exclamation marks and question marks!) within the parentheses. If a sentence appears entirely in parentheses the closing punctuation should appear within the parentheses.

SQUARE BRACKETS

Square brackets are used to indicate that the matter within a quotation has been added by the author or editor.

'Mr Black said, [no, Mr White] he may need to clarify who or what the quotation is about.'

The question mark

This is used as closing punctuation for sentences that asks a question. For expressing incredulity or complete confusion you can use a double (??) or (?!), but use these sparingly: they lose their impact if used too often.

You can also place a question mark in brackets after a word or phrase in a sentence that seems to you questionable. For example:

He said he was delighted (?) that you're reading Teach Yourself Copywriting.

A question mark (unless followed by some other punctuation, such as closing quotation mark or bracket) should always be followed by a capital letter.

The exclamation mark
An exclamation mark (exclamation point in the US) conveys a strong emphasis.

You must be mad to want to join this company!

Your creative brief is a lot of nonsense!

Asterisks (*)
These are used in two instances:

When you don't want to offend the reader by showing a word in full and so likely to cause offence.

You B****y idiot, why don't you just shut your B****y mouth!

When you want to point out that supplementary information is available elsewhere in the document.

Bullet points
Just about every copywriter likes to condense sales messages into bullet points. The reasons speak for themselves:

▶ *It is the most direct way to summarize product benefits or features.*
▶ *It highlights the 'must know' aspects of a service.*
▶ *It helps the reader 'scan' copy.*

I like to restrict bullet point lists to no more than twelve points. Additionally I limit the points to only those that are absolutely relevant to the immediate topic. Bullet points should always be substantiated, either in the preceding paragraph or within the bulleted sentence itself, and should be preceded by a colon. A list of sentence fragments needs no other punctuation than a closing full point. However, if one or more of the points is a complete sentence, each bullet point should start with a capital letter and end with a full stop. Where there is a mixture of complete sentences and sentence fragments, each bullet point should start with a capital letter and end with a full point, rather than mixing punctuation systems.

The slash (/)

This oblique mark has limited uses.

- *To indicate options: An author may sometimes use male and female pronouns in the combination he/she to avoid upsetting his/her audience.*
- *To separate lines of verses when they are run on in the text rather than being set on different lines: Mary, Mary quite contrary/How does your garden grow?/With silver bells…*
- *To abbreviate certain words: a/c means account.*
- *In place of the word 'per' in measures: km/h means kilometres per hour.*
- *To show a 'year' that does not run from 1 Jan to 31 Dec. For example: the 2003/04 football season.*

A space should not be left between the slash and the words either side of it.

The ellipsis (…)

This has three uses:

- *It shows that some material has been left out of a direct quotation: In court, the account director went on and on … explaining this and that …*

- *It shows that the sentence is unfinished: The best movie I ever saw was …*
- *It can show that a series of, say, dates continues following the established pattern: Regular payments at two-month intervals as follows: January, March, May …*

Avoid using the ellipsis mark as well as 'etc.': they both perform the same function, i.e. to show that the list is incomplete. Likewise, never use 'for example' in conjunction with 'etc.'

Capitals
Use for proper nouns and for the beginning of sentences, paragraphs and headings.

Proper nouns are recognized names of people, places and organizations. For example:

Archbishop John Smith

Oxfordshire

Some words can be both a noun (such as 'government', 'police') and a proper noun (*The Tory Government, Metropolitan Police*).

Avoid using capitals for emphasis.

Numbers
Feature words for numbers up to and including ten and numerals for numbers over ten.

Avoid starting a sentence with a numeral even if it is over ten; write the number in words instead.

Use numerals for figures that include a fraction or a decimal (4.75, 33/4). Use words for fractions unless they are attached to whole numbers: two-fifths, but not 2.5, 2²/₃, or two and two-thirds.

Percentages

Use 'per cent' rather than the % symbol. Only use the % symbol in tables, lists, graphs and so on. Avoid expressing numbers such as *50 per cent, 25 per cent, 75 per cent,* too often. Instead write *half, a quarter,* etc.

INTERNATIONAL/US GRAMMAR AND SPELLING

Note, if you are working on something for an international market, please check for any local grammatical variations. For a detailed explanation of grammar and its rules for the US market, please read *Gabay's Copywriters' Compendium* (or see www.gabaywords.com).

Classic copy structure

As explained on pages 27–8, the ideal all-embracing copy structure follows the A-B-C-D principle:

- ▶ *Your headline (Attention – proposition).*
- ▶ *Your lead-in paragraph (Build-in – relating to your proposition).*
- ▶ *Your main argument (Conviction – which can incorporate bullet points to hammer home substantiated benefits).*
- ▶ *Your lead-out paragraph (Deal – relating in some way back to the main proposition).*

In brochure writing, this structure is adapted to become a series of plots within a plot. Each plot has a similar make-up: proposition lead-in, main argument, lead-out, but this time the proposition can be a sub-headline.

HEADLINES AS PICTURE CAPTIONS

Headlines should never be literal explanations of what is clearly visible in pictures. However they can refer indirectly to a picture, drawing attention to certain of its elements.

The headline could answer questions such as these:

▶ *Who's in the picture?*
▶ *What is the person doing?*
▶ *What is the product?*
▶ *In a word or two, what makes it all relevant?*

Virtually everyone reads the first two or three words in a headline. Only 70 per cent of people will read six or seven words. Thereafter attention begins to go astray. The only exception to this rule is direct marketing copy, where the figures are sometimes different.

As you will learn in Chapter 6, response advertising often makes use of time and space to convey a story involving the reader. You will find lots of examples of long copy headlines in direct response material. They offer two advantages over the shorter pithy lines:

1 *There are millions of short, pithy headlines. A longer one helps to make an advertisement outstanding.*
2 *A longer headline can be viewed as an expanded lead-in to the bodycopy, luring the reader deeper into the text.*

For example, I once wrote the following headline:

> 355,024 people aged over 50 didn't plan to check their pension values on our site. Sometimes life doesn't always go to plan ...

This approach enabled me to stir sufficient curiosity to stimulate the reader's interest and to complete the story in the text.

Even if your message is refined to only two or three words, there's no point in writing an arresting headline if it isn't relevant to your message. Create a headline which delivers an immediate and relevant benefit to the consumer: anything else is just icing on the cake (and nine-and-a-half out of ten times make sure you get to the point in your opening paragraph).

Grabbing the market share

Your copy must hold the reader's attention. Let's take a look at what stories appeal to people.

UNIVERSAL FILM PLOTS

According to popular belief, there are only eleven Hollywood scenarios.

1 **Love.** *Boy meets girl, loses girl, wins her back.*
2 **Success.** *The lead character has to succeed at all costs.*
3 **Cinderella.** *An ugly duckling is transformed into a perfect human being.*
4 **Triangle.** *Three characters in a romantic entanglement.*
5 **Return.** *An absent lover, father or spouse returns after wandering off for years.*
6 **Vengeance.** *A lead character seeks revenge.*
7 **Conversion.** *Bad guy turns into a good guy.*
8 **Sacrifice.** *The lead character gives everything up for their or someone else's good.*
9 **Family.** *The interrelationship of characters in a single place or situation (e.g. a hotel, prison, office).*
10 **Jeopardy.** *A life-and-death situation exploiting adeptness and survival instincts of the lead characters.*
11 **Forbidden.** *Liaison gay relationships, incest and other social taboos.*

UNIVERSAL NEWS STORIES

In journalism, the news list is longer, including:

1 *Natural disasters*
2 *Man-made disasters*
3 *Sex*
4 *Commercial gains*
5 *Commercial losses*

6   *Political gains*
7   *Political losses*
8   *Murders*
9   *Suicides*
10 *Law and disorder*
11 *War*
12 *Political rebellion*
13 *Scandal*
14 *Mr or Mrs Good/Bad*
15 *Social struggles*
16 *Royalty*

UNIVERSAL COPY THEMES

Advertising's key list of attention motivators is shorter in length but infinitely greater in substance. There are eleven underlying headline themes:

1   *Question*
2   *Directive*
3   *Comparison*
4   *Challenge*
5   *Invitation*
6   *Promise*
7   *Anticipation*
8   *Location*
9   *Representation*
10 *Demonstration*
11 *News-making*

Using headlines

QUESTION HEADLINES

Who?
There are two ways to use the 'Who?' approach in headlines.

1 *Simply include 'Who' in the headline: who knows what chips kids love best?*

2 *Alternatively think of 'who' in terms of testimonials. Such endorsements can add credence to your copy. However when writing them on behalf of someone, ensure that they sound realistic and always seek permission to include them in your copy.*

CAN I QUOTE YOU ON THAT?

Copywriters often use well-known quotations as an emergency exit out of a difficult project when they cannot find anything original to say.

Sometimes 'Who?' headlines refer to historical or fictitious characters. Use this technique only if it is relevant.

'Why?' 'Which?' and 'How?'

Questions should act as a kind of mental tickling-stick, to tease your audience:

Would you like to get 20,000 euros a week for nothing?

The headline achieves three things:

1 *It poses a question.*

2 *Taking account of human instinct, you can make an intuitive stab at the likely response: 'Yes, but what's the catch?'*

3 *Based on the question you have put and the response you expect, you can proceed with the bodycopy which shows there isn't any catch – just benefits.*

One of the dangers of writing question-led answers is the question that answers itself. For example:

Would you like some life insurance?

Are you overweight?

'Yes' or 'No' answers choke the interest factor at birth. One way to avoid this is to answer the question in a subhead:

> *Are you overweight? Call us on 08700 123 124 - we'll save you pounds the moment you dial.*

Whenever possible try to edit out superfluous words creatively:

> *Overweight? Call 08700 123 124 – save pounds – in more ways than one!*

When questions make answers

You can turn many a bland statement into a powerful sales message, just by adding 'why', 'where' or 'how'.

> *We sell the greatest range of palm-held computers*

Add the word 'Why' and it lifts off the page:

> *Why we sell the greatest range of palm-held computers*

Compare also:

> *Build a 6GB PC*

Versus:

> *Here's how you can easily build your own 6GB PC*

DIRECTIVE HEADLINES

Don't walk on the grass!
Clean your teeth!

Eat your greens!
Stop biting your nails!

What makes people listen to one instruction and ignore another? If you aggressively order people about simply to shock them into doing something, often all you achieve is their doing the opposite – just to spite you.

Use verbs as persuasive tools. Wherever possible, consider the use of verbs in a headline. Not every headline features a verb. You may prefer to imply one.

Here is a headline referring to PenPal's durability and reliability. The text could appear as though it has been written on a piece of paper that stretches for miles:

Yours, PenPod.

Verbs add impact to a headline. For example, ScotsdaleNorth. com announce a new phase of anniversary celebrations. The press release (for more information, see pages 283–93) is headed:

ScotsdaleNorth.com News.

This could be spruced up considerably:

ScotsdaleNorth.com. News that's worth celebrating!

COMPARISON HEADLINES

Historically, comparison headlines work particularly well for diet plans, when the advertiser wishes to demonstrate differences in appearance before and after participating in the plan.

One trick to highlight how the 'after' result has had a dramatic effect for the user of your product or service is to show the 'before' appearance in its worst possible light. If you are promoting a dieting programme, the person in the 'before' shot will be wearing something dull and unattractive. In the 'after' shot, the same person wears something fetching and eye-catching.

Comparison ads work well with inanimate objects too. For example, ScotsdaleNorth.com wants to show how it includes more biscuits in packets than competitors. The ad could feature a substantial pile of Scotsdale biscuits on a plate alongside a plate with the competitor's biscuits.

Similarly, an HD video player manufacturer wishes to demonstrate the durability and quality of its product compared to other manufacturers' players. There are two pictures (a) and (b):

(a) shows a clear TV picture clip of the Titanic; (b) has a fuzzy TV picture clip of the Titanic.

The headline reads:

> Should Titanic leave you feeling all washed up?

A drawback of comparison-type headlines is that they can be construed as 'knocking the competition'. In the UK, such tactics can lead to lawsuits. Of course, you may wish to create a stir in the marketplace and invite public relations coverage (so-called PR advertising).The best way to avoid this is to have evidence ready to support your claim – in case you are challenged.

CHALLENGE HEADLINES

> We bet you that after two weeks of switching to brand X you will forget your regular brand.

The only way a customer can dispute the claim is to pick up the gauntlet and accept your challenge. There are several methods to help you enliven challenge headlines. One is the blindfold test approach in which the identities of the product and that of your competitors are concealed until the results are presented. Often blindfold testing produces surprising results.

For example:

	Open	Blind
Prefer Pepsi	23%	51%
Prefer Coke	65%	44%
Equal/Can't say	12%	5%

(Source: *Relationship Marketing*, by Christopher, Payne and Ballantyne)

Apart from highlighting people's perceptions about the drinks, this table also demonstrates the power of brand loyalty (see 'Give your troops brand names', page 38).

INVITATION HEADLINES

Everyone enjoys an invitation to something special. Invitation headlines work particularly well for launches or in conjunction with demonstration headlines.

> Test drive our latest car.
> Be one of the first to visit our new cyber café.

Invitation headlines can be improved when they incorporate a reward for accepting the invitation.

> *Test drive our latest car and you could win it in a prize draw.*
> *Visit our internet café – next time, your surf'n'turf is on us.*

In these examples the offers are implicit. You could also withhold an element of your offer, either for further explanation within the bodycopy, or to be completely realized when the invitation is accepted:

> *Take it for a spin around the block and keep the keys.*
> *A great deal, a perfect meal, compliments of the chef.*

PROMISE HEADLINES

A promise headline obliges the advertiser to offer guarantees on the product or service. A guarantee is a legal commitment that must be honoured. So, if you decide to make a guarantee, you have to be specific about its duration, value and restrictions. You also have to ensure that any promise doesn't affect standard consumer rights.

Some may say cynically that guarantees create more loopholes than sales. The answer is, it depends on how you phrase your guarantee. You don't want to end up with a headline that is two pages long and includes numerous clauses. Nor do you want to design an advert with more small print than bodycopy.

ANTICIPATION HEADLINES

An old vaudeville magician once said, 'To grab an audience, keep them waiting and they'll come back for more.'

Keeping your advertising audience waiting almost contradicts the 'get the message quick' approach of headlines. But it works! Place your product in an impossible situation. For example:

- ▶ *You want to demonstrate PenPal's amazing strength. So why not drive over it with a Jumbo jet?*
- ▶ *You want to demonstrate the creamy thickness of one of ScotsdaleNorth's yoghurts. Why not 'load' the product with lots of fruit that defies gravity by nestling on the yoghurt's surface?*
- ▶ *You want to demonstrate the strength of a piece of string. Why not suspend a 26-stone woman in a bikini from it?*

Alternatively, feature a headline that can be appreciated by very few – no one else will understand the proposition. Usually these types of headlines have the 'niggling itch effect'. They work well with youth brands or drinks. The consumer sees the advertisement and, not wishing to appear stupid, makes every effort for it to appear to their peers that they understand the message. So the puzzled consumer starts to 'scratch' away at the obscure message.

That's why you may get a beer advert wrapped up in riddles. Then when you go to the pub to order a beer, you will find a certain group of people adopting the beer not just as a refreshing drink, but as a statement that reflects a social attitude.

Another anticipation headline technique is the 'taste of the things to come' approach:

The chocolate bar that looks so good you could eat it off the page. The holiday that looks so relaxing you can't wait to get onto the beach.

Finally, you could try the leading …

… **teaser headline** *(a technique formally known as 'enjambment').*

This works best for mailing pieces where the headline may start on the outer envelope …

… and conclude as you open the envelope.

The technique is similar to a greetings card device – many greetings cards rely on leading headlines:

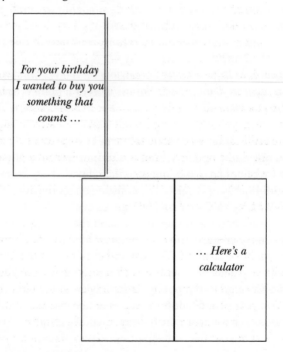

For your birthday I wanted to buy you something that counts …

… Here's a calculator

LOCATION HEADLINES

Perception, like desire, is at first all in the mind, then the heart. Create distinctive imagery (like a world made up of sweets for a confectioner) or actual locations (like an Apple Store) where your brand has the freedom to excel. Location headlines can be useful when you want individual brands to be perceived as being part of a bigger family of products and services.

As you have already learnt (see 'The Elvis factor' and 'The G spot', pages 36–7), brands should be able to stand alone as well as when looked at as part of a whole.

Did you know?

One of the ultimate brand locations must surely be Disneyworld or Disneyland. Here, individual brand items, such as specific film titles with unique characters, club together with carnival rides and attractions to produce a global parent brand with a cultural following all of its own.

Of course, with the economy being what it is these days, you may not be able to spare the odd couple of billion pounds to build a themed location at the moment! In advertising terms, it doesn't matter. Many world leading brands have used advertising to create artificial locations that are just as evocative as the real thing. Alcoholic beverage brands often conjure up a paradise island where their drinks are served all day.

REPRESENTATION HEADLINES

Now you have conjured up your magical land of Oz, show your prospective buyer around. You can either maintain the momentum of imaginary places by inventing a character or feature yourself or your client in the advertising. In general, you should avoid the latter. You and your client may not have appearance or delivery that comes over well, especially on screen. There are exceptions to the rule. For example, a fashion buyer's explanation of why a certain line of suits caught her eye can be effective.

Occasionally, you will come across a client who has what it takes to appear sincere in every medium. However, I advise you to remain cautious. Instead, feature professionals who can arouse a prospective consumer's imagination. An imaginary land gives you the opportunity to paint a vivid picture of a type of utopia; it makes sense to use an imaginary escort to guide consumers through it.

Catering companies invent everything from a person made of dough to one formed from liquorice. Animated characters can show perfect facial characteristics. The combined detachment from reality and precision use of facial expressions as part of the animation process may enhance the impression and message of fun that you want your brand to leave on a prospect.

Did you know?

Highly successful animated characters have included giants, walking milk bottles, dancing credit cards, singing raisins, marching toothbrushes, flying sprays of polish and a variety of others.

Imaginary characters need not be animated. Some of the world's longest-running advertising campaigns have been built around fictitious characters played by actors. For example, advertisements featuring the 'ideal' couple who try to build a sustaining relationship over a cup of coffee.

Did you know?

One of the most famous of all classic advertising characters is the man in the Hathaway shirt. (The eye-patched man has a sophisticated lifestyle that meant he always had to be suitably attired – in a Hathaway branded shirt.)

Fictional and non-fictional brand characters

Captain Birds Eye

Yes, he existed! His name was Clarence 'Bob' Birds Eye and he was a New York furrier.

John West
Yes again! He was Scottish and set up a canning factory in Oregon in 1873.

Uncle Ben
No such person – sorry. The face is that of the maître d' at a Houston hotel.

Captain Morgan
Yes, he existed. He was Governor of Jamaica, was knighted by Charles II and renowned for piracy.

Mr Kipling
He never existed, but he does make exceedingly good cakes.

DEMONSTRATION HEADLINES

Ask vacuum cleaner salespeople how to impress a prospective buyer and they'll tell you to throw a binful of rubbish on your lounge carpet. The real shock for the prospect is that the vacuum cleaner tidies up the mess in minutes, leaving not even a speck of dust behind. Demonstration headlines are closely related to anticipation headlines – they feature the product in an unusual setting. For instance, a brand of glue may be shown as sticking a man to a flying plane.

Did you know?

One of the best forms of media for demonstration headlines is the television. Here you can play out an entire scenario in front of an audience. (See Chapter 8 for more about television.)

NEWS-MAKING HEADLINES

Did you interpret the heading immediately above as 'advertising makes the headlines'? If so, you read it correctly. If not, you are still right. Many believe that advertising sets trends. For 99.9 per cent of the time, this is nonsense. Advertising panders to society's needs by using an understanding of how people see their roles in society. Copywriters listen and watch trends. Topical headlines can either be directly or indirectly connected to a company. Directly topical headlines could refer to specific use of the product in a news-making context.

For example, you supply the oil for a Grand Prix winning vehicle, so you write a headline that refers to the great race.

A topical headline could also be associated with the current news. For instance, a national football team wins the World Cup. ScotsdaleNorth.com could refer to it in the following headline:

> *Congratulations England from one league leader to another.*

Topical headlines give the impression that a company is part of a community. They provide scope for humour, compassion and corporate social responsibility.

I mentioned a 99.9 per cent chance that advertising does not set trends – what about the 0.1 per cent chance that it does? Sometimes advertisers create risky advertising that is meant to be banned and make headlines (so-called PR advertising). At other times advertisers use themes that suddenly become fashionable, such as a particular piece of music. However, even in these cases you generally find that the advert is based on a variation of a published or known theme. When ads are just plainly shocking for their own sake, that is called 'adsterbation'.

HEADS YOU WIN

I can't leave the world of headline propositions without discussing one of its most fascinating aspects: word pictures (metaphors). These impress a product personality on the reader. In addition to highlighting a benefit, they set the agenda for the advertisement's tone of voice.

Here are examples:

▶ *Does your mobile leave your ears ringing?*
▶ *Is your wallet burning a hole in your pocket?*

Word pictures match elements of a product's name or use with the situation or location that you place it within. So, for example, you may wish to present a relaxing ferry journey. Headline:

The not so cross ferry.

(Picture of contented passenger alongside frustrated passenger.)

A variation is a combination of two separate words into one message. Here are some possible examples:

Smoke Ring:
Message: Give up smoking, dial this number.

Action Replay:
Message: Action-packed mobile phone game that you'll want to play time after time.

Air Lift:
Message: New kind of hydraulic elevator system.

Weather Eye:
Message: All-weather eyewear protection.

Ironing Board:
Message: Company's own management tests a new iron.

Vampire Bat:
Message: High-impact cricket bat.

Help Line:
(Picture: Hook and line picking up a phone.)
Message: Fisherman's help line.

Never confuse word pictures with puns (homophones).
Puns are overused and often poor substitutes for clear messages.
Don't toy with sentences for no other purpose than to make
something sound funny when it is clearly not. One of the crudest
puns I have ever seen was for a scaffolding company whose
trade advertisement's headline read: 'Satisfaction guaranteed
with every erection.'

Unlike puns, word pictures open doors to creative writing.
Once you enter into a proposition, bodycopy completes the story.

Nitty-gritty quick tips

- *Design your advertisement to gain the maximum impact on the page.*
- *Invest time in creating a powerful headline.*
- *People read or reject a headline within one-and-a-half seconds.*
- *There are eleven basic film plots.*
- *There are about seventeen journalistic plots.*
- *There are eleven underlining headline themes.*
- *Testimonials must sound realistic.*
- *Quotations can be an excuse to avoid writing something original that's quotable.*
- *Wouldn't you use a leading question to direct a prospect to a sale?*
- *Persuading a prospect is different from pushing a prospect.*
- *Consider writing 'before and after' creative copy.*
- *If a product is difficult to sell set a challenge.*
- *Invite your prospect to view the product before buying it.*
- *All prospects are VIPs – Very Important Prospects.*
- *Guarantee your proposition.*
- *Make your product or service something that's worth waiting for.*
- *Position your product or service in a special unique location.*
- *Add product personality by inventing a unique character.*
- *Demonstrate your product or service.*
- *Advertising doesn't invent, it innovates.*
- *Link words to create pictures.*

Understanding bodycopy

Without bodycopy a firm sales proposition has no substance.

One of the most common questions asked about bodycopy is, 'How long should it be?' There are three interlinked replies:

▶ *As long as it takes to convey all the information.*
▶ *The greater the commitment that is sought, the longer the copy.*
▶ *Finally, as long as it takes until you are bored of writing.*

Let's look at the implications of these answers in more detail.

Your headline, accompanied by a suitable visual, provides the carrot that entices the reader into your message. The bodycopy supplies the detailed reasons why a buyer needs to make a purchase or take appropriate action.

Depending on your requirements, you need either to identify a product or service or to provide information about a product or service. Your bodycopy should be adapted accordingly.

1 *In the case of identifying products or services, strong headlines and visuals usually suffice. Examples are posters and bodycopy for impulse purchases such as sweets or household detergents. In-store posters are specific examples.*
2 *In the case of providing information about a product or service, bodycopy takes the lead from headlines. Informative advertising needs to convey the benefits of a product or service. Good examples of this are web-based or financial products. Often business-to-business advertising also relies on longer copy.*

COPY WITH CONVICTION

Believe me, your mood can always be 'read' in the copy you write. Too often copywriters let themselves and the communication down by writing over-long copy just to fill the space. If you are sincere, the copy will sound sincere. If you are blasé, the copy will appear crass.

Another cause of unbelievable bodycopy is unbelievable claims. Few will suppose that a particular item will change their lives, especially if your bodycopy oversells the product. There is an exception to this rule: in order to draw attention to your product, adopt the technique of overtly overselling. This is often used by American-style car salespeople who may make claims such as:

> *Our deals are so good that if you don't buy we'll eat the car!*

Direct claims from a product supplier or manufacturer can also sound feeble when compared to endorsements from users of the product or service. (Also read the section 'sell vs tell' in the section 'There's no place like home', page 274.)

Here is an extreme example of a manufacturer overselling a product:

> *One sip of our health drink will make you feel pukka.*
> *One sip of our competitor's drink will make you puke.*

For sure, someone somewhere will buy your drink. However most won't touch it. If you want to keep a customer for life, not just the moment, keep your claims credible and people will come back again and again.

BODYCOPY STRUCTURE

The first sentence of your bodycopy (also known as the lead-in sentence) is the second most important part of your main text (the most important is the call to action). The lead-in sentence links your headline with the rest of your piece. It's as if your headline is a shop window and the bodycopy is the showroom that has all the gadgets ready to be discussed by a salesperson. (If you want to go into a lot of further detail, you'll need a brochure.)

Get to the point, lead your prospect to all your benefit points. For example:

> ScotsdaleNorth.com are opening a new chain of cyber cafés
> called Directions.
> Headline:
> Wild West grub?
> Far Eastern chow?
> Southern fried chicken?
> Northern hospitality?
> Subhead:
> it all points to us ...
> Lead-in sentence:
> When you're peckish and just can't decide which food
> matches your mood, head to the one place that has it all:
> Directions.

Here is how *not* to write your lead-in sentence:

> *Fresh food and great surfing can be found in our*
> *new café called Directions.*

COPY PROGRESSION

Copy needs to flow logically. A good test is to remove one of the sentences from a paragraph. If the following sentences still add up to a reasonably plausible message, your copy flow hasn't spilt off the page.

Now, prioritize product benefits in the order you want them read. Here are some of the benefits of ScotsdaleNorth's Directions chain of cyber cafés:

1 *Locations throughout the country.*
2 *Cheap surfing.*
3 *Terminals at every table.*
4 *Diners at tables can email each other.*
5 *Delicious food from all four corners of the world.*

6   *Reasonable prices.*
7   *Special pre-measured portions.*
8   *Excellent service.*
9   *Tempting dishes for the young and not-so young.*
10 *Different speciality menu every day.*
11 *Cool decor.*

Depending on where your advertisement appears, your bodycopy should concentrate on a suitable feature. If your advertisement appears in a family-style publication, benefit 9 in the above list – 'Tempting dishes for the young and not-so young' – may take priority.

Address arguments before the questions start.
Consider how each sentence affects subsequent ones and, more importantly, how each proposition or benefit feature creates a possible response that is against it.

For example, you want to address families using their cars for long journeys:

Headline:

> If you're feeling peckish pull off at
> junction 21and fill the Watford Gap.

(Picture of a family in a car. One of the kids is acting wild. Another looks glum. The front passenger is trying to placate everyone and the driver is looking desperate.)

Bodycopy:

When you're stuck in a five-mile tail-back and the kids are screaming for lunch, you need a new direction – pronto.

What are you going to do about it?
Look out for the special Direction Compass sign and you'll be just a junction away from a satisfying meal that all the family will relish.

What's so satisfying about it?
Directions is the internet café that's right up your street.
Our scrumptious dishes are selected from all four corners
of the world, including Wild West feasts and Far Eastern
specialities.

Is there anything else that's special?
You can choose from three types of order.

The Hearty Filler – ideal for a wholesome snack.

The Big Deal – big on portions, small on price.

The Giant Slayer – a massive portion that will knock your eyes
out and fill even the biggest appetite.

Sounds expensive. What does it cost?
Just because we serve the best choice of food from around the
world, it doesn't mean that our prices are out of this world.
The Hearty Filler costs as little as £6.99. Even our Giant Slayer
starts from only £12.99.

I want some of that. What do I do next?
The next time you're feeling peckish, pull in and fill up at
Directions.

Where can I find it?
(Include a map or list of restaurant locations, web address and
telephone number.)

Writing for a specific audience

All professional copywriters are also copy-readers. Study previous
examples of corporate copy style. There are hundreds of ways in
which you can blend styles of copywriting. To simplify matters,
I have narrowed them down to half a dozen main types.

SIX ELEMENTS OF STYLE

1 **Get on with it.** *This picks up where the headline and visual left off. It prioritizes USP/PODs/ESPs and then explains each one at a time.*
    ▷ *A great panacea for all styles of bodycopy.*
    ▷ *Essential if you have a lot of benefits to convey.*
    ▷ *Maintains momentum.*

2 **View from the top.** *This takes a corporate view of a product or service. It concentrates on the ideology behind an advertised item rather than its immediate specifics.*
    ▷ *Often used by large corporate organizations.*
    ▷ *Helps boost confidence in a company.*
    ▷ *Waves the corporate flag.*
    ▷ *Useful to promote umbrella brands.*
    ▷ *Can be used in conjunction with public relations activities.*
    ▷ *Commonly used to imbue confidence in shareholders or financiers.*
    ▷ *Facts must be totally accurate.*
    ▷ *Exaggerations must be avoided.*

3 **Story line.** *This tells a narrative that develops into a discussion of your salient benefits.*
    ▷ *Ideal for lifestyle copy where feelings associated with a product or services are equal to, if not stronger than, features. For example, gold credit-card advertising often uses a story line (narrative copy) to describe a rich lifestyle.*
    ▷ *Pigeon-holes readers.*
    ▷ *Reinforces a company's corporate image.*
    ▷ *Can be written from the user's viewpoint or can be the writer's description of the user's viewpoint.*
    ▷ *A good story takes longer to express than a short description.*
    ▷ *Adds human interest to products or services.*
    ▷ *Helps you use emotive copy when there are not many benefits.*

4 **Character led.** *This method empowers the characters in your advertisement to introduce your message. Characters may include celebrities, end-users or even characters from comic strips.*
    ▷ *Covers testimonial bodycopy.*
    ▷ *Testimonials must be clear, plain and – above all – sincere.*
    ▷ *With permission, write a testimonial as a person would say it.*
    ▷ *Never write a testimonial that forces the celebrity or end-user to state something that they would not normally know. (e.g. 'I always write with a PenPal. The 30% oil in the ink means that it clings even to non-porous paper.' Yuk! It would sound more credible if you wrote 'This PenPal is great. It works anywhere.' Please refer to page xv.)*
    ▷ *Testimonials can be inferred through bodycopy style; you do not have to include a named person.*
5 **Different strokes.** *This method relies on unusual language such as poetry, humour and foreign words.*
    ▷ *It is rarely used, but particularly potent for bodycopy aimed at the youth sector of the market or when something quirky is required.*

> *There was a young writer from Kirk,*
> *Whose copy never quite worked.*
> *When someone asked why?*
> *He curtly replied,*
> *It's the brief,*
> *Not me, that's the berk.*

6 **Caption captured.** *This uses visuals such as photographs or illustrations, together with appropriate captions.*

Subheads and captions

You may have wondered why I did not include subheads and captions in the previous section about headlines. Well, they act as direction indicators within a bodycopy context rather than as conspicuous 'headline' signposts. Subheads allow you to segment your copy into specific areas of interest. They allow the reader to concentrate on bodycopy from anywhere within the piece of communication without disrupting the copy tracking or flow.

Subheads highlight key points of interest explained by the bodycopy. Captions for visuals either encapsulate the spirit of what is being shown infer an additional benefit. Subheads and captions should be short. They are like breaks beside a motorway. The longer your journey, the greater the need for a refreshment break and direction check. The shorter your journey, the lesser the need.

- ▶ *People read less nowadays than they used to and often rely on subheads or captions to complete the picture.*
- ▶ *If subheads or captions are not brief, they become chunks of bodycopy in their own right.*
- ▶ *As with lead-in copy, it is important that picture captions do not repeat what the visual shows.*
- ▶ *Too many subheads can slow down a message, especially when space is at a premium. So, before including subheads, think about how they will affect your flow of copy.*

Keeping your copy chatty

Too often business-to-business copy may seem stilted or distant. Some writers believe that big corporations deserve aloof, first-person-type language. On the contrary; the bigger the organization, the more intimate you should make your copy.

> *Just because we're big that doesn't mean that we're not personal.*

Actually, that line could be improved – particularly if the context is corporate-style advertising.

> *You are number one. That makes us count.*

If possible avoid using 'we'. Instead, use 'you'. If you have to use 'we', complement it with 'you'. As you will see later, this technique is particularly effective when incorporated in direct mail letters or e-shots.

Closing your bodycopy

Closing your bodycopy requires more than a final full stop. You need to tie up any loose ends and feel confident that your reader will know how to proceed further. If you are after a response, choose options such as website addresses, telephone numbers or coupons (see 'Off-the-page advertising', page 163). On the other hand, you may want to stimulate awareness or want the reader to have a good feeling about the company. Either way, you still have to close your proposition and leave the reader wanting to do something.

One of the best techniques for closing copy is to refer to the headline and lead-in copy. Turn the proposition into a full circle where the beginning leads to a middle, the middle leads to an end, and the end refers to the beginning. By this I do not mean that you should just keep your reader going endlessly around in circles. Instead use a subtle reminder of where the proposition kicked off. For example:

Headline:

We are 1
(Picture of huge birthday cake for the Directions cyber café chain, with a person about to blow out the candles.)

Lead-in copy:

365 days; 45,000 meals; 2,000,000 clicks; and we're still only one year old.

(Contd)

Bodycopy:

(Then, central explanation copy.)

Close:

Directions. First because of you – now that's really worth celebrating.

Straplines, slogans and other pay-offs

A slogan, also sometimes known as a strapline, is the last thing people read. Slogans add continuity to a campaign. They instil public confidence in a company. Finally, they act as a surrogate logo (a company's trademark) when logos are impractical (such as on radio commercials).

Slogans should be short. If possible under seven words, preferably three to five. Slogans are conversational. They need to be memory joggers.

In 2009 a website (adslogans.com) dedicated to studying slogans deconstructed the top 100 American slogans since 1948. They then listed the most common words mentioned in slogans:

1	you	11.15%
2	your	7.94%
3	we	6.03%
4	world	4.18%
5	best	2.67%
6	more	2.54%
7	good	2.43%
8	better	2.12%
9	new	1.90%
10	taste	1.85%

11 people	1.54%
12 our	1.49%
13 first	1.42%
14 like	1.41%
15 don't	1.36%
16 most	1.19%
17 only	1.16%
18 quality	1.15%
19 great	1.13%
20 choice	1.08%

As a fun, yet insightful exercise, I often get students to write a slogan using as many of the top twenty words listed above as possible – try it for yourself!

For my part, over the years, I have noted a dozen different slogan observations.

The twelve slogans of constructive persuasion

1 *Slogans are about you. Successful slogans tend to use the word 'you' somewhere in the copy. Occasionally they may feature 'we', but if they do the overall benefit is still aimed at 'you', the consumer.*
   Directions
   Your friendly cyber café.
   ScotsdaleNorth.com
   We always sell lower.

2 *Slogans make promises.*
   PenPal
   Reliability on paper.
   PenPal
   Quality you can sign your name by.

3 *Slogans call for action.*
   ScotsdaleNorth.com
   Click and enjoy.
   Directions
   com and get it.

4 *Slogans create ideals*
    PenPal
    The little pen that does it all.
    ScotsdaleNorth ice-cream
    Don't you wish every day was a Sundae?
    PenPal
    If only life were this simple.

5 *Slogans may rhyme.*
    ScotsdaleNorth.com
    Top for shops.
    Directions
    Meals that appeal

6 *Slogans are 'it'.*

Go for it.	*Buy it.*
It's here.	*It's now.*
It's more.	*It's less.*
It's forever.	*It's together.*
Stick it.	*You can't lick it.*
You can't beat it.	*You can't touch it.*
It's hot.	*Click it.*
Believe it.	*It's tasty.*
It's cool.	*It's the best.*
It's yours.	*It's everything.*
Try it, you'll like it.	*Be part of it.*
Live it.	*Help it help you.*

7 *Slogans are in a world of their own.*
    PenPal
    Step into a new writing dimension.
    Enter a new world of writing.

8 *Slogans can be full of alliterations.*
    ScotsdaleNorth.com
    Supremely Scottish Salmon.
    Buy better. Buy bigger, by far.

9 *To sell, slogans don't have to be clever.*
> *PenPal*
> *The best pen you can buy.*
> *The writer's choice.*

10 *Slogans conveniently package everything in one sentence.*
> *PenPal*
> *Affordable reliability in your pocket.*
> *ScotsdaleNorth.com*
> *A world of shopping from your PC.*

11 *Slogans repeat key word patterns.*
> *ScotsdaleNorth.com*
> *The right price. The best quality.*
> *PenPal*
> *The writing choice for the right occasion.*

12 *'The' slogan is king.*

The Best.	*The greatest.*
The One.	*The Shape.*
The Answer.	*The experience.*
The genuine article.	*The One you need.*
The industry's choice.	*The Professional's choice.*

Used subtly, slogans reinforce brand values. However, many adverts appear without slogans and are highly successful. (There is an argument that applying a slogan to a one-person business may be considered a little self-indulgent!) If you do have to work on a slogan, remember to keep it short and keep it sweet.

Measuring copy effectiveness

Bodycopy can be an uphill struggle to read. Over the years, various people have come up with methods or formulae to measure the readability of copy.

1 *Academics contributing to this field include C.R. Haas, who produced two significant formulae: one to highlight the readability differences between literary texts and advertising copy, and another to evaluate the effectiveness of advertising copy based on the relative number of verbs and nouns.*
2 *R. Gunning devised the so-called Fog Index. This was based on the average length of sentences and the percentage of words with three or more syllables.*
3 *The Dale-Chall Index was a formula based on a list of 3000 words most easily understood by at least 80 per cent of pupils in the fourth grade of post-World War II American schools. It took into account the average length of sentences.*

THE FLESCH FORMULA

One of the most commonly used readability tests is the Flesch formula, devised by Rudolph Flesch – an Austrian born in the USA (1911–86). Flesch is a good example to look at in greater detail.

Flesch provides a Reading Ease score based on four elements:

1 *The average number of words per sentence.*
2 *The average word length (number of syllables per 100 words).*
3 *Percentage of personal words.*
4 *Percentage of personal sentences.*

The Reading Ease (RE) score can vary between 0 and 100. It is inversely proportionate to the difficulty of the text that is being judged. The relationship between RE and difficulty is shown like this:

Level of difficulty	RE
Very difficult	Below 30
Difficult	30–49
Quite difficult	50–59
Average	60–69
Quite easy	70–79
Easy	80–89
Very easy	90 and above

Flesch's formula, which is adopted by most word processing grammar checkers, takes into account what many writers have always surmised: short sentences with short words are easy to read.

Flesch stressed the use of personal words and sentences to gain added reader interest. Personal words include words like 'guys', 'OK' and 'cheers' as well as personal pronouns and names. Personal sentences include spoken sentences with quotation marks as well as sentences addressed directly to the reader.

There are several drawbacks to Flesch's formula.

▶ *First, it only works if your bodycopy is fairly long.*
▶ *Next, it assumes that every target audience wants to read colloquial copy or that the copy fits within a mass-market category. Just because your copy achieves a high readability score, it doesn't necessarily follow that it is suitable for your target audience. If it did, every writer would produce pithy sentences with short words.*
▶ *Also, the formula doesn't work in broadcast media, where the spoken word reigns supreme.*
▶ *Finally, it fails to judge the sales effectiveness of copy. It may read well, but does it provoke the reader to buy?*

To its credit, the formula is a fair indicator that the bodycopy is either quite readable or too stuffy for most people. It also warns you about imprecise writing – you should use 'the company' rather than 'the team'. Finally, it helps you to keep an eye on the lengths of your sentences.

Copy fitting

There are several ways to ensure that your copy will fit snugly into a specified space. In the old days designers and typographers relied on copy-fitting tables. They were mathematical mazes. First, you had to measure character lengths. Next you had to find the right pica (a unit of measurement used in typesetting) for the selected character. Finally, you multiplied the number of characters to each pica by the length of line to be typeset. Nowadays virtually all writing software will do the job for you.

Body-building quick tips

▶ *Bodycopy should be either as long as the space that you have to write in, or as long as it takes to write a convincing and reasonable argument.*
▶ *A writer must put conviction into their own copy.*
▶ *Never oversell in your bodycopy.*
▶ *The first sentence of bodycopy is called the 'lead-in sentence'.*
▶ *Get quickly to the crux of your bodycopy message.*
▶ *Keep your line of thought on track.*
▶ *Address arguments before they arise.*
▶ *Write for your audience – not yourself.*
▶ *Remember the six elements of style (pages 116–17).*
▶ *Use captions as directions within the bodycopy.*
▶ *Keep your copy user friendly.*
▶ *Present your bodycopy in a logical sequence that relates to the rest of the text.*
▶ *Use one of the twelve slogans for constructive persuasion (see pages 121–3).*
▶ *One way to measure copy readability is to use the Flesch formula (see page 124).*

OVER TO YOU

▶ *List three standard film plots and three standard journalistic plots. Then, using six headline themes, write headlines for the previously listed plots.*

▶ *Apart from slimming products, list six other products or services which could use a 'before and after' technique.*

▶ *Write a list of ten word pictures.*

▶ *Write a headline that captures the spirit of:*
  ▷ *the Mona Lisa*
  ▷ *a traffic light.*

▶ *Write a headline that incorporates a witticism.*

▶ *Write six slogans that describe a friend.*

▶ *List twelve features of your left thumb.*

▶ *Write a linked headline, lead-in sentence and closing sentence about a paper clip.*

▶ *Write an advertisement that never actually hints at any form of direct sale for an encyclopaedia.*

▶ *Write six captions which could be read in sequence – without the support of bodycopy.*

Media and understanding its creative language

In this chapter you will learn:
- *how to gauge the effectiveness of media*
- *how to plan a media campaign*
- *how to write a classified ad*
- *how to write a recruitment ad*
- *how to write b2b copy*
- *how to use incentives*
- *how to write 'off the page' sales copy.*

The table below outlines the features of different sections of the press.

Medium	Creative pros	Creative cons
Trade magazines	Relevant readership. Long shelf-life.	Danger of too many magazines in each sector, which dilutes your creative impact.
	Readers are searching for new ideas and announcements. Opportunity to be endorsed by a market's own official journal.	Some magazines lose editorial credibility by featuring too many adverts – this adversely affects circulation figures.

Medium	Creative pros	Creative cons
	Opportunity to address decision makers in a market sector.	Danger of advertising perceived to be supporting favourable editorial write-ups.
	If the magazine is published monthly, you can take advantage of extra time to submit your final advertisement.	In comparison to some mainstream consumer magazines, some trade magazines may be hindered by inferior reproduction qualities.
	Often the chance to include loose leaflets. (Ideal when you want your copy to stand away from the crowd or when you have a longer story to tell.)	In markets which are represented by one title alone, advertising costs can be relatively high and creative use of space restricted.
Consumer magazines	Ideal for attracting consumer enthusiasts such as car buyers, the health conscious, the fashion conscious, and so on.	Popular magazines may impose long-term copy dates (the copy day is when advertisements must be submitted by).
	At the same time as attracting enthusiasts, you have a chance to broaden your readership.	Compared to newspapers, can be a costly way to reach an audience.
	A chance to blend innovative copy with the latest trendsetting fads and styles.	

(Contd)

Medium	Creative pros	Creative cons
	Often good reproduction for photography.	
	The opportunity to include loose or bound material inside the magazine.	
National press	Your message is reinforced by the credibility and urgency of news items.	You're up against lots of other ads.
	Excellent national coverage.	You need to feature in more than one paper to gain blanket national coverage.
	High believability factor.	
	A better chance of securing an innovative use of creative space on the page.	Depending on your design, creative impact can be enhanced or reduced by predominantly black-and-white advertisements.
		Poor colour reproduction in the main newspaper.
		Messages are flicked through rather than studied (except in week-end newspapers, as the reader has more time to enjoy them).

Medium	Creative pros	Creative cons
Local press	Good for targeting locals.	Reproduction can be poor.
	Loyal readership.	Too many free-circulation local papers hindering your message.
	Copy is often quite friendly in its approach.	
	Adverts can be big on a page while economical in cost.	Limited or non-existent use of colour.
		Editorial is often light in substance. (This has an adverse effect on the general creative quality of advertising.)
The Web	Fastest growing medium of all time. High personalization. Immediacy. Interactivity. Ideal for combining text with audio and video. Enlivens a brand message. The world's biggest direct marketing tool.	Intrusive. Can be difficult to navigate. Needs a PC or GPRS technology. Pages can be relatively slow to download (unless you can be sure your audience has 3G or broadband technology). Hyped up. Banner ads are often totally ignored.
Television	Reaches people directly in their homes.	Production can be incredibly expensive.

(Contd)

Medium	Creative pros	Creative cons
	Viewers are usually relaxed and therefore open minded to creative propositions.	Transmission air time can be equally expensive (although the growth in cable and satellite channels is making it a more financially viable option – see Web TV below).
	Excellent national coverage. Thanks to satellite, excellent for international markets.	
	Immediate short-term results.	Can take several months to make a sustained long-term creative impact.
	Flexibility to target a commercial to appear at a set time and within a specific type of programme schedule (e.g. breakfast cereal commercials can be highly effective when shown during morning television programmes).	Creative messages have to be sensitive to the greater viewing public who may tune in (e.g. children who may watch before the so-called watershed at 9 p.m.).
		Open to wide creative criticism.
	A commercial can be shown regionally.	Too gimmicky.
	The greatest possible opportunity for 'all singing, all dancing' and for especially entertaining creative communications.	

Medium	Creative pros	Creative cons
	Excellent for extending a creative theme into another medium.	
	Can refer to offers in other media (e.g. watch the commercial and clip the coupon in the press).	
	Web TV is highly interactive – combines best of broadcasting with best of narrowcasting, direct to the home.	
Radio	Very loyal listeners.	A danger of too many radio stations diluting the initial creative impact.
	Local and national coverage.	Short creative life.
	Marvellous creative possibilities using sound to stimulate the imagination.	Relies solely on one sense – sound. The listener can't actually see what you are offering
	Far cheaper than television.	
	Immediate impact.	
	Digital broadcasting opens up further opportunities for interactive advertising.	
	Quick production times.	

(Contd)

Medium	Creative pros	Creative cons
Posters	Big, dramatic, colourful images.	You may have to book space several months in advance.
	Excellent for building awareness.	Except regular local traffic, you can never be 100% sure about who sees your creative message.
	Copy can be reduced to one powerful headline.	Image is often more important than copy.
	Mobile billboards ensure precise targeting.	You generally do not have the time to provide detailed copy.
	Special billboards can include anything from 3D objects to Web links.	
Cinema	Ideal for targeting the youth and younger adult market.	Audience attendance is variable.
	Good for attracting locals.	You have to rely on a 'big' movie to pull in substantial audiences.
	Big screen excitement.	
	Ideal for reinforcing awareness to an audience in relaxed frame of mind.	Production costs can be as high as advertising costs.
	Unique audience ambience.	

The advertising industry map can be divided into three territories.

1 *The first is ruled by the advertiser. The servants are the agencies and media.*
2 *The second territory is governed by the agencies. Here, associated suppliers like web content producers, commercial producers and printers group together with media owners to sell their wares to the advertising agencies.*
3 *The final territory is dominated by media owners who take decisions according to the needs of their audience – readers, surfers, viewers and listeners. They rely on advertisers' budgets to serve those needs and extend their territory to accommodate an even larger audience.*

Together, all three make up a thriving community whose members depend on each other for survival. The advertisers want to reach the maximum number of appropriate people. So a medium has to be editorially as well as commercially attractive to a specific audience. This requires investment, which calls for more advertising.

Advertising feeds the media with the financial support to attract a bigger readership. The media feed the audience with editorial that attracts greater interest.

The audience feeds the advertiser with sales leads which attract a bigger percentage of an advertising budget.

The media are split into two categories: above-the-line media and below-the-line media. The 'line' originally referred to the commission paid to advertising agencies for booking advertisements in mainstream media like the press, television, cinema, posters and radio.

- *All above-the-line media paid commission directly to the agencies.*
- *Below-the-line suppliers – such as direct mailing companies, design agencies, incentive brokers and sales promotion specialists – did not pay commission, so the agencies invoiced a service charge to clients.*

Today, most suppliers are willing to pay commissions to agencies, and areas such as direct marketing use above-the-line media such as television and radio. So the term 'through-the-line' has been created. It covers any aspect of communication media. (See Chapter 6.)

Did you know?

Your choice of above-the-line media is staggering. To take websites alone, there are in excess of two billion pages on the web, with more being added as you read this sentence.

Deciding which media to select for an advertising campaign can be daunting. Each working day, thousands of media salespeople contact companies aiming to sell the virtues of a particular medium. Countless deals are struck, offering everything from full-page discounts to discounts for multiple Webvert impressions.

So how do you draw up a short list of media?

- *First, look at your bank account. How much money can you invest in communicating your message?*
- *Next, return to your targeting parameters. Which media offer the greatest number of appropriate readers, viewers or listeners for the project? You should remember that mass-market media like TV and the national press may offer lots of readers or viewers. However, you have to ask how many of those people will actually be interested in your product or service. (The web offers both a mass market and a direct market – particular care is needed when deciding where you advertise.) It boils down to quality as well as quantity. Which media offer the greatest value for money, dollar for prospect?*

- ▶ *The tighter your budget, the narrower you or your client's media choice. Small budgets tend to direct advertisers towards concentrating all their buying power (often termed 'media spend') into one specific media title. The broader your budget, the wider your media potential. Often larger-scale advertisers with substantial budgets target media in an upside-down funnel-like formation: the high-cost items (TV, cinema) at the wide opening of the funnel, the lower-cost items at the neck.*
- ▶ *Broad awareness is needed to launch a product or to speak to the mass population. The more a budget is concentrated into one tight target area, the greater the chance of making that area profitable.*

ScotsdaleNorth's traditional retailing may promote its range of coffees in a broad awareness campaign. However, it may also promote its special Italian super-strength coffee to targeted coffee drinkers.

Each level in the funnel complements the next. The copy in a TV commercial may refer a consumer to a press advertisement, a press advertisement may refer the consumer to a sales promotion and so on. In order to re-enforce the strength of the message, creative elements used in one medium are often shared with another. For example, a poster may feature a specific scene from a TV commercial. Through doing this, the power of the commercial is reinforced by the strength of the poster and vice versa. One reminds the consumer of the other.

Getting the right mix of media is as essential as pruning the creative solution to its core benefit. After all, it would be fruitless to produce a stunning piece of creativity if it were communicated via an unsuitable medium. (Refer to *Teach Yourself Marketing* for more information.)

Arguably, media planning is beyond the realm of the responsibility held by a copywriter. However, given the fact that poor media selection can ruin a great piece of creative work, it is important to understand the basic process of media planning. That way you can avoid pitfalls before they appear.

The eight steps to effective media planning

1 **Will it enhance the creative work?** *Can you answer 'Yes' to the following?*
   ▷ *Is it targeted at the group that is addressed by the copy and visual?*
   ▷ *Does the medium allow for elements like colour or coupons?*
   ▷ *Will the general editorial style be in keeping with the copy's tone of voice?*

2 **Media penetration.** *Does the medium deliver fewer people who are unlikely to become customers?*

3 **Prove it.** *Consider the medium's track record. Have other advertisers who produce similar products used it? If so, and most importantly if they used it consistently, the chances are strong that it is a good vehicle. You can track the type of advertiser who has appeared in a medium through contacting an organization called the Media Register. They can supply relevant data showing who has advertised in which media, including TV and radio as well as some overseas media.*

4 **What's the 'hit' rate like?** *How often can your target audience see your advertisement? Opportunity to see (known as OTS) isn't a quality-led judgement. It doesn't consider whether an audience pays particular attention to the contents of a magazine and style of copy, for example. It is more concerned with the number of times the audience is able to see the advertisement. Specific interest would be governed by the type of reader and whether that person identifies with the content and style of the magazine.*

If you plan to write an advertisement to appear in a specific magazine, how do you choose the publication? Is it the kind of magazine that is published only every now and again but is constantly referred to by the readership? A good example of this kind is the type of magazine you find in a dentist's surgery – great for longer bodycopy. Do you want your product to be repeatedly seen by an audience or is your message more suitable for a one-off appearance, perhaps in a national newspaper?

The share of the web targeted audience is sometimes called MindShare or Eyeball Share. You can learn more about this in Chapter 12.

5 **Does it whisper or does it shout?** *How targeted is the medium? For instance, if you are writing about vegetarian restaurant dining, would it be appropriate to place an advertisement in a regional paper which covers the restaurant's locale? Or would it be better to place the advertisement in a magazine?*

6 **Back to back, who comes out front?** *Compared to another medium, list the proposed medium's advantages. Don't get confused into comparing one title against another – for example two magazines.*

7 **Describe the audience.** *Precisely whom is the medium targeted towards? List their ages, sex, income, job type and social grading. (Refer to 'Social categorization', page 60.) You could take the media owner's word about the audience profile or you could refer to figures supplied by an organization such as JICNARS (the Joint Industry Committee for National Readership Surveys). Refer to 'social categorization', page 60.*

8 **Add more ingredients for success.** *You may wish to use more than one medium. Although your product is aimed at a particular person (user), the potential buyer may be someone else. For example, if ScotsdaleNorth wants to promote its own brand of healthy foods, it could place the advertisement in a woman's magazine, yet your copy could discuss the health benefits for men with high cholesterol.*

Additional media also enhance the funnel effect discussed at the start of this section. In the example of the ScotsdaleNorth healthy-eating campaign, during the course of a typical day the housewife may be exposed to a message several times via several media.

Wakes up
Hears a radio commercial
Sees a TV commercial on the web or on TV
Reads a press advertisement
Receives an e-shot

Takes the kids to school
Hears another radio commercial
Drives past a roadside poster

Mid-morning
Sees a TV commercial
Hears a radio commercial

Lunch
Reads a magazine advertisement
Surfs the web – spots a banner ad

Afternoon
Goes shopping
Sees an in-store promotion

Picks the kids up from school
Hears a radio commercial
Passes a poster

Evening
Sees a TV commercial
Participates in web TV contest
Serves the healthy meal

The press up close

This section deals with different aspects of specialized press advertising.

RECRUITMENT ADVERTISING

It is surprising just how many great copywriters started their craft in the recruitment advertising industry. Person-wanted ads are more than simple employment announcements. Every newly advertised job is an example of how the organization is helping the community through providing job opportunities and how it is investing for the future.

Recruitment advertising falls into four categories:

1 *The first is the standard line advertisement which you often find towards the back of publications or on job websites.*
2 *The second is the box or classified ad which literally boxes in the copy, thereby giving the advertisement a much greater page presence.*
3 *The third is the display advertisement. This provides the greatest creative opportunities – but at the greatest advertising placement cost.*
4 *The fourth is the multi-media approach. This often utilizes radio and web in addition to press advertising.*

All job adverts have to consider equal opportunities which span age, experience and ethnicity.

Steps to ensure equality in recruitment advertising copy (based on Equality Commission guidelines)

1 *Advertise widely so that the maximum number of suitably qualified candidates can apply.*
2 *Don't just publish your advertisement to a niche audience.*
3 *Write in clear and simple English. Avoid vague or abstract words. For example:* young; mature; dynamic; energetic.

(Contd)

4 *Where possible, avoid distinctly male or female job titles:* waiter/waitress; salesman/salesgirl; postman; stewardess; handyman; craftsman; manageress; foreman; storeman; matron; chairman/chairwoman; headmaster/headmistress.
Instead, try: waiting staff; sales assistant; postal worker; manager; storesperson; supervisor; chairperson; nurse; manager; headteacher.

5 *If you really can't avoid using a job title or description add a clear equal opportunities statement to show you welcome applications from all suitably qualified men and women.*

6 *Where your advertisement features a photograph or picture, aim to portray a balance of men and women and persons of different racial groups and persons of different ages performing a variety of jobs. At the very least incorporate an equal opportunities statement welcoming applications from all suitably qualified persons.*

7 *Don't perpetuate stereotypes by showing pictures of workers traditionally associated with one or other of the sexes (e.g. women nurses and stewardesses or male lorry drivers and mechanics).*

8 *Unless indicating a jobholder's position in an organization's hierarchy, where possible avoid age-related job titles:* junior or senior.

9 *Be careful not to exclude persons with definite characteristics. For example, minimum height or physical fitness requirements may exclude women and disabled persons. If such criteria can't be objectively justified then it is recommended that you don't write copy that excludes certain candidates. An advertisement that states* 'young person wanted' *or* 'mature person wanted' *may be directly discriminatory, or copy such as* 'recent graduates' *may be indirectly discriminatory against persons over the age of 25 years.*

Equal opportunities copy examples

> We are an equal opportunities employer and we welcome applications from all suitably qualified men and women.

> We are an equal opportunities employer and we welcome applications from all suitably qualified persons regardless of their religious beliefs or political opinions, sex, marital or family statuses, races, sexual orientations, ages or whether they are disabled.

> We are an equal opportunities employer. We welcome applications from all suitably qualified persons. However, as women are currently under-represented in our workforce, we would particularly welcome applications from women. All appointments will be made on merit.

> This post is open to women only. For this post, being a woman is a genuine occupational requirement in accordance with Article 10(2)(b)(i) of the Sex Discrimination (NI) Order 1976 (as amended).

LINE ADS

Line ads usually accommodate two to three lines (up to thirty words) of copy describing the job opportunity. With such tight restrictions you have to make sure that your requirements are clear and to the point.

First, assuming that you have thirty words to work with, deduct the copy that provides response details (like your email address). Never feature a lengthy address as this is a waste of words; instead feature a telephone number and website. Allowing for telephone codes, that reduces the words to 27. Is it essential that you include a name to contact? If it is, you have to deduct one or two more words. Now you are left with only 25 words to convey your message.

Let's assume that ScotsdaleNorth.com is looking for a warehouse manager. Before you write any bodycopy, consider the main requirements that you are looking for in a candidate. For example:

1 *Aged 25 to 50 years*
2 *Experienced*
3 *Fit*
4 *Good manager*
5 *Qualified*
6 *Available for shift duties*

Out of these six attributes, how many are essential for the job? Are you being discriminatory? Perhaps you are able to narrow the list down to:

▶ *Good manager*
▶ *Available for shift duties*

Next, think about three key adjectives that describe the kind of person you want. For example:

1 *Thorough*
2 *Cheerful*
3 *Conscientious*

Finally, think of three key adjectives that describe the kind of work lifestyle that the warehouse manager would experience. For example:

1 *Hectic*
2 *Rewarding*
3 *Enjoyable*

Combine the two:

Conscientious, experienced shift Warehouse Manager for a busy yet rewarding ScotsdaleNorth.com depot. Call 123 4567 or download an application form from (web address)

The finishing touch is to embolden the job title and perhaps the contact details:

> Conscientious, experienced shift **Warehouse Manager**
> for a busy yet rewarding ScotsdaleNorth.com depot.
> **Call 123 4567 or email [address].**

If you simply cannot accommodate all your message in a small space, you can either move up to a classified box advertisement or opt for an alternative solution that is becoming popular. I call it the 'read 'n' click' recruitment advertisement. Explained simply, your advertisement includes the most basic details and then invites the reader to either call a special number for a complete job specification or surf onto a microsite.

For example:

> Have you heard about the new rewarding **Warehouse**
> **Management** opportunities with one of the country's leading
> retail chains? **Call 123 4567** for a profitable word in your ear.

Or :

> A **Warehouse Management** career with one of the country's
> leading retail chains is unlike any other fast-track opportunity
> of its kind. **See for yourself (www.address.com)**.

THE BOX OR CLASSIFIED ADVERTISEMENT

Box advertisements provide and deliver even greater impact. Although they allow for more words, they actually work best when not jammed to the edges with copy.

THE DISPLAY ADVERTISEMENT

Display recruitment advertisements provide the space, scope and positioning to make the maximum impact on a recruitment page.

This gives candidates – as well as any competitive organization seeing the advertisement – a favourable impression.

The display advertisement has three features essential for success:

- ▶ *Consistent and dynamic borders*
- ▶ *Relevant graphics*
- ▶ *Succinct copy*

Borders

The importance of consistency in borders is particularly relevant in recruitment advertising, which has to make each display-format recruitment advertisement achieve several tasks:

- ▶ *Advertise the job vacancy.*
- ▶ *Reinforce presence in the marketplace.*
- ▶ *In some cases, demonstrate to shareholders and the public alike that an organisation is prospering.*

Borders can incorporate logos, twisted perimeter lines – in fact, as long as they operate within the space available on the page, borders can be stretched to the limits of your imagination and the frontiers of style dictated by those concerned. In order to make a recruitment advertisement as distinctive as possible, always try to use typography creatively. (See comment in the 'Did you know' box on page 207.)

Relevant graphics

Poor graphics spoil an otherwise well-planned display advertisement. A common mistake is to show people at work. It is obvious that people work at the organisation. Why not show fringe benefits of their job? An air stewardess could be shown enjoying her free time in the big city.

Succinct copy

Copy needs to be succinct. Traditionally, display recruitment advertising follows a formal order of contents. These are set out below.

Display recruitment advertising's order of contents

1 *Headline featuring job title, geographical location of office and, depending on the salary, the salary level. Usually the bigger the financial reward, the greater the need to include it in the headline.*
2 *Introduction paragraph of approximately 45 words about the company and its caring attitude towards employees, as well as its success story to date.*
3 *Whom the candidate reports to and who in the company reports to the candidate. This provides an idea of seniority of the role.*
4 *What the key tasks involve.*
5 *What key attributes are needed to perform the tasks.*
6 *How the job will help the candidate achieve something personally as well as contribute something corporately.*
7 *A summary of the educational qualifications, work experience and personal qualities required.*
8 *Instructions on whom to contact and where to send a CV.*
9 *The contact address details.*

THE MULTI-MEDIA APPROACH

Traditionally this approach combines press advertising and radio commercials. Depending on the general state of the economy, this kind of recruitment advertising falls in and out of fashion. Currently, the mode is to list various jobs in press adverts and provide complete details, including the option to send a CV, via the web.

Chapter 9 provides details about producing an effective radio commercial. Great radio commercials work in tandem with press advertising. The close of the commercial should refer the listener to the appropriate advertisements in the press. Also, the copy technique of including:

▶ *who is wanted ...*
▶ *where ...*
▶ *for what reward ...*

should be applied on the radio as well as within the press advertisement.

Surfers like succinct copy. On the web, never write more than an 80-word three-paragraph description of the job and if possible, try to design your website to give a sense of a recruiter's employer/ employee values.

Recruitment advertising quick tips

- *State the job title clearly in the headline.*
- *Make sure your copy is not discriminatory.*
- *Check which media produce the best response. (Incorporate a reference code in the advertisement.)*
- *Highlight the company's achievements and goals.*
- *Refer to salary, experience and qualifications.*
- *Consider testing your advertisement in several media.*
- *Make your copy appealing and enthusiastic.*
- *Target possible employees through job recruitment websites.*
- *Convey the excitement of working for an employer as well as that organization's employment values.*
- *Set out the potential employee's long-term career and additional financial benefits.*

Business-to-business press advertising

There are thousands of specialist trade publications dealing with everything from accountancy to zoo management. Advertisers who use trade publications fall into three broad categories:

1 **Sellers of materials and products or of the equipment to process those materials.** *This first category uses business and industry-specific magazines either to highlight a new product or endorse the credibility of an existing one. This kind of advertising tactically influences a specific professional sector. Once you can prove that those within an industry choose your product or service above another, you can influence others such as distributors and retailers as well as the end consumer.*

2 **Sellers of services to help run a company's operations.** *These include software, accountancy and office equipment. This category typically employs business magazines and specialist websites to inform one industry sector about another industry's products or services. For example, a financial software company advertises an accountancy computer program for accountants in the relevant business press.*

3 **Resellers (the sales channel, i.e. the resellers and retailers of goods and services).** *The third category is aimed at resellers. This audience is the front-line interface between you or your client and the ultimate consumer. Their creative message should incorporate product or added value service enhancements which encourage loyalty through ongoing promotions.*

Traditionally highly targeted business-to-business campaigns often feature direct mail. It offers precise targeting and can even be filed away for future reference.

Trade magazines are excellent for:

▶ *Creating awareness.*
▶ *Inviting a response for further information.*

KEEP AN 'I' ON BUSINESS COPY

To solicit an appropriate response your copy has to:

▶ *Influence the decision makers.*
▶ *Inform those people about your product or service benefits.*
▶ *Instruct those people on how to contact you.*

Trade advertising encourages distributors and retailers to specify your brand. Copy pushes one of the following:

▶ *The commodity or product.*
▶ *The promotional offer.*
▶ *The bottom-line profit margin.*

JOB SPECIFICATION CATEGORIES

Typically, business-to-business advertising copy addresses:

1 **Users** – *like secretaries or mechanical operators who want to try out a product.*
2 **Choosers** – *like purchasing managers who have the power to place an order.*
3 **Proprietors** – *like directors who have the authority to sign the cheques.*
4 **Investors** – *like shareholders who are addressed in corporate advertising.*

> **The User** wants to read copy that shows how your product works or service operates.
>
> **The Chooser** wants to read copy that demonstrates affordability.
>
> **The Proprietor** wants to read copy that highlights trust and integrity.
>
> **The Investor** wants reassurance that the company is making the right profit-driven decisions.

Job title	Target group	'I' want	Your copy offers
Secretary/ administrator	User	Efficiency Supply Reliability	Competence Willingness Trust
Sales person	User	Support Results Credibility	Encouragement Reassurance Qualification
Technician	User	Performance Adaptability Maintenance	Demonstration Tailor-made for you Guarantees

Job title	Target group	'I' want	Your copy offers
Manager	Chooser	Service Speed Economy	Dependability Proficiency Competitiveness
Director	Proprietor	Trust Stability Control	Integrity Certainty Character
(Corporate advertising) Shareholder	Investor	Experience Direction Profit	Knowledge Objectivity Optimism

The smaller your business, the greater the chance that Users are also Choosers.

In all advertising, readers, surfers, listeners or viewers ask: 'What's in it for me?' In business-to-business advertising your creative challenge is to combine the hard corporate commercial messages with softer mass-market appeal.

▶ *The headline 'PenPal means business' offers a promise of further business but it lacks direct association with a specific promotion.*
▶ *'Pick up a PenPal' is a neater message, but it isn't relevant to the retailer.*
▶ *However, 'Business picks up with PenPal', combines the two messages and motivates the retailer.*

Show the industry that you mean business. Just because you or your client may spend a great sum of money directing your advertising towards the consumer by using, for example, TV, the web or the press, you can't ignore trade advertising. The trade is your support. The people behind the counter ultimately sway the people in front.

Every written sentence will be studied in detail and for accuracy. (Business audiences are particularly cynical and demanding.)

However, that doesn't mean that you have to be a world-renown expert in a product or service to write about it. Conduct as much research as is reasonably possible and never be afraid to ask further questions. Nine times out of ten, people will respect you for asking and berate you for not. Never try to fob off the trade reader with clever prose rather than hard commercial facts.

Each business sector has its own vocabulary. Professionals within a specific area prefer their particular industry language. Nevertheless, however much jargon you use, you should always balance it with user-friendly copy, within the sector's acceptable creative bounds.

Did you know?

During my copywriting courses, I collect examples of so-called 'management speak'. See how many expressions you can recognize from your work:

At this moment in time, if you've got a moment, between a rock, a hard place and pushing the envelope with the cards on the table, I simply sing from the hymn sheet, with due respect to horses and courses, this is absolutely the most irritating sentence I could write, basically by close of play, to be frank, as I see it, keeping in the loop I myself hear what you are saying about the tidy little nest egg which can go up as well as down, all things being equal; at the end of the day, putting collateral customers first and going forward by moving the goal posts and lining all our ducks in row to see how they fly, passing the monkey, avoiding the low hanging fruit, let's suck it and see, touching base and applying blue sky thinking to this thingy: It's not rocket science, but, naming and shaming, innit?

Pictures and illustrations should be industry friendly and not automatically chosen from a picture library full of clichéd images. Only show what is relevant to your message. If, for example, you want to demonstrate a printing machine to a printer, feature its mechanics rather than gleaming body work. (Sparkling machines don't necessarily add up to dazzling results.)

KEEP YOUR BUSINESS COPY HUMAN

Often corporate-type business-to-business copy is directed towards a person who, assuming that they are interested in what you are saying, will pass it on to a colleague whose job is to delve further. These 'gate-keepers' want facts, not chat. Avoid humour. If you can't take your own product or service seriously, how can you expect anyone else to do so? Balance a friendly tone of voice with a powerful and convincing fact-led commercial proposition.

Examples of specialized industries that have specific vocabulary include:

- ▶ *Financial sector*
- ▶ *Medical sector*
- ▶ *Legal profession*
- ▶ *Chemical and mechanical engineering*
- ▶ *Information Technology.*

Allow your creative language to enhance rather than engulf a factual message. For example:

An advertisement directed towards doctors treating asthma

Headline (creative approach):
Asilaz.
A breath of fresh air for doctors.

Bodycopy (factual):
The combined active ingredients of silbutalmol, bricanontl and sodium cromoglycate in Asilaz deliver immediate relief for asthma sufferers. Recent tests carried out by the British Pharmacy Association show that when compared to traditional asthmatic treatments containing compounds
(Contd)

such as droxy 7 or betamac, Asilaz delivers a relieving 20% improvement in bronchial congestion. As with all similar products, it is recommended that patients follow dosage and treatment instructions as specified on the label.
Logo

Asilaz
Recommended dosage – one spray twice a day.

Strapline (creative):
Delivering relief.

RETAINING YOUR TRADE READER'S INTEREST

Don't delude yourself, business is about making money. That requires speculation; an investment in time and effort. Time the immediacy of your message to match a business person's busy lifestyle. Don't waste people's time by forcing them to grapple with unclear, yet clever headlines or subheads. If your proposition is relevant, the reader will read further. If not, like spam, they will filter it out.

HANDLING FALLING SALES

Trade advertising can combat declining sales. For example, it is not uncommon for one brand of toothpaste to be found less effective than a newer brand. Sales decline. Market share decays.

Use copy to challenge the findings of the newer brand indirectly through organizing an independent research project. The manufacturer could inform the trade that latest tests prove the effectiveness of brushing with the original brand as opposed to the newer brand. Of course, the research has to be conclusive and indisputable.

If you can't beat 'em, another way to combat falling sales is to announce modified toothpaste.

For example:

> With an even bigger bite of the market
> more customers than ever are saying Aah!

The bodycopy would explain that the company has improved the toothpaste's ingredients and has great trade offers.

With your toothpaste relaunched, adapt the new Point of Difference – POD (in this case, unbeatable cleaning power, better trade discounts) throughout the entire trade campaign. You could include point-of-sale material such as cardboard cut-outs, price-reduction coupons for distribution to the public and so on. (Also see the 'Reply device' on page 195.)

Product or service value doesn't always relate to money. In fact, the best value could come through the way of added-services or cutomer care, range of products, distribution and so on.

Sometimes when a product can't be sufficiently differentiated from other similar competitive products, sales promotion can instead concentrate on incentives and display material available to the reseller.

> Leaflet to trade about toothpaste brand:
> 10% more in every tube for you and your customers
> Point-of-sale for the counter:
> 10% more in every tube

The toothpaste may be just one of literally scores of products produced by a company. Advertising each brand separately in the trade press would be costly and frankly a waste of three invaluable business commodities: time, effort and money.

Why not consider advertising the umbrella brand within which the toothpaste is a successful product in its own right? Try to position the product as part of a bigger picture.

> Tingle toothpaste – from ScotsdaleNorth.com – the people's choice.

What if your own product is neither part of a multi-national company's portfolio of brands nor fits neatly into the category of 'me too' types of product? An example of this is PenPal. In this case, the trade needs to be reassured that apart from being innovative, the product has distribution and marketing support that makes it a viable product to stock. Above all, you need to produce trade advertising that anticipates genuine potential profit. For example:

> PenPal. We're investing £800,000 worth of media spend to get your customers writing off more.

In Chapter 4 (see page 114) we looked at how to stay one step ahead of your reader by tackling difficult questions before they arise. This is particularly helpful when you want to placate a fussy business user. Your ultimate customer may be concerned with everything from security to durability. You can address these concerns effectively by highlighting a possible problem up front. For example:

> Headline:
> Inferior USB sticks can cause you to lose more than just a good night's sleep.
> Subhead:
> XYZ sticks are guaranteed never to let you down.
> Bodycopy:
> Losing data is a nightmare. Now you can sleep easy. XYZ have produced the most powerful USB sticks ever. They are certified 100% error free under our 10-year warranty ...

Corporate-style press advertising

Corporate advertising has to achieve much more than just announcing products or educating a market about product use. It can:

1 **Explain a company's policy direction.** *It may be important to demonstrate a company's open culture of discussing its exciting plans for ever-expanding market penetration with the people who will be responsible for helping the organization implement those schemes (retailers, wholesalers, distributors and so on).*

   The recession of 2009 saw many companies merging and demerging with other businesses. Changes may typically entail announcing joint ventures with companies that make products complementary to the ones that you or your client already produce. (An example could be a digital camera manufacturer which links up with a memory card manufacturer.) You may plan to expand into new markets by enhancing the features of an existing product or service. For example:

Teach Yourself Books (professional division); Teach Yourself Audio; Teach Yourself Starter Kits; Teach Yourself Away Days; Teach Yourself DVDs.

2 **Endorse sub-brands.** *Creative corporate endorsement copy comes into its own when promoting umbrella brands. Such advertisements need not be directed solely at the trade. For example:*

Headline:
Since first selling a pound of butter from a barrel 100 years ago, we've added some extra weight to our shelves.

(Picture of original interior of small ScotsdaleNorth corner shop with proud shop-keeper in front of barrel.)
Lead-in bodycopy:
To be exact, 37,481 own-brand products ...

3 Instil confidence. *Discuss outstanding service and value, as in this PenPal advertisement:*

Headline:
> After 9 days, 2 cartridge refills and 1km of ink, Bob decided to exchange his PenPal for another model.
> (No questions asked.)

Lead-in copy:
> Bob loved using his flexible PenPal. Thanks to our no-nonsense 10 days' money-back guarantee promise, if he wanted to change it for another model he could – no questions asked and we even replaced his cartridge.

Another method is to discuss a company's excellent track record:

An advertisement for ScotsdaleNorth.com

Headline:

1959

Mrs Jones insists on doing all her shopping at Scotsdale Northside

(Picture of Mrs Jones shopping at her local ScotsdaleNorth corner shop.)

2011

Her granddaughter, Mrs Smith, can't find any reason to change a family tradition.

(Picture of her granddaughter in 2011, surfing website.)

Lead-in copy:
> The Smiths do their weekly shopping at the local ScotsdaleNorth.
> True – over the years, our product range has improved radically. However, some things remain the same today as they have always been: great food, discount prices, terrific service ...

4 Show ability. *Copy can demonstrate how a company professionally fulfilled the tallest of orders:*

An advertisement for PenPal

Headline:

When the British Antarctic Team order PenPals
They don't want to be left on ice

Lead-in copy:
On 9th February 2009 we received an email for 50 PenPals to be dispatched post haste to the South Pole.

It was from the British Antarctic Team. They chose PenPal because of its proven reliability even at –60°F. Captain Johnson, the team leader, needed supplies within 48 hours. He didn't want excuses.

We put our skates on and met the demand ...

An advertisement for ScotsdaleNorth – traditional

Headline:

Everything checks out perfectly – just ask Sandra.

(Picture of housewife at check-out with Sandra, the check-out girl.)

Lead-in copy:

Sandra ensures that our customers' groceries are speedily and efficiently packed and priced, saving them time and hassle.

5 Empathize with a businessperson's own goals and concerns.
*Business people are beset by daily challenges. Ideally, each
problem should be turned into an opportunity. Your copy
should demonstrate how a product or service can help turn
those opportunities into profits:*

Give business people a break

Most business people want to be ...	Creatively, your message should demonstrate ...
Rich	Financial credibility
Efficient	Business support
Confident	The ability to meet deadlines
Respected	A tried and tested heritage
Innovative	Investment in the future
Competitive	Market understanding
A leader	The choice of the professional
Successful	A sound track record
Popular	The preferred choice
Technically competent	Leading-edge products or services

Typical key creative corporate feel-good phrases often sound a little
cheesy. They may include:

▶ *We're on your side.*
▶ *We want you to win.*
▶ *We react to your needs.*
▶ *Your partner in (the industry not crime!)*
▶ *Helping you to help your customers.*
▶ *By your side.*
▶ *The right choice.*
▶ *Committed to your success.*
▶ *Just call, we'll answer.*
▶ *We help you make it happen.*

Addressing managers

Managers need to keep in touch with industrial news as well as international news. They read leading newspapers, surf the web, browse trade journals ... They are influenced by trends. They set standards.

Accordingly, your copy has to be sharp, appreciative of their needs and modern. Visuals should be dynamic and people-centric. Bodycopy content frequently incorporates a promise of achievement: *to become the all-round, totally professional person* (thanks to whatever the product or service may be).

Management- and executive-targeted copy needs to demonstrate that you are on 'their' side without sounding grovelling or insincere. It has to present a goal and provide the facts by way of the product or service. For example

(Picture of luxurious executive car cruising along a motorway at sunrise.)

Headline:
The meeting is at 7.30 a.m.
For the discerning few, whilst the conversation ahead promises to be 'bumpy' the journey will be exceptionally smooth.

However turbulent the meeting ahead, the eco-driven Pastiche 398 means you can face the music in considerable style.

Car Choice magazine described the new Pastiche 2001 series as 'the ultimate Executive car'.

Everything about it is special. Beneath the bonnet sits a razor-sharp 2.3 litre multi-valve engine. Frugal on petrol,
(Contd)

could pounce at exhilarating speeds of up to 130 mph within a cat's whisker of 0–60 in 8 seconds. Unruffled acceleration is never compromised by ambient noise. Fuel is sipped, never guzzled – providing an astounding 61.2 mpg at a steady 56 mph.

Relax in one of the luxurious leather-upholstered colour co-ordinated seats. Each features computer-controlled air-sprung cushioned support as well as side impact air cushions.

The driver's console is clearly defined, combining hi-specification features like air conditioning, multi-play all-round speakers, voice controlled Sat-Nav, CD drive, central door locking and electric window power – all at finger-tip reach.

Your passengers will feel equally at home with on-board integrated seat-mounted television. There is even a fold-away courtesy work desk for any last-minute paperwork.

Other captivating features include alloy wheels, heat-sensitive electronic sunroof and ABS braking, all fitted as standard.

Why not arrange for a test drive today? Just call 0800 00 200 or visit our website. It could be one of the smoothest management decisions you've ever made.

This type of macho-management creative approach was popular in the 1990s. During the 'noughties' (the first decade of this century), management attitudes changed radically. Expressions like 'hands-on management' (meaning a manager who gets physically involved with the business at all levels) were replaced with terms like 'hands-off management' (meaning everything is delegated to someone else). Advertising reacted by addressing issues in a different way. Of course copywriters never took this too far; if they had, their copy would have sounded 'suboptimal' (lousy). The serious point to all this is that the Caring Nineties was a period in which creative advertising typically followed, rather than set, trends.

Business-to-business quick tips

▶ *Trade magazines create awareness and provide an educational platform.*
▶ *Copy needs to push your product, push your offer and push your client's own profits.*
▶ *Always ask yourself, 'What's in this offer for my clients?'*
▶ *Never assume that consumer advertising alone will satisfy the business market. Integrate with the web and other media.*
▶ *Meet the people who sell your client's product or service to the consumer.*
▶ *Get to grips with the business language and jargon of a specific business sector.*
▶ *Keep your copy professional but accessible*
▶ *Never allow your creative message to dilute your product or service facts.*
▶ *Get to the point.*
▶ *Use research to substantiate claims.*
▶ *Always stay one step ahead of your buyer's questions.*
▶ *Reward managers with the tools to save time and earn respect.*
▶ *Address declining sales positively.*

Off-the-page advertising

Off-the-page (selling directly from an advertisement) words need to leap out and pull (not drag) customers all the way to your doorstep. Customers need to be encouraged to react immediately by contacting a company through a response device.

Off-the-page selling offers two creative copy steps towards securing a sale:

1 *Make an offer, ask for payment and then dispatch the product.*
2 *Make an offer, provide some outline details about the product or service and then offer to email or post back further information. The final purchase is made through either mail order or another avenue of distribution.*

Examples include:

▶ *Selling property off the page – read the ad, ask for a brochure, see the property, sign the contract.*
▶ *Selling insurance off the page – read the ad, call for advice, surf for more details. see a financial adviser, sign the contract.*

The acid test to measure the effectiveness of an off-the-page advertisement is whether it generates a sale as well as encourage continued future purchases from the same buyer.

Off-the-page copy needs to be backed throughout with messages of reassurance. Provide as much descriptive detail as possible. For example, If you are advertising a classic hits download collection, list every single track. Someone somewhere will want the entire collection – just because of one special track. If you are writing about a dress, discuss its texture, how it flows, how it feels, its colours and so on:

> Its pretty pastel is as delicate as the silk that wove it.

If you are selling something that is large, explain in an original way just how *big* that really is:

> The travel bag can carry two suits, three dresses, six pairs of shoes, twenty shirts, three scarves …

And if the product is small, describe just how small it is:

> … it's so incy-wincy – you'll never know it's there.

(This would be a good copy line for a hearing aid.)

If, for example, you are selling an artistic collection, like bone china plates, provide details of their actual size, the work that went into crafting the piece and so on:

> This beautiful collector's piece has been specially commissioned by leading artist Bob Jones. Every vase is hand made. Each flower is hand painted. So each piece is peerless.

For even greater urgency, consider the limited edition technique:

> Only 1000 ever made. Your piece is individually numbered.
> Once we've sold the 999th piece, we'll break the mould.

The role of incentives

Having read about the many product benefits and features of your client's product, the potential buyers may still need one final creative push before taking the plunge and responding. This could be some kind of reward for prompt action:

> Answer in 10 days and claim a free gift.
> Reply today and save 10% off your bill.
> Respond now and you could win a holiday for two.
> Reply soon and we'll pay your first month's insurance premium.

Or feature a time limit:

> Hurry. This offer only lasts 5 days.
> Hurry. Stocks are limited.
> Hurry. Frst come, first served.
> Hurry. Avoid disappointment by replying today.
> Hurry. There are only 20 shopping days till xmas.

Next to the web, coupons and telephone are the most popular response devices. Whichever you decide to take, make it as simple as possible for a prospect to get in touch.

COUPONS

Strategically, your copy should refer to how easy it is to use a featured coupon. As with web responses, like www addresses and email addresses, the closer the prospect gets to the coupon, the greater the creative emphasis given to just how easy it is for them to get in touch.

Over the years, designers have tried various ways to balance urgency with style. Coupon captions have been reversed out of boxes, run along the coupon's edge, 'splashed' with colour, enlarged, reduced ... the list is endless. As in many aspects of creative copy and design, as long as you try to tone down the trite and keep everything sounding as well as looking credible and in keeping with the overall creative tone, your coupon should get clipped.

Here are some typical coupon captions:

> Can you answer 'Yes' to these questions?
> Complete and reply today.
> Hurry. 14 days to respond.
> Order today.
> Order now.
> Cut out the wait. Cut out the coupon.
> All you need to do is sign.
> Reserve your order now.
> Secure your order without delay.
> This coupon saves you money.
> It just takes a couple of 'ticks' to reply.

Making coupons user friendly

As with an online form, a good coupon is simple – not just for the benefit of the person who has to complete it, but also for the good of the person who has to process all the written information. Avoid questions requiring optional answers. I have yet to meet anyone who actually enjoys completing forms on or offline. Wherever possible, in coupons guide the prospect to completing things in legible CAPITAL LETTERS. Think about how one question should logically be followed by the next. Consider the person in the back room who has to process all of the coupons.

Hopefully, sacks full of coupons will arrive. Someone should gauge the effectiveness of the various media in which the coupons appeared. Here's how:

▶ *Incorporate a discreet publication code that indicates a publication's title and date.*
▶ *Create an artificial order department. One publication features coupons addressed to a certain department, whilst another features a different department. This is useful for very large-scale, even international campaigns.*

Coupons should be positive:

> YES! I am interested in what you have to offer.

They should minimize laborious writing:

> Ordering is as easy as 1.2.3.
>
> **1** *What is your name?*_____
> **2** *What is your postcode?*_____
> **3** *What is your house number or name?*_____
> **4** *How much would you like to spend?*_____
>
> Please send me a:
> RED ☐
> PINK ☐
> BLUE ☐
>
> dress (just tick the relevant box).
>
> Please charge my
> VISA ☐
> ACCESS ☐
>
> credit card
> My account number is _____
> The expiry date is _____

Explain what happens after the person sends in the coupon. How long will it take to process the order? Say when the offer expires.

Coupon information can be used again and again for selling other products or services in the future. This technique is called cross-selling.

It is illegal to pass on the information contained within a coupon to another company without permission. Likewise, when emailing a prospect, ask to confirm their details before you sell anything to them. (This is called 'a double-opt in'.) In the UK, The Data Protection Act 1998 instructs advertisers to cease direct mailing to any company or person who asks them to stop. This means a complete 'halt' request would affect ALL kinds of advertising response including, email, phone and direct mail.

Think about the confidentiality of the information contained within your coupon. Offer a FREEPOST address in which you pick up the postage costs. All the prospect has to do is pop the coupon in an envelope and then post it.

CALL NOW!

Telephone response copy adds further urgency to a creative message. A strong telephone graphic accompanied by copy, such as:

Call now
Act now
Dial Free
Call our Hotline
Dial anytime
We're waiting for your call

... tells your prospect that you mean business and are ready and waiting for their call. This may be essential for organizations such as charities that need to raise money quickly.

> One phone call can save this girl's life.
> To save her the twenty-mile trek for a cup of water
> just walk to the phone.
> Your phone is her lifeline.

You'll notice that one of the copy lines above the charity examples includes the word 'Hotline'. Hotlines are nothing particularly new. To get around this why drop the word 'hot', in 'hotline' and replace it with the product name or company name. This makes your phone response number even more memorable.

In the case of PenPal variations could include:

> The PenPal Hotline Line
> The PenPal Line
> The Cartridge Line

If ScotsdaleNorth (traditional) wanted to promote a particular own-brand service (say, nappies) and sales line they could call it:

> ScotsdaleNorth Nappy Line
> The Nappy Advice Line
> Nappies Direct Line

A further creative way of including a telephone response number is to use an existing enquiry phone directory service such as 118 which caters for lots of companies, on one externally promoted number.

> Find your local dealer at the end of the phone – Just dial
> 118–225

Probably the most popular phone-based response method is texting. SMS (Short Message Service) is rife throughout the world. SMS Text Advertising companies have collected a great number of mobile numbers from their users on an opt-in basis, with permission to send them SMS text advertising messages. The company will have also collected profile information such as age, sex, income, location etc. A phone user provides the company with your chosen message and any profile targeting and in return the advertiser sends an SMS text advertising message.

Another growing trend is for social networking sites via mobile phones. In these cases, the user provides their contact details in return for receiving offers via SMS as well as free access to social networking sites via their mobile phone.

Assuming you are not using the web and still cannot decide between featuring a telephone or coupon response, you could always feature both:

Clip the coupon, or for an even faster service
call 0800 00 123 or click www.gabaynet.com

Whichever route you choose, ensure that you or your client can handle the anticipated response. There's not much point in producing a great advertisement if the consequent enquiries are ignored.

As mentioned above, not all off-the-page advertisements complete sales transactions immediately off the page. For example, medical or financial services may require further information. High-priced items may call for further creative reassurance that can only be provided by a next step: either a salesperson or a brochure.

Getting your prospect to make the next step often relies on the only form of advertising which offers the creative opportunity to be as intimate as the law allows with your target audience. This is covered in Chapter 6.

Off-the-page quick tips

▶ *Decide whether you want to sell directly or indirectly off the page.*

- *Encourage future as well as immediate sales. (Buy today and start a collection.)*
- *Describe everything about your product, from its size to its material – even down to the plug, if applicable.*
- *Reward response (e.g. discounts).*
- *Feature a time limit for responses.*
- *Endorse the simplicity of responding.*
- *Keep coupons concise and easy to complete.*
- *Track the effectiveness of a publication by incorporating a special coupon code.*
- *Encourage action with directive headlines.*
- *Add urgency by offering hotlines.*
- *Consider 'opt-in' SMS campaigns.*
- *Integrate your campaigns with popular social media networking sites.*
- *Test response by telephone or coupons or both.*

OVER TO YOU

▶ *Write a recruitment advertisement for the job of prime minister.*

▶ *Name an advantage and a disadvantage of television advertising.*

▶ *What are the three media territories of the advertising industry?*

▶ *Plan an integrated web/press employment campaign – how would you adapt your copy?*

▶ *Design and write a coupon to be used in an off-the-page advertisement for PenPal.*

▶ *List twelve different directive headlines.*

▶ *List six business benefits offered by a photocopier machine.*

▶ *Write an advertisement that highlights the business benefits of an old second-hand car.*

▶ *Write four versions of a headline that announces a business merger:*
   ▷ *to Users*
   ▷ *to Choosers*
   ▷ *to Proprietors*
   ▷ *to Investors.*

▶ *PenPal has a big competitor with a better product. Write an advertisement which supports PenPal's position.*

6

....

Selling through the letterbox

In this chapter you will learn how to:
- *understand the role of direct marketing*
- *construct the perfect direct mail letter*
- *and when to use direct mail gadgets*
- *draw inspiration for classic direct mail ideas*
- *write catalogue copy.*

Above-the-line advertising gets you a hold on a market (i.e. increases your market share). Direct marketing increases your share of the individual's buying decisions. To achieve this, you need to know as much as possible about your client – more than just why a buying decision is made. This requires extensive data – which is why direct marketing is sometimes referred to as 'database marketing'. It has many other names too:

- ▶ *Relationship marketing*
- ▶ *One-to-one marketing*
- ▶ *Response marketing*
- ▶ *Through-the-line marketing*
- ▶ *Quantitative marketing*
- ▶ *NSM marketing (Non-Specific Media marketing)*

Whatever you call it, direct marketing builds sustainable relationships between a company and its audience. Using direct mail or other integrated marketing channels, including the web, direct marketing reaches a client through websites or the letterbox to lead them to your point of sale. Reaching the appropriate letterboxes or email addresses calls for accurate lists. These can be purchased from list brokers or generated from completed sales promotion coupons, press advertising coupons and telephone research – or even questionnaire mailings. The problem with email in particular can be demonstrated with this mild joke that was circulating around the web during the Swine pandemic of 2009: 'Don't open any tins of pork – they could be spam.'

The days of reaching prospects via one media alone are sadly gone forever. Equally, with direct mail in particular, if you try to reach everyone … you'll touch no one. That's because today's prospects are worldly wise and, in terms of marketing, highly sophisticated. They have greater choice, and more ways of choosing: *they know what they want and why you want them.*

Integrated direct marketing encourages a sustainable relationship between you and your customer – that is why it is sometimes referred to as 'relationship marketing' or 'one-to-one marketing'. This relationship can become so strong that eventually, through keeping in touch at appropriate times with relevant information and incentives, the customer remains loyal and recommends you to others. The person's value to your company is doubled with every new customer they introduce.

This is demonstrated in a classic sales model originally conceived by Ray Consada, an American salesperson, and then developed by authors Ray Considine and Murray Raphael in their book *The Great Brain Robbery: Business Tips* (published by The Marketer's Bookshelf, Philadelphia, 1986). The model is still commonly used throughout the marketing industry. It is called the Loyalty Ladder.

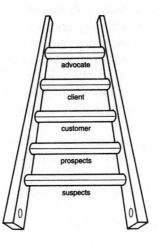

The loyalty ladder.

When correctly implemented, direct mail can:

1 *Target a message in a controlled campaign.*
2 *Personalize a message to a specific audience.*
3 *Prioritize a message by delivering it directly into the hands of a specific audience.*
4 *Time a message to coincide with an email campaign.*
5 *Explain a message in detail by including enclosures such as brochures and leaflets.*
6 *Offer confidentiality when a message is sensitive.*
7 *Hasten a message through using first-class postage.*
8 *Stimulate sales leads by following up messages by phone or post.*
9 *Offer outstanding value in terms of cost for each reply when compared to other media such as pure awareness advertising.*
10 *Test the effectiveness of a message by segmentation of your mailing's distribution.*
11 *Update your message by content or distribution.*
12 *Allow for unusual formats such as pop-ups, video mailers and large or small size envelopes.*

13 *Keep customers in touch with company developments and stimulate interest in future offers.*
14 *Ask customers for views and opinions.*
15 *Stimulate sales by offering special vouchers against new or ageing products.*
16 *Fight competition quickly by promoting revised prices.*
17 *Increase store traffic by inviting consumers to special retailer or distributor events.*
18 *Tie-in with other media such as the press which may feature an awareness/information-type advertisement.*
19 *Cross-sell with other direct mail users. (For example, the ScotsdaleNorth.com's cyber café, Directions, could share a mailing list with a restaurant guide publisher.)*
20 *Cover sales areas not readily accessible by sales staff.*

In addition to competing with many other enveloped items, ranging from utility bills to birthday cards, your mailing has to compete with endless email campaigns. It's hardly surprising that many suggest dropping direct mail altogether and just using email. However, I think that's missing a trick. The more people use email, the less will use d-mail; opening a window of opportunity to use one of the oldest forms of one-to-one marketing ever devised. So let's go back to basics.

Your envelope should indicate, at a glance, that its contents are:

▶ *interesting*
▶ *relevant*
▶ *worth the effort of opening the envelope.*

Above all, your mailing has to be involving. The more you can involve a reader with your creative proposition, the higher the likelihood that they will follow your copy all the way to a sales conclusion (if you are selling).

The envelope's copy and design need to reflect the mailing's contents and your commitment to caring about the community. So in addition to being printed on recycled paper and if possible vegetable ink, your envelope copy needs to entice the reader. In its hey-day one of the strongest words you could write on promotional direct mail was, 'free'. Today, with the exceptions of bargain-basement consumer promotions, whilst still attractive, the word FREE suggests junk mail, or in the case of email, spam.

You could opt instead for an added-value proposition:

> Open now and save 25% off your next grocery bill.

Another technique is to give the recipient a peek at what's inside the envelope. This is achieved through having one or more transparent windows on the envelope. One may show part of a picture from the brochure inside, whilst another shows part of the message on a sales letter – such as details of a cash prize.

Why not use a 'zipper' envelope? The recipient is asked to pull a tab on the envelope which zips it open. As the tag is pulled, a message is revealed on its reverse side. Here are possibilities:

> Pull open for great news.
> Exercise for a healthier lifestyle: start by pulling open here.

A further idea is to announce that there is a secret message inside:

> Are you a millionaire?
> Inside this envelope is your key to success.
> Can you find the hidden message worth £500,000?

You can personalize an envelope with the recipient's name:

> Your table is waiting, Mr Jones, at Directions café ...

Envelopes are ideal for short teaser copy lines. Such copy lines are particularly effective when you do not want to plaster your envelope with brash illustrations or use unusually large envelopes, which again may give the appearance of tacky junk mail.

Teaser envelope copy lines are invariably unanswered questions.
To find the answer, the recipient is obliged to open the envelope:

> Directions
> Would you prefer a creamy prawn cocktail or a filling
> minestrone soup?
> Does £9.99 sound appetizing for a three-course meal?
> PenPal
> Business-to-business mailing:
> *Isn't it annoying when taking an order your pen runs out just as*

People often open envelopes from the back rather than the front,
so use the reverse side. The minimum you can do is feature a return
address for use if the mailing is undelivered. Strengthen the offer
by featuring further details about the product or service inside.
Alternatively highlight an incentive – such as a holiday weekend or
complimentary travel bag.

Gabay's tips to guarantee your envelope gets opened

Follow at least three of the ideas in the following list and I
guarantee that your direct mail envelope will be opened:

- *Feature a hand-written address – this is up to twenty times
  more powerful than using a confidential or urgent stamp.*
- *Feature a thick package.*
- *Don't use a clear envelope.*
- *Consider using a real stamp on a reply-paid envelope.*
- *Make sure your copy approach matches your audience's
  mind-set and the setting in which they will open your
  envelope.*
- *Be warned that bar codes and other forms of electronic
  postal tagging make it clear that a piece of direct mail is
  just that.*

YOUR LETTER

There are scores of copywriting techniques that can help
improve the effectiveness of letters. A good rule of thumb is to
write your letter as if you are writing to a friend or colleague –
formally enough to be credible yet informally enough to
be sincere.

Letters should be as long as it takes you to write them – by this, I
mean either until you run out of permissible space (e.g. one side of
A4 paper) or until you have nothing else to discuss.

Long copy letters take time to read but short copy letters may
not be adequate. The ideal compromise is to structure your letter
copy with several entry points. Whether your copy is long or
short, that means that the reader can dip in at key points. If your
message is interesting, the reader will read on or return to the letter
at a later stage. (Just because you sent a direct mail piece by
first-class mail, it doesn't necessarily follow that it will receive
prompt attention.)

A step-by-step guide to letters

LETTER STRUCTURE: STRIPE

Salutation
Topic (headline)
Reason
Information
Prompt to action
End

The shorter steps: O-M-A
First paragraph. Overview interest copy.

Second paragraph. Meaning – putting your offer in context. For example, in a letter inviting the prospect to a trade show, explaining what you will be demonstrating at the show.

Third paragraph, call to Action, including email, coupon etc.

(For email copy, remember the 'James Bond' rule of writing: just as James Bond movies open with a big 'bang', open your email with your proposition, including details of intriguing benefits and features, and then close with your big 'bang' offer.)

LAYOUT FOR EMAILS: CRABS

Chunk your paragraphs into blocks of no more than two sentences.

Relevance. Ensure your tone and style is appropriate.

Accuracy. Check your facts and if possible drop jargon.

Brevity. Get the message distilled into the first paragraph and make each bulleted item less than eight words.

Scanability. Make headings, first words in paragraphs and calls to action stand out.

OVERALL APPEARANCE

Your letter should be clearly laid out on good-quality, preferably environmentally friendly paper. Your company logo adds to the overall credibility as well as increasing recognition.

Don't force all your text onto one side of paper. Readers tend to scan text (as they do when reading websites). In long letters, they skip to the reverse side. Try to keep the copy on just one side.

Wherever possible, give your copy the space to breathe. Crammed sentences are difficult to read.

Type styles (fonts) should also be easy to read – save the creative flourishes for your message not the typeface.

Think about how the eye tracks your letter. If your layout is generally messy, the whole mailing could end up as a fruitless exercise.

Unless you are writing for the Middle-East market, which reads from right to left, or the Far-East market, which reads from top to bottom, structure your letter with its headline and any leading subheads or illustrations at top left. Then flow the copy neatly left to right, with your final push at the bottom right-hand side of the page. (This is only a basis for your letter layout, not the template for every letter.)

Never staple or clip your sheets of paper together. This can tear the letter and staples and clips may get caught on fingernails. Even paperless staples bulk-up letters.

Your letter is a person-to-person affair. Make it appear as personal as possible. Photocopied letters look and feel tacky. Printer typeset letters look like printer typeset letters. It is a waste of everyone's time and effort preparing a letter to a named person, and then wiping out all the elements of individuality through inappropriate production techniques.

DEAR ...

Address your reader by their name. (Remember that direct mail is also called 'one-to-one' marketing.) Check that you have spelled the recipient's name correctly and included the correct address details. If you don't know the person's name, address them by job title. If this isn't possible, address them by category (e.g. Dear Diner, Dear Shop-keeper, Dear Fellow Director).

HEADLINE

Wherever possible, capture your main proposition in a headline. Although they are vulgar, include copy words that stimulate involvement or action. For example:

> At last here's a restaurant that caters for all the family.
> Announcing ScotsdaleNorth.com's brand new site.
> 12 Reasons to pick up a PenPal.
> Don't buy anything until you have read this.
> Yours free ...
> Everything you ever wanted to know about ...

OPENING PARAGRAPH

When writing email, limit your subject box copy to six words or less. This is because many browsers cut off the text in subject boxes after six letters.

If you haven't included it yet, now is a good time to use the word 'you'. (Remember both email and direct mail are personalized, targeted forms of communication.) For example:

> You appreciate the finer things in life ...
>
> Your continued support for the local action group is really appreciated ...
>
> Our records show that you are a keen reader of Teach Yourself books. You already know how the series features fascinating insights into everything from marketing to copywriting . Each title is written by a respected expert in his or her field. Now you can extend your library knowledge by taking advantage of our exclusive reader's Teach Yourself book club.
>
> Each month you can select another Teach Yourself title that will be sent direct to your home at a price that is guaranteed to be at least 25% off our recommended retail price.

> Just think. All that invaluable information available when you
> want it.
>
> School projects are made even more fascinating. Hobbies come
> to life ...

Your opening paragraph needs to grab the reader's attention
and be succinct. Opening paragraphs should contain no more than
three to four sentences. Vary the length of paragraphs so that the
copy looks lively on the page. Too often, overloaded copy leads
to overloaded readers. Remember that a sentence is a thought.
Thoughts make up ideas. An idea is a paragraph. Once you have
explained your idea, close the paragraph and start with a fresh
thought. Keep sentences (average 14–16 words in each) short.
Limit paragraphs to three – or at the most – four per paragraph.
In email copy those figures are reduced down to one to three
sentences per paragraph at the very most.

BENEFITS

As tacky as it sounds, even in our sophisticated world, people
adore a great offer. Hammer home your benefits. Tease your reader
with further details of benefits (e.g. a free mystery gift) which will
be revealed later within the copy. Highlight your benefits with
bullet points. Stress the benefits:

> ▶ *Believe me when I say ...*
> ▶ *When they told me, I couldn't believe it.*
> ▶ *What do you think?*

Incorporate benefits in captions:

> (Picture of PenPal)
>
> Stainless steel casing, tungsten tip and tested to write for
> kilometre upon kilometre.

Explain why the reader needs the product or service. Show examples of how the product or service can enhance their lives:

> Compared to many other credit cards, the ScotsdaleNorth credit card can save you up to 25% off purchases and an additional 5% off every bill totalling over £50 each and every time you shop at ScotsdaleNorth.

GET INVOLVED FROM THE START

A letter is special. After all, apart from birthdays and anniversaries, people are sending less and less personal post. So make sure your letter is:

- *intriguing*
- *charming*
- *surprising*
- *rewarding.*

To achieve all this both letters and emails should be:

- *relevant*
- *personal*
- *tactful*
- *courteous*
- *clear*
- *conversational*
- *interesting*
- *right length.*

So put yourself in your reader's shoes:

- *People are procrastinators – give them a reason to respond.*
- *People are sceptical – offer a believable message.*
- *People are lazy – make it easy to reply.*
- *People worry about making the wrong decision – use case histories to offer assurance.*
- *People avoid risk. Give them a guarantee.*

▶ *People think 'I can't read all this.' Provide what they need to make a decision and not a word more.*

Another way of highlighting benefits is the Grim Reaper approach. Within reason and certainly without compromising any regulatory rules, discuss the consequences of not making a commitment. In the past, life assurance companies used this technique:

Should the worst happen, your dependants could be left to cope with financial burdens such as funeral expenses and mortgage repayments.

The Protection Plan helps to ensure that even if your existing life policies from work have matured or been cashed in, you can still leave a significant cash sum to the ones you love.

IT PAYS TO REPLY TODAY

Offer an incentive for a quick response and describe the reason for a quick answer in full.

✓ Reply today because …
✓ We can't hold this price forever.
✓ Stocks are low.
✓ We'll give you a 'cashback' for your old product.
✓ The bigger your order, the more you save.
✓ We want to demonstrate it in the comfort of your own home.
✓ This offer is exclusive to you.
✓ We want you to try it before you buy it.
✓ We want to offer you a personalized quotation.
✓ This is only a small sample of something even better.
✓ If you buy it we'll give you a second one free.
✓ If you buy the bread, we'll give you the butter.
✓ If you don't like it, you can exchange it for something else.
✓ It's delivered free.
✓ We don't want your money until next year.
✓ We're always here to service it.
✓ You can sample the entire range for a special price.

(Contd)

- ✓ *You have our guarantee on it.*
- ✓ *Buy it today and we'll extend our guarantee.*
- ✓ *We'll also send one to your friend.*
- ✓ *We'll enter your name in our prize draw.*
- ✓ *Every applicant wins a prize.*
- ✓ *We'll match every penny with a donation to charity.*
- ✓ *We'll pay the extra costs.*
- ✓ *We'll eat our hat if you don't like it.*

Guarantee your guarantee

Don't just make an ordinary guarantee. Offer an extraordinary level of assurance – after all, an amazing product or service such as yours is perfect:

14 days no-questions-asked money back guarantee.
365 days no-quibble service guarantee.
30 days part-exchange guarantee.

- Up to £10,000 BIG value life
- From just 30p a day
- No awkward medical
- No intrusive health questions
- Up to £50 cash back on your
- Free first month's premium
- Guaranteed

SAVE THE BEST TILL LAST

Just as the reader thinks that you couldn't possibly offer more – Bang! You fire off your dynamic closing shot. Perhaps this could be covered in a PS (post script) or embolden type face: Urge them to 'act now'. Quick! Before it's too late!

IT'S SO EASY TO ORDER

Nothing could be easier than saying 'Yes' to your terrific offer. All they have to do is complete the simple reply device that either is attached or can be found in the mailing package.

YOURS SINCERELY

Every letter should be signed – if not in person, at least the signature should be printed in blue ink so it looks as if it was individually signed.

DON'T FORGET THE PS

The PS is your last opportunity in your letter to reinforce your sales argument. You can use it in a number of ways, including:

▶ *Adding a last-minute benefit.*
▶ *Reminding the reader about a special free gift.*
▶ *Drawing the reader's attention to one of the key points made within your copy.*

PPS – JUST IN CASE YOU DIDN'T HEAR THE FIRST TIME

The postscript is one of the most powerful creative elements in a letter. Keep your postscript short. Response may be further increased if you enclose your postscript in a box or simulate a hand-written typeface.

THE OPTIONAL GIZMO

Gadgets help give a mailing an extra creative dimension. For example, you could include a pair of 3-D glasses to view a specially printed leaflet, or a pen to sign the order form. One interesting idea is to attach a dime or a 10 pence piece to your sales letter, then ask the reader to use it to scratch out a panel revealing whether or not a prize has been won. (This technique is sometimes called 'coin rub'.)

The OK guidelines for including gadgets
It's not OK to:

▶ *include anything that can be squashed or melts in the post*
▶ *include anything that's perishable*

- *include a gadget that may offend (e.g. a key ring holding a condom)*
- *include a particularly bulky or heavy gadget*
- *treat a live animal as a gadget – never include anything that's live.*

It's OK to:

- *attach your gadget to one secure spot*
- *try and tie your gadget in with the copy*
- *strengthen your envelope so that the gadget doesn't rip it to bits.*

Let's see how some of the above techniques can be incorporated into the text of a typical direct mail letter:

Relevant gadget

[packet of seeds stuck to letter]
Cultivate these seeds for a beautiful
display of flowers.

Strong headline:

Buy this book and cultivate your gardening knowledge at a never to be repeated price
Personalized salutation:
Dear Mr Jones,

Intriguing opening paragraph:

John Willis once said that the 'essence of caring for a garden starts with appreciating the simple seed'.
(Now show how all of this is directly relevant to the reader.)
The longer you spend caring for and nurturing a garden, the greater your horticultural knowledge becomes.
Now, you can develop your skills and understanding and so gain even greater satisfaction from gardening.

Note the use of the words 'you' and 'yours' in the example above.
Now introduce the three Ws.

What is it?

The Gardening Almanac is the most authoritative work of its kind.

What does it offer?

It draws on the highly respected experience of over 100 world-leading botanists and horticulturalists. The Gardening Almanac plant classification standards are practised internationally. The Gardening Almanac classifies and describes practically every plant species in the world.

- Everything you'll ever need in one volume.
- Over 10,000 ornamental and economical plants.
- 350 specially commissioned, beautifully accurate line drawings.
- In-depth facts that help you accurately identify and name even the rarest plants.
- Practical guidelines that will help you achieve spectacular results with your own plants.
- The 'inside secrets' of creating spectacular plants.
- Those are just a few examples of a world of answers that can be found inside the extraordinary 2,200 page Gardening Almanac.

Wow! – save the best until last.

You can own this simply ingenious book for just £99. That's a saving of £60 off the recommended retail price.

It pays to reply today.

Be sure to place your order before 31st May. Please do so – as a token of thanks, we will send you a complimentary copy of 'Gardening Secrets'.

It's easy to order.

Ordering your Almanac is easy. Simply complete the enclosed order form and return it with payment in the pre-paid envelope provided. Alternatively you can order online or over the phone with your credit card. Just call our 24-hour customer Hotline on 1234 5678, quoting reference number 'one' or visit www. gardening-genius.com
I look forward to sending your Almanac and hope you enjoy the complimentary packet of seeds.
Yours sincerely
Name
Title
PS Remember, this offer will never be repeated. You must respond before 31st May.

Email styles

Many send emails far too quickly. Apart from being full of typos (especially if sent when angry), they can be full of spite. (Not a great idea when sending an email to a boss or customer.) Often called 'e-shots' or 'e-blasts', great email campaigns deliver:

▶ *A direct offer ('sell')*
▶ *An indirect offer ('tell', as in providing service information)*
▶ *News (as in sending out an e-zine (electronic newsletter).*

They may also pose a question which is answered when linked to a website. They may be assertive, commanding people to take immediate action, for example when instructing web users to protect themselves from a web-virus.

They may offer reasons to do something. For example: *'12 reasons to read Teach Yourself'* or *'How to fix your roof in three hours …*'. Another great technique in emails is to incorporate testimonials from people with similar needs to those of readers. This can also include linking the email to specialized blogs or micro-blogs such as Twitter.

Apart from mis-spelling a recipient's name, or sending your email from an impersonal email address (such as info@ or mail@) one of the most common mistakes made when writing emails is to reduce the content to either piffy sentences or bullet point lists.

Look at these 'before and after' examples:

> Dear Mr Smith,
>
> Thank you for your email of 9th March. Regrettably, we are unable to accommodate your request, but remain most interested to hear from you at your own convenience if, and when you should have any similar requirements.
> Yours sincerely
> Timothy M. Timms

(Too formal.)

> Dear Mr Smith. Sorry, but we can't help on this occasion. Thanks for the enquiry.

(Perhaps too friendly.)

> Bob – thanks for your email. Sorry, we can't help, but you could try Wackos in Wakefield. All the best, Tim Timms.

(Too gruff.)

> *Hi Bob. We don't do it . But be happy – TT.*

(Too flippant.)

> Dear Mr Smith,
>
> Thanks for your enquiry. I've checked with the various
> departments and I'm sorry to report that, for now at least, we
> can't help. You could try Wackos of Wakefield who I understand
> might have what you need.
> Please try us again next time - we're always updating our range.
> All the best,
> Tim Timms
> Sales Manager

(Ah – just right!)

Leaflets

Leaflets highlight a few more details of your offer – just enough to
'seal a deal'. They often feature illustrations to show how a product
is used or a service operates. A common leaflet format is 'roll fold'.
This type of leaflet is folded up to six times. As the reader unfolds
each page, the creative message is explained in greater detail.

> *If you thought that was a great idea ...*

(Unfold the page to the next 'reveal'.)

> *... then look at this:*

As with advertisements, allow subheads to direct the reader
through your leaflet copy. If the product is particularly technical,
consider including a question-and-answer panel towards the end.
These help you to address legal requirements:

> • How long will this service operate?
> • Who is eligible to apply?

and so on.

A one-page leaflet encapsulates your benefits on a double-sided sheet of paper. One-page leaflets are ideal for recapping the benefits of an early reply – for example:

> *Reply early and receive a free travel holdall*
> *Yours FREE if you apply in 10 days.*

(The tighter your advertised deadline, the keener the response. The more distant your deadline the more lack-lustre the initial response. So 10 days is better than 14 days and 24 hours is better than a week.)

> *This handy travel holdall doesn't only look great...*
> *... but helps lighten the load when out on your travels ...*

Actually, let's use this opportunity to demonstrate the power of a positive over a negative headline:

Original (negative):

> *This handy travel holdall doesn't only look great...*
> *... but helps lighten the load when out on your travels ...*

Improved (positive):

> *This handy travel holdall looks great ...*
> *... and lightens the load ...*

Feature a picture of the incentive and, if practicable, close-up pictures of certain special details. In the case of the travel holdall these might be double zips, hidden pockets, rubber-grip handles ...

GIVE YOUR COPY A LITTLE LIFT

Lift letters are small note-like memos which enhance a sales message or reassure the reader about a purchasing choice. Often, lift letters are 'written' by someone other than the writer

of the main letter copy. This creates an individual endorsement.
For example:

Dear Mr Jones,

Can't make up your mind?

When I first looked through the Gardening Almanac I was
amazed at the kind of detail that each entry went into. The
illustrations are, to say the least, impressive. The technical data
reveal fascinating facts that will help you get the most from
your plants and flowers.

Best of all, the price of just £99 means that you save £60 off the
recommended retail price.

Take it from me, if you only ever buy one gardening reference
book in your lifetime, you should make sure it's the Gardening
Almanac.

Yours sincerely

Before progressing further, once again let's consider a 'before
and after' copy approach to this piece. Compare the following
version which, through the use of shorter sentences, inclusion of
substantiation, 'active' verbs and pertinent adjectives, all help make
it sound much more punchier:

Dear Mr Jones,

Exploring the extraordinary fact-packed Gardening Almanac
I was hooked from cover to cover. The expert gardeners'
attention is simply amazing. For example, impressive
illustrations offer a bee's eye view of flora and forna. Technical
data reveal fascinating tips on how and when to plant plants
and flowers.

Best of all, for just £99 you get an extraordinary £60 off the
recommended retail price. Take it from me, if you only ever buy
one gardening reference book, make sure it's the Gardening
Almanac.

Yours sincerely

The reply device

Like coupons in press advertisements, the mailing reply device needs to be clearly designed. Include details such as your email, website and telephone number. You could also consider completing an example order form (great for mail order catalogues, including online versions).

Always repeat the response incentive offer, if only in a couple of key words.

If you want to try a classic 'old school' direct mail copywriting idea, consider including a 'YES' and 'NO' sticker for your reply device. This encourages the reader to select a sticker and then put it on the response device. Research shows that in the case of a free prize draw, if you offer people a choice of stickers, most people choose the YES sticker in preference to the NO sticker as that appears to influence their chance of winning in the draw. (Of course, this is not what necessarily happens.)

Alternatively, you could include a 'MAYBE' sticker. A MAYBE response back to your company can be passed on to other departments which could offer the respondent an item that is more suitable for their needs.

Finally, try to include the powerful YES word within the copy for the reply device:

YES – I want to know more.
YES – please send me my Almanac today.

Twenty-six 'old school' creative mailing ideas

1 PEELABLE APPEALS

Stickers add intrigue and involvement. They are infinitely versatile. Peel them and you can reveal part of the contents of the package. Why not give a sticker additional value by asking the recipient to use it on a free gift voucher?

> Stick this onto the coupon inside and you could win a free holiday to Jerusalem.

2 DISTINCTIVE ENVELOPES

Unusually shaped envelopes make your mailing more distinctive. However, circles can be quite expensive to produce as they take up a lot of paper stock (not a great idea for environmentally aware organizations). Other similar possibilities include triangular-shaped envelopes, extra large envelopes and extra small envelopes.

3 CARD DECKS

These are also known as 'postcard decks' or 'foil card decks'. The idea is to share a mailing with other advertisers. All contribute special cards which fit in either a foil, plastic or paper pouch. Product details are presented in the form of a postcard. One side details the product whilst the other features a response device. A variation is a postcard distributed to relevant hotel, cinema or restaurant chains. Tourists, cinema goers or diners, pick up a complimentary postcard usually featuring an interesting visual device or graphic promoting ... you!

4 MEMORY STICK AND POD MAILERS

Instead of a printed mail piece, why not produce a short downloadable podcast linked to an email or an interesting short film published on YouTube. Consider a downloadable slide presentation on a site like slideshare. Some organizations send memory stick presentations, however I have found that a growing number of companies are averse to using them. An up and coming trend is to electronically offer an 'App' that can be downloaded to a mobile phone. Alternatively, for something a bit more in keeping with the 'old school' theme, if you are promoting a product like a fitness programme, a short DVD preview may get your prospects reaching out for more.

5 *THE NO-NAME MAILER*

Leave out the product name on the envelope. This works well when your product is financially sensitive or has already been mass-mailed several times. (I once had to do this for a credit card company that had previously been mailed to 12 million households!)

6 *THE JACK-IN-THE-BOX MAILER*

Breaking open a seal – usually at the edge of the outside envelope, the reader pulls out a concertina-type mailer in which each sheet is attached to another.

7 *THE DOOR-DROP MAILER*

Circulate your mailing with a letterbox distribution company, working door to door. You can be very precise about which households receive your mailing and you gain greater control over timing its arrival.

8 *THE BANGTAIL ENVELOPE*

Include a special envelope featuring a perforated 'tail' of paper near the sealing flap that can be used as an auxiliary order form.

9 *BILL STUFFER*

Add a leaflet or separate letter along with your invoices or statements. If your budget doesn't stretch to a separate leaflet, you can use space available on the invoice or statement to highlight a creative message:

> Total now due £220
> HAVE YOU APPLIED FOR YOUR PLUS CARD YET?
> IT COULD SAVE ££££s ON YOUR SHOPPING AT SCOTSDALE
> NORTHSIDE – FOR FURTHER DETAILS CONTACT THE
> PLUS CARD HOTLINE ON 080012345

10 *BIRTHDAY MAILING*

Wish someone happy birthday or congratulate them on the anniversary of first using your product or service. This is regularly used by insurance companies, who choose the anniversary of an insurance policy (e.g. a motor insurance policy) to remind the policyholder of the company's great contract renew deals:

> 12 months' additional peace of mind at last year's prices.
> Hurry – you must renew your policy within the next 11 days!

11 *BOUNCE-BACK MAILING*

Congratulations! You have successfully sold your product using direct mail. Now include a second special offer sent along with the product itself. For example:

> Now you own a PenPal – use this coupon to write off 50% on a
> PenPal gift set.

12 *MEMBER-GET-MEMBER MAILERS*

These are also known as 'MGM', 'Friend-get-a-Friend' or 'Introduce-a-Friend'. They are one of the most effective ways of enhancing your customer database.

The technique often relies on a small incentive-led leaflet which details an additional free gift offered to the recipient for recommending a friend. This can be strengthened even further by offering an extra gift if the friend signs up for a product or service:

> This connoisseur's Guide to Fine Wines is yours FREE just for recommending a friend.

> This box of six specially selected wines is yours FREE once your friend starts to enjoy the benefits of our club.

(Again, let's rewrite that last sentence to offer a sense of urgency:

> *This box of six specially selected wines is yours FREE as soon as your friend starts to enjoy the benefits of our club.*

Even if you only have a limited budget for an MGM, it is still worth your while to include space for a recommendation within a reply device.

13 *POP-UPS*

Pop-ups include anything from a pop-up letter to a pop-up coupon that places the order form directly into the recipient's hand.

14 *AUDIO MAILING*

Audio mailings include pre-recorded CD discs or, when used as emails, links to podcasts. 'Old school' writers used to feature envelopes with pre-recorded microchips. When the recipient opened the envelope, a tiny speaker inside the envelope was activated playing a voice heard from inside the envelope!

Whatever kind of audio technology you use, take complete advantage of music, sound effects and a compelling story.

15 *EMBOSSED MEMBERSHIP CARDS*

The technique of including a plastic credit card-type membership card – complete with the recipient's name embossed on it – was particularly popular during the 1980s. With people's wallets bulging with more plastic than actually cash, its use is waning. However it can still encourage custom and enhance personalization. For example:

Here's your ScotsdaleNorth.com PLUS CARD

↓

PLUS CARD

5% on line DISCOUNT

Ms Ann Jones
SHOPPER VALUE CODE 1234

Keep it safe, Ms Jones. The more you use it,
the bigger your discounts.

Here's your ScotsdaleNorth.com PLUS CARD – click on and type in your online membership number to claim your shopping discount.

16 *PRE-MAILER MAILER*

Also known as a pre-announcement mailer, this technique provides advance notification of a major mailing campaign. It works well when you want to announce something like a major prize draw or to 'warm' up an email prospect in stages leading to a campaign. (These stages can be supported offline in the press as well as traditional post.)

> Watch your post – this time next week you could be wiser and richer in more ways than one.

(Be careful though, the more an email or direct mail heading or subject box line sounds 'crass' the less chance it will have to work.)

Like birthday mailings, pre-mailers can be strengthened by including personalized details unique to the recipient:

> We've only sent this notice to 23 people in Queenstown.
>
> Alison, you are one of only 4 people in your road who will receive it. By this time next week you could be our next millionaire!

17 *KEEP UP WITH THE JONESES MAILERS*

This is an example of database management working closely with copywriters. Assuming your product or service is mass-market, check the geographical area that you intend to mail. Then produce a company list of all nearby organizations who have previously purchased a specific product or service. This kind of list is called a 'cluster list'. Then:

> Right now your competitors are making great savings with a Plus Card for retailers. Why not join them?

18 *TWO HALVES ARE BETTER THAN ONE MAILERS*

Dear Mr Jones,

Last August you kindly purchased a 6mega pixel mobile phone from us. As a valued customer, you can now take advantage of a hands-free car adaptor kit at 75% off the manufacturer's recommended retail price. All you have to do is complete and send the second half of this letter off to us today.
We look forward to hearing from you.
Yours sincerely

Dear Mr Jones,

Have you ever been at the wheel when, 'ring' 'ring', someone calls on your mobile?
You can't pull over. It's illegal. Even if you could, just as you park, the phone stops ringing. Boy, it's frustrating! Well now you can pick up that call without picking up the phone. All you need is our our free car adaptor kit. Simply complete the following and return it to us today. You'll even save 75% off the usual price.
Your name _____
Your mobile number _____
Your credit card number

_____

Type _____
Expiry date _____
Signature _____

Thank you.
Yours sincerely

19 *CHEQUE-BOOK MAILERS*

Cheque-book mailers feature an 'old school' cheque-book type format in which each 'cheque' is a valuable voucher against an incentive such as an additional entry into a prize draw.

The 'cheque stub' section of the book incorporates text copy. Each page of text refers to that section's personalized 'cheque' offer.

20 SNIFF AND BUY MAILERS

Spice up a mailing by incorporating scent strips alongside the copy. The overall sensation (or scentsation!) is conveyed in a letter that you read and smell as you go along:

> You can smell the summer meadows in a ScotsdaleNorth air freshener.

21 GO GREEN

Fact: our planet is running out of natural resources. Direct mail advertisers need to be responsible marketers by using options such as recycled paper. The downside is that certain recycled paper may be detrimental to print quality. The upside is that this effect demonstrates that an organization cares about our planet. However, shop for recycled stock carefully; it has been known to be more expensive than ordinary paper!

22 POST AND PHONE

Send a simple mailing containing nothing more than a postcard. It features an intriguing headline directing the recipient to make a phone call or visiting a website – when all will be revealed.

Depending on your type of organization and the length of telephone message, this technique can be made even more cost effective by using a self-financing commercial phone number.

23 THE OVERSEAS LETTER

Curiosity can be further enhanced if you mail your piece from an overseas address. In certain circumstances, this may even save on postal costs.

24 FAX MAILERS

Every office has a .com address and virtually all consumers are so used to email that for many the thought of a fax mailer will just sound ludicrous. However, before completely writing off the idea, keep in mind that most PCs have fax machine software or at least access to scanning devices, mostly for business-to-business purposes. By using fax mailers sparingly – asking for permission first – you have access to a different communications channel that promotes officialdom, immediacy and impact. Try to keep your message on one page. Use large and bold typefaces and always provide details of how you can be contacted.

25 *QUESTIONNAIRE MAILERS*

Questionnaires test a market or build a new database. They show existing customers that you care about their opinion. They give you an ideal opportunity to contact customers and strengthen the dialogue with them. You should write questionnaires with simplicity in mind. Questions should be clear, copy should be precise, and terminology should be kept to a minimum. Each question should require either one direct answer or one choice from a pre-determined set of multiple-choice answers.

Copy tips for questionnaires
▶ *Explain why you are sending the questionnaire. Use a covering letter (or, if linked to a web-based questionnaire, a covering email) to explain why you are seeking a response. Reassure your respondent that answers are confidential. (If you intend to use the answers for other companies, give the respondent the opportunity to decline the option to share data with other organizations.)*
▶ *Consider the merits of rewarding answers with a free gift (although be careful not to influence specific answers).*
▶ *Complete a sample question to show how the respondent is intended to answer the rest of the questionnaire.*
▶ *Whenever possible avoid open-ended questions: 'Why do you think …?'; 'Explain your views …'*
▶ *Include a 'Don't know' option. Otherwise the respondent may think that the question is too difficult and give up with the rest of the questionnaire. (A good technique for web-based questionnaires is to feature a question line chart showing how*

many questions are left to be answered. This is question 9 of 20 – only 11 to go! This helps reassure people that the whole process really wont take that long to complete.)

▶ *Assure your respondent that the questionnaire is not an intelligence test. There are no 'right' answers. The only thing being tested is your product or service.*

▶ *Don't cram too many possible answers into one question. Instead of: Typically, how many own-label products do you buy at ScotsdaleNorth.com? ask about each category, one at a time, and then:*

> *In a week do you buy*
> one [□] two [□] three [□] *cans of ScotsdaleNorth vegetables?*
> *Which can of vegetables do you buy?*
> Mushrooms [□] Corn [□] Carrots [□]

▶ *If possible avoid personal questions. Instead of: 'How much do you earn?' try:*

> *Is your income between*
> £20,000 – £30,000 [□]
> £31,000 – £35,000 [□]
> Over £36,000 [□]

▶ *If you really cannot avoid direct intimate questions, explain why you are asking them. Avoid: 'Have you ever had an extra-marital affair?' Instead try:*

> *To establish how our service can best provide confidential counselling to couples, please answer the following:*
> *In the last year, have you had more than one sexual partner?*
> Yes [□] No [□]
> *If yes, how many?* 1–2 [□] 3–4 [□] Over 5 [□]

▶ *Include a pre-paid postage device – sealable and overprinted with the word 'Confidential'.*

(Refer also to *Make a Difference with Your Marketing*.)

26 PRIZE DRAW MAILINGS AND COMPETITIONS

Prize draw mailings and competitions add excitement and energy to a product or service offer. In the UK, these may be:

- *Charitable lotteries.*
- *Draw for which no skill or purchase required; selection of a pre-determined number of tickets.*
- *Competitions calling for a fair degree of physical or mental skill or judgement, and with the proviso that a purchase must be made.*
- *Competition for which no purchase is needed, no payment is required, and there is no call for great skill or judgement.*

So, ScotsdaleNorth could:

- *Ask customers to make a purchase and enter a competition to identify the country of origin of four types of canned fruit and complete a tie-breaker.*
- *Ask any person to enter a hundredth anniversary free prize draw by completing a coupon and returning it by post. (No purchase needed.)*
- *Ask customers to purchase a lottery ticket for £2, with part of the proceeds going to a charity and a top prize of £20,000-worth of shopping (as long as the company was registered as part of a voluntary body giving proceeds to the charity and followed the restrictions imposed by the Lotteries and Amusement Act).*
- *Ask anyone to play a shopping game and win a holiday (as long as the game was based on the rules for a draw and incorporated in the Gaming Act restrictions).*

Prize draws and competitions should lead with the big prize:

We'll pay your shopping bills for life.

Are there any runner-up prizes? If so, list them. The more prizes, the more chances to win! What's the total amount of prize money or prize value? Excite your readers:

> All in all, we're giving away an incredible £105,000,000 worth of prizes!!!

The bigger the figures, both in financial terms and appearance on the page, the better. Again, referring to the classical school of copywriting, you could also feature the big numbers on valuable-looking prize draw certificates.

Did you know?

One art director that I used to work with collected old bonds. He adapted the borders on each bond and used them to give an impression of value on prize draw certificates. (Today for many cynical consumers such certificates appear artificial.)

If there are any previous winners, give their names – with their permission. People like to see real people winning prizes. Always discuss how easy it is to enter and win.

Incorporate 'dream copy' into your text:

> Just imagine; this time next month you could be relaxing by the pool of the five-star Holiday Hut hotel in Dimona. Fancy a drink? Your bar steward will be delighted to serve you anything from a tropical Pina Colada to a long, cool and refreshing Tequila Sunrise.
>
> Come the evening and you can step out in style. We'll lay on a chauffeur-driven limousine that will whisk you and your partner away to the sensational Charedi's night-club where you can really let your hair down and swing ...

Or:

> What would you do if you won £20,000,000?
> Buy a mansion in the country? A perky Porsche? Your own light aircraft? ... Why not start up that business you've always promised yourself?
> Take a year-long cruise around the world ...

Always list your rules simply and clearly:

1 *Entrants must be residents of the UK and over the age of 18, but not employees (or members of their families) or anyone connected with the draw.*

2 *All entries to be received by [date]. The draw for a Porsche car will be made on [date].*

3 *Only one entry per person is allowed.*

4 *Entry to the draw is free. No purchase required. Proof of posting will not be accepted as proof of delivery. Responsibility cannot be accepted for lost or mislaid entries. Damaged or defaced entries will be disqualified. No correspondence will be entered into.*

5 *The winner will be notified by post. The name and area of the prize draw winner will be available after [date] to anyone sending a stamped self addressed envelope to [address].*

6 *No cash alternative will be offered.*

7 *The draw will be made by an independent body.*

8 *Entry to the prize draw is deemed to imply acceptance of these rules.*

Always seek legal advice for advertising regulations from your local country's ruling body such as the Advertising Standards Association (www.asa.org.uk) or Institute of Sales Promotion (www.isp.org.uk).

A word about catalogues

Until the proliferation of direct sales websites, mass-marketed direct mail made considerable profits from mailing catalogues of goods and services.

Did you know?

Incidentally, the first-ever mail order business was incorporated on 15 September 1871 as the Army & Navy Co-operative. The society published its first mail order catalogue in February 1872. It had 112 pages and included goodies such as Ladies' Merino Drawers at 5s 9d a pair.

As with writing descriptive product copy on the web, rules of detailing everything about a product are particularly relevant for catalogue writing. Yet don't over-write. Your style has to be direct. Captions need to be benefits led.

Example from fashion catalogue:

> (Picture of a blouse – close-up of buttons.)
>
> *Pretty colour co-ordinated buttons that add an extra touch of elegance.*

Explain how things look and feel, how they will make the user feel or cook or read or write... better than ever before.

> Feeling cozy doesn't mean feeling trapped under a rough blanket of wool. These bold cable-knit crew neck sweaters are durable enough for even the toughest Scottish North Sea conditions. Yet they feel wonderfully soft and delicate on your skin.

Again as on a web page, copy needs to work alongside the visual layout and style of a catalogue. It should be enthusiastic and personal, assuming the role of a shopper's companion. The companion points to a special product detail: '*look at this ... notice that ...*'.

If you offer a credit facility, include a small panel after each product description showing how little needs to be spent over how long in order to buy the product.

Once again as with web pages, catalogue and brochure pages need to be accessible and welcoming rather than stuffed with words. Colour code to differentiate between categories. Consider various forms of indexing including heavy board section dividers. Incorporate extra details in boxes about the history of goods and size of clothes.

100% PURE TRIPLE-WEIGHT CASHMERE

YOUR CHOICE OF COLOURS
MUSHROOM• MID GREY• TARTAN GREEN
AVAILABLE SIZES S.M.L.XL.
Our direct price from Scotland:
ONLY £xxx (UK & EEC)
ONLY £xxx (OVERSEAS TAX FREE)
JUST QUOTE CODE xxxx

Add interest and authenticity by including background titbits about, for example, where a silk dress comes from, or outline the manufacturing process:

It's not just a PenPal owner who could write a compelling life story
This mild-mannered pen has been stamped upon, burnt, smashed and even drowned before getting our written seal of approval.

Other methods are to incorporate a testimonial from a happy user, or include a guarantee panel.

Many catalogues also feature an introduction piece or letter. For this, follow the general rules of writing a direct response letter, with the copy acting as an all embracing guide that explains:

▶ *What makes this catalogue so special.*
▶ *The effort that went into its production.*
▶ *The range within.*
▶ *The easy ways to order.*
▶ *Any credit facilities.*
▶ *Reiteration of the easy ways to order. (Shaded boxes or panels highlighting order hotlines, perhaps featuring a telephone salesperson, are a good idea to incorporate throughout the catalogue.)*

Direct mail quick tips

▶ *Direct mail builds customer relationships.*
▶ *Direct mail is a personal business.*
▶ *Good copy with bad targeting is wasted copy.*
▶ *Mailings need to inform.*
▶ *Mailings need to involve.*
▶ *Envelopes and copy should reflect a creative tone of voice.*
▶ *When appropriate use the words free and you in copy.*
▶ *Entice recipients to open an envelope now.*
▶ *Letters should be easy on the eye and simple to understand.*
▶ *Letters should feature multiple entry points.*
▶ *Letters should be personalized.*
▶ *Letters should be benefit led.*
▶ *Use the three Ws.*
▶ *Explain why someone should reply.*
▶ *Make replying easy.*
▶ *Make replying fun.*
▶ *Offer guarantees.*
▶ *Use postscripts.*
▶ *Feature relevant gadgets only.*
▶ *Consider different creative formats.*
▶ *Use leaflets to tell a fuller story.*
▶ *Use questionnaires to discover more about a prospect and enhance service to a customer.*
▶ *Use prize draws and competitions to add energy to a mailing.*
▶ *Know your aim.*
▶ *Get to know your prospects.*
▶ *Talk about them – not you.*
▶ *Focus on benefits.*
▶ *Get to the point.*
▶ *Keep it simple.*
▶ *Have a strong opening and theme.*
▶ *Be specific – not vague.*
▶ *Reflect the language of your brand.*

- *Offer believable arguments.*
- *Edit, edit, edit your copy.*
- *Ask for action.*

COMMON SALES LETTER MISTAKES

- *Too chummy with reader (insincerity).*
- *Making clichéd statements.*
- *Too many features – not enough single-minded benefits.*
- *Bad-mouthing the competition.*
- *Making 'over-the-top' claims.*
- *Relying too much on the brochure.*

OVER TO YOU

▶ *Write copy for three different types of zipper envelope.*

▶ *Write a lead-in paragraph for a sales letter selling this book.*

▶ *Write a lift letter from Hodder Headline urging people to buy this book.*

▶ *Look at any example of direct mail and highlight the three Ws in the text.*

▶ *Look in your wardrobe. Write a 60-word direct mail catalogue description for an article of clothing.*

▶ *List six alternative ways to communicate the word 'free'.*

7

Direct mail and charity

In this chapter you will learn:
- **how to use celebrities**
- **how to develop charity copy tactics**
- **how to identify donors.**

One of the most emotive uses of direct mail is the charity mailing. Certain creative criteria which have been shown to be intrinsically motivating for charities:

▶ *Goal orientated – appeals for a specific tangible cause (e.g. human rights in China) or for the provision of an essential service (e.g. blood transfusion).*
▶ *For the helpless – appeals for charities associated with children, animals, the sick or disabled; all regarded as good causes.*

Kinds of donor

1 **The committed giver.** *Gives generously/often. Decides carefully which charity/charities to support. Is concerned about social problems. May offer voluntary work or know a disabled person. They may have a religious commitment.*
2 **The occasional giver.** *Gives less often, usually when asked directly. Is concerned about social problems, but more passively. May provide voluntary work or know a disabled person. Characterized by an ambivalent attitude towards charities/disability, based on ignorance and guilt feelings – 'Should I be doing more?'*

Both types of giver are sensitive to the point of resentment to high-pressure tactics. Many would spurn being approached on the street by aggressive charity workers known as 'chuggers' (Charity-muggers).

WHAT TURNS AN OCCASIONAL DONOR INTO A FREQUENT GIVER?

- *Change of lifestyle – often having children.*
- *Close contact with illness or disability.*
- *Maturing – becoming less self-orientated and more secure about their role in society.*

WHAT MOTIVATES PEOPLE TO GIVE?

There are two main types of trigger:

1 **Direct behavioural trigger** – *for example, pushing a collection box under someone's nose. When not over forceful (as in the case of 'chuggers') this tends to cause an involuntary donation since it is often harder not to give than to give.*
2 **Indirect behavioural trigger** – *based on rational and emotional evaluation of the cause. Seeing a photograph of a sick child in an advertisement may encourage someone to appraise the cause rationally before they are moved to contribute.*

Both routes help charities be more effective. The level of direct fund raising activity is as important as the indirect promotion of the charity's image and appeal.

Committed charity givers are likely to respond to a worthy cause, regardless of its relevance to them personally. In other words, they are willing to give to others in need.

Occasional givers are likely to be motivated by a personally relevant cause – in other words, they want to know what's in it for them (e.g. they may support safe sex information to limit the spread of HIV).

Recognize the type of donor you are writing to and adapt your creative approach accordingly.

Attitudes towards charities using advertising and direct mail

Increasing competition in the charity market means that professional marketing of the worthy or good cause is becoming increasingly vital for survival. Charities adopt professional creative standards used in the marketing of consumer goods. However, charity advertising, including direct mail, remains a sensitive area. Your copy should therefore recognize and respect the feelings of the reader. It is a waste of time to write copy that over-dramatises to such a point that some readers feel subjected to intolerable emotional pressure. Having said this, your copy should be realistic and may not always be pleasant. Sympathetic realism is permissible, emotional blackmail is not.

Flamboyant television or press advertising which clearly costs a lot of money may be perceived as a wasteful use of funds. When using direct mail, a good impression can be given by use of materials such as recycled paper and simple two-colour leaflets.

If one charity helps another through sharing the names of their supporters, that can save money in buying lists and improve responses. However, contributors to charities may object strongly to this and must be given an opportunity to refuse to have their details passed on.

TYPES OF CREATIVE MESSAGE AND SPECIFIC ATTITUDES

Types of charity advertising can be broadly categorized.

1 **Shock.** *This type of copy message ranges from starving kids to frightening statistics. The first creative port of call for charity copywriters is often the shock story. However overtly shocking visuals can actually make a reader turn away.*

2   **Case histories.** *Charities have great stories of courage and*
    hope to tell. Explain about how people have benefited
    from a cause. Provide an emotive dimension (children are
    especially good for this) or show how previous donations have
    transformed a particular person's life:

> £20 will give this girl the gift of a better life

Use of personalities

Endorsement of a cause by a popular and respected personality
increases the awareness of the charity and adds to the credibility
of the cause. The key thing is to choose a celebrity whose persona
either reflects the general tone of voice of a given cause, or who
has a personal story to tell which has been affected by the specific
issues handled by the given charity.

Legacy-direct mail

This kind of direct mail often arises from the results of small-space
advertisements placed near the wills and deaths columns in daily
newspapers by those charities connected with the fight against
terminal diseases (and with old age). For example:

> 1,000,000 children killed each year by malaria.
> No flowers please, but you can make a legacy donation
> to Malaria NetAid
> www.malariahelp.org

Tone

Neither an aggressive attack nor a feeble begging request for
money is going to motivate someone to tap in their credit card

details. This is especially true for the major charities, which must communicate an authoritative image to retain their level of credibility. Whilst it is important to show how reliant you are on donations, the tone in which you do so is crucial.

DIAL 911 NOW!

The Action 911 approach turns an ongoing crisis into an emergency. It concentrates on just one aspect of a specific need. For example, the overall cause may be a particular country but your Action 911 approach can be shelter in that country:

> $10 will shelter this child from hurricanes, freezing rain and frost bite.
> Take action.
> Please give to the Emergency Malawi Appeal today.

Time your Action 911 approach to coincide with a 'giving' period of the year. Christmas is the firm favourite. You could also choose Diwali, Rosh Hashanah, Chinese New Year, Easter and so on.

WE CAN'T DO ANYTHING WITHOUT YOU

These creative messages explain exactly what the charity does and how it spends its money:

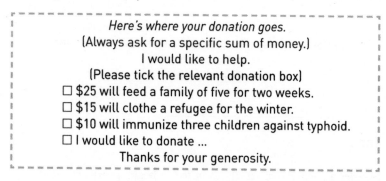

> *Here's where your donation goes.*
> (Always ask for a specific sum of money.)
> I would like to help.
> (Please tick the relevant donation box)
> ☐ $25 will feed a family of five for two weeks.
> ☐ $15 will clothe a refugee for the winter.
> ☐ $10 will immunize three children against typhoid.
> ☐ I would like to donate ...
> Thanks for your generosity.

Notice that the largest sum was shown first and none of the sums is excessive. Also note the option for the donor to give a sum of their own choice.

Whenever possible, steer your copy towards helping people, not conditions. By all means use visual supports to show the scope of a problem, but centre both your copy and visual on individual cases within an overall problem.

Never make a request that makes the problem sound so vast that any donation would appear to be a drop in a bottomless ocean. Avoid this:

> Each year it costs $12 million to keep children off the streets. Can you help?

Did you know?
Broadly, there are two categories of charity of advertising: 'shock' and 'case histories'. Of these, 'case histories' is often the strongest creative approach. If using a personality or celebrity to endorse your charitable message, make sure their personality either reflects the general tone of voice of a given cause, or is someone directly affected by the cause.

OVER TO YOU

▶ *What are the two main types of 'trigger' to motivate donations? Which do you think is most effective and why?*

▶ *Which of these two pieces of copy would be likely to attract greater interest and why?*
  ▷ *Please send £10 to help this blind person see again.*
  ▷ *Please do whatever you can to save this village from destruction.*

▶ *When would be ideal times during the year to run a charity campaign and why?*

▶ *Consider two well-known charities. Now think of the most unlikely celebrities that could endorse each. Write a testimonial from each celebrity that convinces people to donate to the specific cause.*

8

....

Moving pictures

In this chapter you will learn
- *about the development of copy for TV*
- *how to attract viewers*
- *how to write direct response TV ads*
- *how to handle sex in TV advertising*
- *how and when to use TV celebrities*
- *how to use animation.*

TV and cinema

Since the 1950s, television has played a major role in communicating sales messages. Today it is streamed over many devices – making it ideal to reach consumers just about anyway and at any time which suits them.

Originally, television copy was directed to vast mass markets. Today rather than 'broadcast' messages, 'narrowcasting' – reaching specific audiences on mass – requires more definitive messages appealing to more discriminating viewers. Web enabled devices offering on-demand programmes and user-defined scheduling, have given rise to so-called 'METV', in which the viewer mixes and chooses from a smorgasbord of digitally enhanced, interactive channels. With hundreds of channels to choose from, people 'flick 'n' mix'. Quick judgements are based on what the viewer initially sees as they zap channels.

This results in:

1. *TV commercials giving greater emphasis to visual content rather than to word content. (At a glance, does this look interesting? Either 'yes', 'no' or 'zap'.)*
2. *Copy has to be trimmed down to the most basic information – viewers' attention span is quite short. A fairly elaborate picture takes 1.5 to 2 seconds to process. (That is the time in which the brain processes the words of this sentence.)*

As viewers become more and more desensitized to TV, the task for copywriters to produce highly memorable TV commercials becomes increasingly difficult. So products or phone numbers or website addresses need to be featured throughout the commercial.

WHAT MAKES PEOPLE WATCH TV COMMERCIALS?

Your mind constantly processes various stimuli. When that process is interrupted, the brain starts to concentrate on the source of the interruption. In the case of television commercials, when a sight or sound attracts attention, the pupil of the eye dilates. This in turn causes the lens to focus on the television screen. So a bridge is established between the viewer and the TV commercial.

Diverting the mind to one specific area of attention takes less than a second to establish itself. During that time, a decision has to be made about whether to allow the bridge to stand, enabling more detail from the source of distraction (i.e. the television commercial) to be processed; or to ignore the stimulus and go on to something more interesting.

With so many other possible distractions that demand attention from the viewer (such as a hot cup of coffee that demands drinking), this process is virtually impossible to control. However, by understanding which stimuli are likely to arrest attention in the first place, it is possible to influence the viewer's propensity to becoming distracted by a television commercial.

The good news is that if the commercial is broadcast during a programme that is already of interest to the viewer, the chances are good that they will not be distracted from the screen during a television break. Also, the sooner the commercial appears after the start of the break, the higher the probability that the viewer won't be distracted by something else.

Yo! You!

Possible routes to attracting attention include the following.

1   **Material meanings**
    ▷ *Colours – vivid colours alert; pastel colours pacify.*
    ▷ *Sounds – overtly loud or unusually muffled both stimulate interest.*
    ▷ *Movement – a moving object is often more 'moving' than a stationary one.*
    ▷ *Size – unusual sizes and shapes attract interest.*
    ▷ *Light – contrast stimulates.*
2   **Social interpretations**
    ▷ *Eyes – express feeling and depth (very good for close-up shots).*
    ▷ *Facial expressions – provide further details of emotions.*
    ▷ *Hands – accentuate key points.*
    ▷ *Posture – helps set the mood: casual, attentive, professional, laid back.*
    ▷ *Sexual undertones – incredibly strong attention distracters – but designed within the parameters of decency and ethics.*
    ▷ *Children or pets – bring out natural paternal or maternal protective instincts.*

NOW YOU'VE GOT THE VIEWER'S ATTENTION, 'PULL THE TRIGGER'

Once you have attracted the viewer's attention and constructed a bridge, think how to trigger the right types of emotions for a product or service. Consider how you present the basic attention stimuli. For example:

▶ *Movement – animated.*
▶ *Size – huge shopping trolley.*
▶ *Sound – music.*
▶ *Behaviour – incongruent, novel or surprising.*
▶ *Hands – expressive.*
▶ *Face – animated.*
▶ *Posture – lively.*

The television image could be of a tin of ScotsdaleNorth (traditional) baked beans pacing up and down in a shopping trolley singing to the tune of 'Please Release Me':

> Please release me, let me go.
> Your kids will love the way I taste.
> At a mere 90 pence a tin.
> Value my freedom,
> Or I'll be a has-bean.

The commercial above ends with a mother removing the tin of baked beans from the shopping trolley and handing it over to an eager child.

This cheerful approach to selling baked beans sets off a wider and deeper range of psychological triggers. In this case the triggers could include:

▶ *fun*
▶ *cheap*
▶ *cute*
▶ *children.*

The viewer processes this information and draws a conclusion: the product is fun to eat, cheap to buy and will keep the kids happy.

Remember to show the company logo and any contact information either throughout the commercial or at the close of the commercial, or both. In this way the viewer is stimulated to associate an image with the product. (Also refer to Chapter 2.)

Practical creative approaches

Unlike press advertising or direct mail, television – and, to a lesser extent, its cousin radio – is an entertainment centre. Your television commercial must entertain as well as inform. Your commercial acts as a catalyst for creative concepts to be embraced rather than endured.

LIFE'S A PITCH

The sales style or spiel of an old-fashioned market tradesperson reveals great 'how to ...' TV commercial copy techniques. The trader shows you:

- ▶ *What it does.*
- ▶ *What is for sale.*
- ▶ *How durable it is.*
- ▶ *How it compares with similar goods.*
- ▶ *Why he has to sell it now.*
- ▶ *How cheap it is.*
- ▶ *Why you'd be crazy not to buy it.*
- ▶ *What you should do to get it.*

The sales shtick is confident. The trader uses sales gimmicks – from throwing an unbreakable china plate on the ground to chopping a variety of vegetables with one simple cutting device. The customer is repeatedly shown the virtues of the product. One benefit rapidly follows another... All climaxing in an orgy of customer demands to buy this product *now*!

In just the same way, step by step, the 'how to ...' commercial explains how something can be done quicker, slower, easier, softer, cleaner, cheaper and so on. Nothing is left to speculation.

Every aspect is assured and substantiated, mostly through practical examples. In the United States it is commonplace to put the market trader in a studio, give him television air time and get him to sell. The problem with this approach is that for a good sales pitch the seller needs time to warm up an audience until they are driven into a heated frenzy to buy, buy, buy!

One method of stirring up interest, demonstrating a product attribute and stimulating sales in a limited time is to use an unusual, even far-fetched demonstration.

Here is an example for PenPal:

Visual	Audio
Man sits in a demolition truck. He is about to swing the wrecking ball against the wall of an old building.	(Male, aged 35 plus, voice over (VO), very confident.) PenPal is the strongest, most reliable pen you can buy.
(Close-up.) PenPal adhered to a brick wall.	But don't take my word for it.
It is stuck on the bull's-eye of a painted target. Ball swings and hits the pen at full impact. The wall collapses.	(Sound effect [SFX] Crash!)
Man walks through the rubble and uncovers the PenPal. It is in perfect shape. He dusts it down, opens it and begins to write on a piece of paper.	Hmmm, well that's all write then.
(PenPal logo super imposed on the screen.) You'd be lost for words without it.	

When writing a successful demonstration commercial put your product through the mill. Defy speculation.

> Before washing this T-shirt in ScotsdaleNorth Brilliance
> Powder it looked like this. [grimy]
> Now it looks like this! [shiny]

Proudly show off every detail. A working engine can be shown from inside. A plank of wood that's treated with fire-resistant paint can be lowered and retrieved in one piece from the mouth of a volcano.

GET IN THE DRIVING SEAT

Car commercials can embrace one or more of the following aspects:

▸ *Show the car in action.*
▸ *Show someone driving the car.*
▸ *Show the environmental advantages of the car.*
▸ *Show interior and exterior of the car. Exterior footage should feature the body highlights and the lines and curves of the vehicle.*
▸ *Show the type of person who drives the car.*
▸ *Show the type of person who typically drives the car driving the car.*
▸ *Concentrate on specific mechanical and technical enhancements – e.g. safety.*
▸ *Encourage a test drive.*

One of the most popular approaches is to film the car in HD format in a suitably dramatic landscape. Such commercials rely more on art direction than copywriting. Here, lighting, music and scenery take centre stage. The downside of this kind of TV commercial is that you can spend vast sums of money just searching ('recceing') for a suitable location before you get to film anything. Special effects ranging from clever use of lighting to computer aided visual procedures are all well and good. Finishing touches such as film type, sound, set design, lighting, make-up, wardrobe and locations all come under the term 'production values'. The more time and effort taken over each production value, the more expensive the final presentation of the commercial will be.

Most special effects are inspired by music videos and cinema production effects. (Advertising usually follows trends – it does not set them.) However, no effect can ever replace a strong, single-minded message. Anything else distracts from the simple, big idea if you are not careful and is simply icing on the cake.

> ## Did you know?
> The first gay relationship commercial ever broadcast in the UK was shown during December 1995, for Guinness: A great example of advertising following social trends rather than setting precedents.

SLICE OF LIFE

Soap operas were originally called 'soap operas' because they were sponsored by soap powder manufacturers. Viewers continue to identify with soap characters. As you have seen, television commercials take a sales message directly to the heart of a family home, providing a great opportunity to introduce the viewer's family to a product's fictitious family.

The 'slice of life' technique helps establish a product or service as something that is accessible to ordinary everyday people. More importantly, showing the product being used by real people – people like the viewers – gives the product additional street-cred.

Slice of life commercials can feature any person in a family:

- *The kids*
- *Mum and dad*
- *Grandparents*
- *The kids and mum*
- *Mum, dad and the kids*
- *Grandparents and any of the above*

Slice of life commercials can also feature:

- ▶ *Friends*
- ▶ *Friends of the family*
- ▶ *Would-be lovers*

As you are writing for everyday people, your dialogue should be written colloquially. Think of your copy as a transcript of conversation heard by eavesdropping on people in situations like these:

- ▶ *at work*
- ▶ *at the bus stop*
- ▶ *at the dinner table*
- ▶ *whilst shopping and so on.*

Subjects should be based on everyday occurrences or (given acceptable creative licence) possible everyday occurrences. The best slice of life commercial campaigns have an ongoing theme that spins out across several TV commercials. For example:

- ▶ *Will the girl ever get the boy?*
- ▶ *Will the parents ever understand their kids?*
- ▶ *Will she ever get a promotion?*

The slice of life scenario should revolve around the product – not vice versa. For instance, if you produced a slice of life commercial for a PenPal, the pen would act as an anchor point for the action.

First commercial:

Character B passes by the window of a shop selling a PenPal and daydreams about Character A, who is on business 1000 miles away.
Character A wants to write a letter to Character B and looks for a pen, but can't find one.
Beautiful Character C enters the scenario and offers to lend Character A her PenPal.

(Contd)

> The first commercial ends leaving a question in the viewer's mind:
> 'Who is Character C?'
> The end title reads:
> Get the full message with PenPal

Second commercial:

> Character B receives the letter from Character A and writes
> a love letter back to Character A.
> Meanwhile, Character C (who is at home) is seen writing
> something with her PenPal, signing it and then posting it.
> Character A receives a letter, opens it and smiles.
> Character B, in her location, smiles.
> Character C, in her location, smiles.
> The second commercial ends, leaving the question
> 'Who wrote what to whom?'
> The end title reads:
> Get the full message with PenPal

And so on.

INTIMATE MOMENTS – HANDLING SEX ON TV

Sex on television is a divisive issue. There are many who argue that sex actually doesn't sell that well. On the other hand, what would a perfume commercial be like without including the fragrance of seduction?

Clearly, sex doesn't sell everything and today's audiences, exposed to so many commercials, would probably see through the fluff and puffery of titillating imagery over a clear and useful product message. Moreover any commercial must comply to television broadcast regulations on decency. That said, if you want to consider the notion of sex in commercials, ideal product candidates include:

- *ice-cream*
- *chocolates*
- *body care products like foam baths*
- *keep-fit equipment.*

Sexual undertones can be really subtle yet powerfully effective. One common creative trick is to endow an inanimate object with a phallic symbol. For example:

▶ *A woman snuggles up against a rolled-up towel and says how soft it feels against her skin.*
▶ *A model wearing luscious lipstick licks and then takes a sensuous bite into a ripe apple.*
▶ *A man caresses a bottle of aftershave with a female shape.*
▶ *A woman drinks from a stream of clear, frothy water cascading out of a long-necked bottle.*

Another type of intimate-moment TV commercial is the secret sex approach. This can include an intimate confession about:

▶ *Cleavage-enhancing bras.*
▶ *Sports and leisure activity supportive underwear.*
▶ *Leg-caressing tights.*
▶ *Passion-arousing perfume.*

The big star on the small screen

'I'm still as big a star as ever. It's only the screen that got smaller.'

(Gloria Swanson)

If you are going to hire a celebrity to endorse a product or service on television, first ask yourself who is going to be the real star of the production: The celebrity or the product?

As in testimonials used in press advertising (see 'Question headlines', page 97), write as the person would speak. A popular strategic creative option is to use TV stars rather than big-screen stars. They are usually more affordable and, more importantly, they are more familiar regular visitors to the viewer's home (via streamed TV programmes or regular broadcast channels). That makes them appear more credible with the ordinary person. Such stars may include soap opera players.

Stars needn't come from the show-business galaxy of glitz and glitter. Industry-specific 'stars' add extra credibility. Try these:

- ▶ *A policeman endorsing a safety belt.*
- ▶ *A web business person endorsing a website.*
- ▶ *A celebrity chef endorsing a food product.*
- ▶ *An author endorsing a pen.*

The combination of cheaper-than-ever video editing software, cameras and the web, reaching specific audiences is far easier than ever. (Although on social media sites, it is always better to avoid direct hard-sell, as people generally don't like to be marketed to by brands.) Thanks to reality TV shows, today just about anyone can enjoy their fifteen minutes worth of fame. Rather than invest in a major star, an alternative idea is to get ordinary people to endorse products or services. This approach makes a product appear practical. To add aspiration to the mix, why not feature ordinary people using the product and stars introducing the product to the ordinary person.

Creative techniques include:

- ▶ *On-the-street interviews/doorstep interviews in which the star interviews people outside their homes about a specific product or service.*
- ▶ *Extreme close-ups of people discussing the product (known as 'talking heads').*
- ▶ *Ordinary people acting like stars because of the glamour associated with the product in question. (One taste of ice-cream makes the housewife enter a fantasy world where she takes on the appearance of a well-known, actress or singer.)*
- ▶ *Company directors demonstrating their own product and confidence in their company.*

Animation

Animated characters are cute. They have been since the first English-language cartoon film appeared in 1906. However, just how cute is the image that you wish to convey?

Cartoon characters can make:

- *a weighty subject lighter*
- *a 'me too' item lively*
- *a toy more desirable*
- *a boring subject interesting*
- *a brand name person-friendly.*

They can become the spokesperson for the brand. For example:

- *Peter PenPal could be a talking, walking PenPal who demonstrates the product.*
- *The Fruities could be a pop band made up of ScotsdaleNorth fruit yoghurt characters.*

Never become entrapped into writing an entertaining commercial that happens to sponsor a product rather than a sales commercial that is entertaining. Animated TV commercials should be uncomplicated. The more you can incorporate exaggerated human qualities into a character, the more charming the character appears on screen.

CRASH! BANG WALLOP!

Sound effects and music can make or break a piece of animation. Take as much care and spend as much time choosing suitable sound tracks as you do in choosing an animator. Music sound tracks can be parodies of existing pieces of music adapted to suit an individual piece of music. Parodies of 1950s–1990s music are especially popular.

Sung to Elvis Presley's 'Hound Dog':
(Animated dog, dressed in 1950s suit, singing to a can of dog food.)
You ain't nothing to a hound dog
Your meat is just brine.
You ain't nothing to a hound dog
Your taste just ain't prime.
So hand me back my Scotsdale
And that'll be just fine...
(Spoken in Elvis's voice.) You might step on my suedes, but never mess with my meal, man.

Alternatively, feature extracts from existing mood-enhancing themes and songs.

I once adapted the original Addams Family TV series theme tune to promote the animated cartoon series of the Addams Family:

Title: Lurch sings	**Duration:** 30 seconds
Notes: Lurch sings the whole commercial to the Addams Family theme tune. Each scene enters screen from top to left, bottom, right and so on, in sequence.	
Video	**Audio**
(cartoon channel logo) (animated explosion reveals action)	They're
Bear looks shocked and jumps out of picture (2 seconds)	Kooky (SFX – bear in shock)
American presidential statues have a shock (3 seconds)	and they're spooky. (SFX – crumbling rocks)
All the family dancing (9 seconds) ID of all the family (2 seconds)	You'll find them on the telly. So tune in, be there early for the Addams Family.
Boy makes boggle eyes (2 seconds)	It's on the cartoon channel. (SFX – 'boing, boing')
Uncle Fester eats a chain (1 second) Lurch thumping his chest like Tarzan (2 seconds)	Uncle Fester (SFX – 'crunch') and me, Lurch,
Mr and Mrs Addams and Uncle Fester get groovy with electricity (4 seconds)	we'll welcome you to join us. (SFX – electricity buzz) on the Addams Family.
Rain cloud appears and fills moat around the car (3 seconds)	If you think my voice is weird, (SFX – thunder clap) like a soprano with a beard,

| Grandma cooking up a brew (4 seconds) | it's nothing as bizarre (SFX – bubbling stew) |
| Cartoon channel credits fall from top of screen. | as the Addams Family. (Spoken to himself) With my musical talent, maybe I should get an agent. |

When writing copy for a cartoon character, watch the clock. (Notice how the script for the Addams Family showed how long it took for each piece of action to be acted out.) In the case of a 30-second commercial, reduce your word count from 60–70 (usual for live action commercials) to 40–50 (right for cartoon commercials). This allows the cartoon to animate into life without being shackled by too many words. As with all television and radio commercials, act out your animated sequence to see if it fits within your allocated time slot.

Animation does not simply mean cartoons. You can consider animation as part of a live commercial to demonstrate the mechanics of a product, enliven a company logo or add emphasis to a sales message. For example:

▶ *A housewife pours detergent down a kitchen sink and the plug hole animates into a smile.*

Animation can also be used as a special effect. For example you could:

▶ *Stretch a person's face in awkward directions, using part live action and part animation.*
▶ *Use stop frame animation to transform an ordinary scene into a Keystone Cops-style flickered image.*
▶ *Fly people on a magic carpet or even have them dance with an animated product.*

The possibilities are endless.

The last laugh

Humorous TV copy offers a fading brand a bit of shine.

> **Did you know?**
> Where possible, you should not apply overt humour to new
> brands as there is a danger that the humour will distract
> viewers from the sales benefits.

Viewers like to laugh. If you can make them laugh, hopefully they will
pay greater attention to your message. Of course, if your humorous
message is too hilarious, credibility may be affected. The viewer will
spend too much time laughing at the gag rather than thinking about
the product or service. On the other hand, a great joke can distract the
viewer's attention from any arguments against making a purchase.

With so many possible directions it is not surprising that this type
of commercial is one of the hardest to write. Even if you do get
the gag right, there are only a finite number of times that you can
broadcast the same joke. One of the main difficulties with managing
humour for a TV commercial or even cinema commercial is that
a good joke needs time to make an impact. Most TV commercials
are 30 seconds in length. Seven of those seconds are taken up with
establishing a scene and end-of-sequence logo branding.

Assuming you are convinced that a humorous commercial is the
best way to sell a product or service, you have to consider what to
base the humour upon.

A good gag with bite calls for:

▶ *a well-structured plot*
▶ *an easily accessible set up*
▶ *an interesting character*
▶ *a precision-timed delivery*
▶ *and an unexpected punch line.*

All in 30 seconds!

One of the best ways to look for something funny is to look at yourself. Observe your own frailties and shortcomings and list them, honestly – warts and all. Use the same technique on friends and family. Eventually a pattern of similarities will emerge. Use the most striking of those similarities to add dimension to a central character. Creating empathy with a character takes time. There are two ways to address this:

1 *Borrow a character from a comedian, a comic strip or an amusing piece of animation.*
2 *Build a long-term campaign revolving around the central character.*

Give the character a task which, try as they might, it seems that the entire world is ganged up on to foil. The problem is solved, thanks to a particular product or service. This helps create sympathy with the characters who are trying so hard to do something in order to make a point.

Video	Audio
Shop assistant builds a traditional pyramid of tins of baked beans as an end-of-aisle sales promotion device. She balances the last tin on top of the pyramid.	(Male Voice Over – MVO) Nobody can stop our prices from falling.
The pyramid collapses. She replaces the tin. The pyramid collapses again.	
Flustered, she replaces the tin. Again the pyramid collapses- and so this continues.	
Graphic – animated ink stamp thuds onto the screen. ScotsdaleNorth Price Savers.	
Caption: Good food has never been better value.	

Consider making your character talk to inanimate objects or treat awkward objects (such as something incredibly large like a grand piano, or tiny like a microchip, or absurd like a false leg) as if they were alive. You could place your character and product or service in an unfamiliar surrounding, such as:

- *a different country*
- *a different time*
- *a different place*
- *a different planet.*

You could also:

- *mingle new technology with traditional ideas*
- *use upside-down logic (instead of hitting a nail in the wall, hit the wall into the nail)*
- *draw illogical conclusions from logical summations.*

Consider introducing your character to other characters with peculiar afflictions, like a nervous twitch or a compulsion to squawk like a parrot – the stranger, the better.

Don't just settle for small problems. Give your character vast problems – exaggerate the predicament, exaggerate a solution, by finding the answer using the most convoluted of routes. If things have to go wrong, make them go disastrously wrong, allowing the product or service to act as the catalyst that saves the day.

Above all, remember that it's OK to see the funny side of life as long as that image insults neither the integrity of a product or service nor the viewer's instinctive perception of what is politically, socially and morally acceptable.

Video	Audio
Sombre, moodily lit room In the centre is a psychiatrist talking to a patient (whom we can't see).	(Psychiatrist) It's down to you. Things appear dark now. You really have to want to change.

The doctor sits on the edge of his large leather chair, looking concerned – clearly involved with his patient's case.	It needn't always be that way.
Close-up of the psychiatrist, trying to reason with the patient.	(Light bulb) OK already.
The psychiatrist stands up and walks to the other side of the room.	
Close-up of the patient, who turns out to be an animated, branded light bulb.	
Titles appear on the screen – logo is a light bulb which a hand switches on; as the switch clicks so the words, *Have you seen the light?* appear	

TV you read

One way of driving a message home is to turn a TV commercial into a graphic bulletin board. Instead of relying purely on a powerful image accompanied by memorable music and convincing dialogue, why not go all the way and add graphically designed titles that reinforce key benefits?

A PenPal TV commercial could show a beautiful actress in a romantic setting, writing with a PenPal. At the same time the dialogue (or voice over) could be saying: '*The stylish way to write – right from the heart.*'

The superimposed titles could animate out of the apparent love letter, varying in shape and length, reading:

TV jingles

Contrary to popular belief, jingles are not meant to 'sing out' the end of a commercial. If that were their sole purpose, they would be self-defeating. Every jingle, no matter how melodious, would only serve as a sign to the viewer that it is time to lose interest in the commercial. All jingles, including radio jingles, provide instant recognition of a brand. In the case of radio, a jingle helps establish a brand logo and embellish it with 'sound' values. (See 'Music', page 256.) It is a musical reminder combining the evocative pull of a score with the selling clout of a persuasive piece of copy. The craft of jingle composition may seem simple, even trivial. However, catchy jingles, like catchy headlines, are not easy to write.

A jingle has to:

▸ *reinforce a product or brand name*
▸ *inform and add personality as well as amuse*

I've never had a pen friend like a PenPal.

▸ *make sense and at the same time rhyme*

It's the one for me – a written guarantee.

▶ summarize everything in one simple statement:

> Get the message – pick up a PenPal.

One of the product categories for which jingles are especially popular is toys. Jingles can have an important role in children's own play time. Each time a game is played, the child may think of the jingle associated with a toy character involved in the game. Even everyday tasks can be turned into play. Every time Mum or Dad serves the breakfast cereal, the child may think of a character in a TV commercial who uses the jingle.

Did you know?

In the UK the Ovalteenies jingle was still going strong in the late 1980s – some fifty years after first being broadcast. The oldest American jingle that was still in use in the 1990s was first broadcast in the 1920s – for a cereal called Wheeties.

Get the picture?

Standard 35 mm or 16 mm film runs through a projector at 1440 frames per minute. A story board, (so called because as children, Walt, and his brother Roy, Disney drew scenes for cartoons on boards of wood which they nailed onto trees in scene sequence) is a vital tool to assist commercial directors with creative aspects such as lighting, mood, camera angle and general character positioning. It can show you or your client how the commercial will appear on the screen. However, a story board can only capture the basic creative essence of a commercial, including shot continuity and the general flow of action. In order to accurately represent the entire (30-second) production, it would have to feature 720 separately illustrated frames! One version of a story board is called an 'animatic'. This is a crude animation of the commercial, sometimes used for research purposes.

Ask yourself whether you really need an expensive animatic or story board. If so, at what stage of the creative process?

I recommend that you save a story board until you have settled for a typed TV script. You could always act out your script to a client. Read it aloud, get colleagues to read parts. Titillate your audience.

Play the commercial in your mind before committing it to paper. Aim to capture what you see in your mind on paper, then develop what's on the paper through discussion.Once you have arrived at an agreed script, think about story boards, especially if you are going to sub-contract the actual production to a producer and director. Rather than dictate what you want – which restricts creativity – a story board will help provide you with peace of mind. What you originally played in your mind will be better understood by the person who has to put the image on the final version.

As for writing a script, don't worry too much about technical jargon. If you like to use buzz words, the following list should be all you need to ensure that in terms of mechanics your final picture is seen and understood by everyone. If you want to describe a more complicated camera angle or technical aspect, do so in words – but never forget that a director should have the imagination to take your words and turn them into a moving experience.

Ad lib	Spontaneous dialogue – not scripted (ideal for on-the-street interviews).
Animate	To arrange an inanimate object or graphic in a way that, when seen as part of a finished film, gives the impression of movement.
CU	Close-up.
Cut	Change camera angle or scene.
Dissolve	Fade out of one picture or scene into another.
Editpoint	The point at which a scene change is planned.
Eyeline	The position of a subject's eyes on the screen.
Fade in	Brighten the illumination of a scene (usually at the start of a scene).

Fade out	Darken the illumination of a scene (usually at the end of a scene).
Freeze	Stop the action by freezing it in time.
FVO	Female Voice Over.
Lead-in	Initial words spoken by the VO at the start of the action.
MCU	Medium close-up shot – the person is seen from the chest upwards.
MS	Medium shot in which a person on screen is seen from just below the waist upwards.
MVO	Male Voice Over.
SFX	Sound effects.
Super	Superimpose one action or scene on top of another.
Track shot	Horizontal camera movement which zooms in or follows something.
VO	Voice Over.
Wipe	Change of scene from A to B, using a graphic device (e.g. scene B wipes diagonally across scene A).
Zoom in/out	Increase/decrease magnification of a subject.

If you are going to hand your script over to a director eventually, then you have two possible ways to write it:

1 *If you are totally confident in the director's abilities, just write the dialogue and describe the action.*
   ▷ **Pro** – *the director has the chance to enhance a production by giving the commercial an angle that you may not have considered.*
   ▷ **Con** – *are you seriously going to leave your 'baby' in another person's hands?*
2 *If you want to have greater control over the actual interpretation, also include the camera angles.*
   ▷ **Pro** – *you know what you put down on paper will end up in the can.*
   ▷ **Con** – *how would you like to have your creativity shackled and, more importantly, how do you think that will affect the final results?*

Direct response television

In the UK, the original DRTVs (direct response TV commercials) lasted about two minutes. The copy style was usually led by demonstration techniques with a great deal of emphasis given to the response details. However, broader-stream advertisers who preferred repeated short, sharp 30-second commercials persuaded the TV networks to put a stop to these as all the best prime-time commercial spots were being lost.

The copy style of direct response commercials still tends to rely on the here's what it does and here's how you respond approach. Continuous graphics showing telephone numbers and website addresses are vital to reinforce the response mechanism. Weave the telephone number, email address and website details into the presenter's dialogue. By all means use clever techniques like talking telephones or music to give the response device even greater impact – as long as the technique doesn't distract from a clearly understood explanation of why the product or service is beneficial and how to get in touch:

Quick jot down this number: 08700 123 456.
(Graphic shows the number)
It connects you to the cheapest, yet best, cover policy money can buy.
Bob is 21. His regular motor insurance company quoted him over £1000 for his policy. A couple of clicks at www.insurecompare could have saved him £200.
That's right. Just a couple of clicks at insurecompare.com could have cut his premium in half!
and so on.

Always use DRTV to wake up the viewer to take some kind of action. However, a presenter shouting or even singing a telephone number would only encourage the viewer to switch off the noise. A good DRTV commercial has to:

Demonstrate Stimulate Activate

Combine a convincing message with a credible, not overtly pressurised setting. Target a specific audience and urge them to call a response number (particularly a DRTV ad for charity).

BEYOND TEMPTATION

Based on the seven deadly sins, here are sure-fire ways to stimulate a response from your TV copy:

Sloth	Your product makes life easy, the viewer can do less hard work.
Greed	Why wait to boost your earning power?
Envy	Your friends will go green with jealousy when they see your brand new…
Gluttony	It's so low fat, you can eat as much as you like.
Pride	Display your collection with pride.
Lust	Wear this and drive your partner wild!
Vanity	You will look a million dollars.

I hope that entertained you – now, here's the bill

There's no denying it. Television can be costly.

TV commercial costs are based on ratings, position, demographics and time. 'Rating' is another way of saying 'percentage of chosen type of audience'. If you want to attract (or reach) a proportion of housewives in South-East England aged 35+ in socio-economic group A1, you would want a rating of perhaps 90.

Timing depends on the time of day when a commercial is shown. Daytime television or very late-night/early-morning television is generally cheaper than prime-time television, when most viewers watch.

Then you have to consider the popularity of a programme and, more specifically, how popular a programme is with the type of person that you wish to reach. Finally, you have to consider the position within a commercial break that your commercial appears in:

- ▶ *First during the first break?*
- ▶ *Last during the middle break?*

Another option is not to produce a commercial but a sponsorship message which appears at the start of a programme. The beauty of this is that your product or services becomes associated with the programme's theme or message. On the other hand, if the sponsored message gives too much emphasis on your brand's role in the production of the programme, it could affect not only your brand (being seen as a paymaster rather than supporter) but the programme (being seen as losing its independence).

It is usually wise to purchase your TV time through a television airtime media broker with a large portfolio of clients. If you are particularly effective as a negotiator as well as being an effective copywriter and have a highly marketable product to advertise, you could get a very reasonable commercial rate. However, it is better to direct your creative skills to raising viewers' interest by offering entertaining and compelling informative copy than negotiating a higher viewing rate at a lower budget cost.

Did you know?

Before you worry about the cost of airing your masterpiece, consider the cost of producing it. Remember, never let razzmatazz get in the way of a simple, single-minded idea.

A straightforward single scene, employing one camera angle and one actor, may be just as powerful as an all-singing, all-dancing Hollywood-style production. Why not substitute for the dancers a couple of pairs of hands with little skirts tied around the fists and a face drawn on the back of each hand? Providing the creative treatment matches the style of product and the tastes of a market sector, anything goes.

Budget allowing, recruit an independent producer who can negotiate on your behalf and 'marry' you with an appropriate commercial director – often easier said than done. (They will want to make the commercial one way whilst you may have other ideas.)

TV commercial advertising quick tips

▶ *Commercials have to entertain as well as inform.*
▶ *Demonstration commercials work well with extreme examples.*
▶ *Special effects should enhance rather than distract from a single-thought message.*
▶ *People like people – 'slice of life' television is effective.*
▶ *Sexy commercials can turn guilt into desire.*
▶ *Although a celebrity may be a star in their own right, their appearance in a TV commercial is that of a guest – the lead vehicle remains the product or service.*
▶ *Animation can be cute. It must be relevant.*
▶ *Cartoons speak clearer if you make them say less.*
▶ *Never laugh at a product or service. Laugh with it.*
▶ *TV graphics of copy make messages more memorable.*
▶ *TV jingles should say 'buy me' rather than signify the end of a commercial.*
▶ *Story boards can only capture the essence of a commercial, not the soul.*
▶ *DRTV sells off the screen as you would sell off the page.*
▶ *DRTV commercials should strongly feature a website supported by a voice over that repeats contact details.*
▶ *If you produce a DRTV commercial, be sure that you have the ability to handle the response.*
▶ *Generally speaking, the longer the DRTV commercial, the greater the chance of a good level of response.*
▶ *TV airtime costs can be expensive. Satellite TV stations or streamed content web TV stations may be more cost effective than terrestrial ones.*

OVER TO YOU

▶ The brand-new Pastiche 200 series car has a sun roof that
when open disperses rainwater away from the car so that
driver and passengers always remain dry – whatever the
weather. Write three TV commercial treatments in script or
story board formats which advertise this useful feature.

▶ Write a 20-second TV commercial that encourages motorists
to be extra nice to traffic wardens during a special 'Hug a
warden' week.

▶ Write a 60-second dialogue between two housewives discussing
a new kind of washing powder that helps them iron out
creases.
  ▷ Keeping all the essential parts of the dialogue, cut the
    script down to 30 seconds.
  ▷ Keeping all the essential parts of the dialogue, cut the
    script down to 20 seconds.
  ▷ Keeping all the essential parts of the dialogue, cut the
    script down to 10 seconds.

▶ From your own choice of pop singles, adapt a lyric to sell a
PenPal.
  ▷ Without changing any lyrics, choose two well-known
    songs that could be used to convey the right atmosphere
    and message for a PenPal TV commercial.
  ▷ In no more than fifty words for each, describe the action
    of the two commercials devised in 4a.

▶ List six different ways to write: CALL NOW ON 0500 123 123.

▶ Video two TV commercials, then rewrite the commercials,
conveying the same messages without dialogue, using just vision.

▶ List eight different ways to write: NOT AVAILABLE IN
THE SHOPS.

9

Listen to this!

In this chapter you will learn:
- *how to turn a casual listener into an avid supporter*
- *how to use music with copy*
- *how to choose a voice over*
- *how to use and choose SFX.*

Unquestionably, television broadens the mind. (Up to its screen width.) Radio, on the other hand, can stretch the imagination far wider. You can listen to the radio just about anywhere, whilst TV demands you are visually as well as audibly connected. Radio is portable, intrusive and accessible.

Radio commercials are heard by ordinary people doing ordinary things like eating (a good opportunity to target a snack food) or shaving (a good opportunity to target a shaving product). Your audience is there. As long as your copy is realistic, accessible and believable you can be certain that when your copy 'talks' your audience will hear.

Academic research has shown that '[Radio] as a secondary medium accompanying its users while they are engaged in primary activities, can infiltrate their view of the world in a way which is all the more powerful for being half-conscious' (*Understanding Radio* by Andrew Crissel, published by Methuen).

In the UK, one-third of households have five or more radios in their homes. During the late 1990s, now a classic piece of research carried out by CIA Sensor asked: 'If you were marooned on a desert island, which ONE of these things would you want to have with you?:

▶ *A radio that works?*
▶ *A subscription to your favourite magazine?*
▶ *A subscription to your favourite national newspaper?'*

You can guess the most popular answer.

Radio can bring a listener closer to a product or service:

(MVO)

The nib on this PenPal is so smooth that the ink (Whooooah!) slides down and through it effortlessly.

(SFX – MVO brushes himself down)

So giving a smoother, more professional finish to everything you write.

When writing a radio commercial 'paint' evocative visual images. There is absolutely nothing that the eye can see that the mind cannot 'see' even clearer. You have a powerful arsenal of creative weaponry at your disposal to hammer home a picture. These include:

1 **Choice of voice overs (VOs)** – *young, old, male, female, rich, poor, indifferent, professional, zany, serious, happy, sad ... and so on. (Unlike TV what the VO looks like is irrelevant. It is what they sound like in the mind that is important.)*
2 **Sound effects (SFX)** – *a good SFX can add humour and drama and, above all, 'show' a minute yet essential detail that builds tension and delivers credence to your commercial.*

Would you like to 'show' the listener a shopper choosing something from a superstore? Here is an example:

(MVO – young professional man, thinking to himself)

(SFX)

(Busy ScotsdaleNorth store)

Hmmm. Sue wanted something special tonight ... Fisherman's Pie only £1.50. Not bad.

(SFX)

(Places pie in trolley.)

Hmmm. Something to wash it down? Ah, just the job – ScotsdaleNorth's own-brand Muscatel, just £5.99 a bottle. That should do nicely.

As for desserts ... (giggles to herself) Well the night is still young.

(FVO)

ScotsdaleNorth. Good food, terrific value.

Or 'show' the listener the shopper at home:

(SFX – busy meal time at home, TV in background, general household pandemonium)

(Very young son)
Mum! What's for dinner?

(Husband)
Hello, luv.

(Very young son)
Sue won't let me play with the football.

(Young teenage daughter)
Any chance of getting this blouse done for tonight?

(MVO – warm, friendly)
Busy mums lead busy lives. So we've created the healthy Meal Maker range. Each tasty meal is nutritionally balanced, with only the freshest of ingredients. Just pop a Meal Maker in the microwave and, within minutes, you can serve up a little masterpiece.

(Contd)

Delve deeper, turn up the creative volume

Radio has often been considered as the poor and distant relation to TV. While DRTV is one of the most dynamic ways to measure a creative campaign as well as the most sustainable way to nurture client relationships, radio is one of the most exciting opportunities for pure copywriting.

But does it work? For one piece of research an advertising agency invited over 300 housewives to test out a new ironing product. Whilst they were ironing, the agency made sure that a radio was being played in the background – ostensibly to make the atmosphere informal. In fact the purpose of the exercise wasn't to test the iron, but the power of radio.

The housewives later recalled a specific radio commercial that was played while they were ironing – right down to the brand name and details of what was said about the product. Significantly, creative treatment played a major role in recall.

Listeners are loyal and, compared to many other media, targeting is incredibly sharp – apart from very early crude experiments, such as in 1925 when Selfridges sponsored a fashion talk from the Eiffel Tower.

In the early days of radio there were only three commercial stations
in the UK:

- *London Broadcasting Company (the first, which on 8 October
  1973 transmitted the first commercial, a 60-second spot at
  06.08 for Birds Eye Fish Fingers)*
- *Capital*
- *Clyde in Scotland.*

Now, hardly a year, sometimes hardly a month, goes by without
another specialist radio station entering the airways – and then
of course there are thousands of podcasts. You can target anyone
from a jazz enthusiast to a newshound by choosing your station
and your programme. And the more stations there are, the greater
the choice for the listener.

As you have seen from the commercial for ScotsdaleNorth, radio
is a medium that allows you to describe a thought as well as an
action. It is ideal for the kind of commercial that delves deep into a
narrator's psyche. For example:

(MVO – grumpy, slightly zany)

What kind of a name is PenPal? Pen, pod. I can see it now.
Hot summer's afternoon, big farm. Lots of strawberries.
Lots of girls picking the fruit.

(SFX – summer day in the background)

Girls. She's nice. 'Hello ... (Hmm) ... How's it going?' She asks.

'Oh, fine,' I reply. 'Lovely day for it. Look I've picked hundreds
and hundreds of ripe pens off the pod.'

'That looks tasty,' she replies.

(Contd)

Delivering the message

Radio is ideal for conveying complex information. Just tune into a
Talk Radio show – there is news, weather, sports, traffic updates,
guests talking about different subjects. Like all messages, as long as
your creative message is single-minded, radio will deliver it direct
to the consumer's mind.

As with television, it is vital that you use your first few seconds
to attract the listener's attention. Address your audience. Make
your commercial lead into or out of a scheduled announcement.
You could use a weather forecast:

(SFX – hot summer's day)

(FVO)

Weather like this is something to write home about.

Your forecast from PenPal.

(During a music chart show)

(Male rapper)

Yo! Listen up. You can get a pack of 12 Colas from
ScotsdaleNorth at a price that's as cool as it is clean.

Also consider 'link sentences':

Want to know more? listen to this ...

but that's not all ...

Proven creative listener-grabbing devices include music, SFX and scripts that are read quickly. By digitally compressing a commercial radio recording, you can speed up the commercial by as much as 15 per cent without having a detrimental effect on its quality. That means you can literally squeeze thirty-eight seconds of scripting into thirty seconds. In the United States, tests have shown that this creative technique delivers up to a 40 per cent improvement of aided recall over commercials read at normal speeds.

Another attention-grabbing technique is to record the commercial at a slightly higher volume than normally required. This method is also commonly used in TV commercials.

Radio commercials are considerably cheaper to produce than TV commercials. This means that longer-length commercials are relatively affordable. A normally spoken radio commercial allows for about seventy words in thirty seconds. One minute gives you about 150 words. However, depending on the mood of the commercial, you could easily double those figures (for a quickly spoken, 'Hurry, hurry, hurry' type of delivery) or halve that figure (for a slow, seductive commercial that makes the listener savour every single moment).

I once heard that the only accurate way to time a commercial is to measure the script in syllables – up to five = one second. However, I believe that the only way to time a radio commercial accurately is to buy a stop-watch!

Another radio attention-grabber is the question teaser:

> Where can you download over 3 hours of soul music for just £19.99?

> Wouldn't you want less time on your hands?
> With our gentle anti-wrinkle hand-cream, you can.

Music

(Also see 'TV jingles', pages 240–1). If you decide to choose to use music (and why not? – most radio stations are built on music) make sure that you have permission to use a track.

For example, there's no point featuring the Beatles' song 'Paperback Writer' for a PenPal commercial if you can't afford the music rights. So you may decide to parody a relevant track. Instead of 'Paperback Writer', you could feature the words 'PenPal writer'.

Whenever you write a lyric, make sure the words and sentences are short. A simple sentence that can be understood first time is always preferable to a more complicated, longer version.

Perhaps you have decided to go for securing the rights for a piece of music. If so, budget for the air play royalties. A great idea could end up costing a great deal. There are companies who will take publicly available music (known as public domain music) and edit it into usable five- or ten-second segments (known as pre-recorded needle-drop music). You can also purchase existing music in commercial chunks from specialized commercial music libraries.

There are two schools of thought about music parodies.

1 Pros
   ▷ *Music is very evocative.*
   ▷ *You can vary lyrics and even styles.*
   ▷ *You can vary singers.*

2 Cons
   ▷ *What is 'in' today is 'out' tomorrow.*
   ▷ *Music parodies can be a poor excuse for an unoriginal creative idea.*
   ▷ *The royalty costs may outstrip your sales generated by the campaign.*

Involve your listeners – it's to their advantage

Ensure that your creative idea is single-minded. Don't let complicated production enhancements get in the way of an easy-to-grasp message. Your brand name should be repeated throughout the commercial and, of course, listeners should be told how to get hold of the product or service – either by phone or in person.

Consider setting a time limit for your offer:

> This Friday at 5 p.m., we're closing the offer for good.

Notice 5 p.m. rather than simply Friday. This adds even greater urgency. The shorter your deadline, the higher your response. Make it 5.35 p.m. and you'll add even greater urgency. (As in TV, it's the small details that help build the bigger picture.)

You can also consider celebrity endorsements – especially radio presenters. This is quite common in the United States where presenters discuss products or services during the course of programmes. Unless for charities, in most instances such disguised endorsements are not allowed in the UK. However, you can still use the presenter during an obvious commercial break. As with all forms of dialogue copy, make sure that your copy sounds real and that what is said reflects how the presenter would normally speak.

One way around the UK radio regulations is to make your commercial part of a broader promotional package. It could be part of a competition to win a major prize. Competitions are always in demand by breakfast DJs looking for new ways to stimulate their early-morning listeners to get up and go without encouraging them to stand up and leave.

One of radio's greatest strengths is that it encourages listeners to participate in activities:

> Listen to this, then ring this number.

Any promotion featuring interactive ideas like a vote line or a quiz, a music dedication and so on, helps increase interest and response. Studies show that 27 per cent of local radio listeners physically interact with the station in some way – they phone in, have a dedication read out, enter a competition, attend a road show.

ScotsdaleNorth.com could run this kind of promotion. For example, the breakfast DJ could give away £100 worth of shopping vouchers every day for a week, as part of ScotsdaleNorth's centenary celebrations. This could be reinforced with a ScotsdaleNorth commercial.

Radio production

Some of the greatest fun you can have as a copywriter is in a radio commercial production suite. Unlike television, it is usual for copywriters to direct as well as write an entire production.

AIB I am always impressed by the versatility of radio voice overs. One good actor can deliver several distinctive voices – saving you time and the cost of employing lots of actors for one script.

Did you know?

Once I asked an actor to deliver a line in different ways. He obliged, brilliantly performing the line: '*What, are you joking? I've really won a hundred thousand pounds!*' Try the line yourself!

Make sure you have enough scripts for everyone. Tell the actors everything about the product. Who's going to buy it? Why would they want to buy it? What did you have in mind when you wrote the commercial? A good actor needs a sound brief to make words work. Give all the help they need, down to advising them about emphasis of key words in the script:

▶ *What, are you joking? I've* really *won a hundred thousand pounds!*
▶ *What, are you joking? I've really won* a hundred thousand *pounds!*

Whenever possible, plan your commercial with enough time to get the best actors to read your script and research the most relevant creative enhancements such as music, jingles and sound effects.

If a commercial lasts thirty seconds, allow for a minimum of two hours in the studio: half an hour for recording and the rest for production. Ideally, book three hours. If the commercial is complicated or requires more than three actors, this may need to be increased to even longer.

Radio commercials quick tips

▶ *Write a mind picture, not a sound track.*
▶ *Concentrate on a single thought.*
▶ *Target your audience.*
▶ *Allow your copy to talk one to one.*
▶ *Capitalize on a radio spot – e.g. the weather, a particular type of programme.*
▶ *Consider writing two radio commercials for one commercial break – one that leads into the break and one that leads out.*
▶ *Making your advertisement part of a broader promotion such as an on-air competition.*
▶ *SFX builds interest and reinforces believability.*
▶ *Don't overwrite a commercial. If you have to describe a detail, let an SFX provide it.*
▶ *Radio is cost effective. Consider producing two versions of a commercial – this avoids people getting bored with*

hearing the same thing and can be used as a form of creative testing.

▶ *If you need longer than thirty seconds to convey a message, use longer (and vice versa).*

▶ *Choose actors to reflect your product and its audience.*

▶ *Involve your audience.*

▶ *Repeat the product name throughout the commercial.*

▶ *Radio is intimate – speak directly to your listener, in the bath, in the garden, in the car, at work.*

▶ *Write as people speak.*

▶ *Capitalise on the trust and faith which people have in radio.*

▶ *Use music prudently and watch costs.*

▶ *Actors can be incredibly versatile – use them.*

▶ *The more time you take over recording your commercial, the greater the energy you can expend into ensuring it features high production values.*

▶ *Pre-plan all jingles and music.*

▶ *Remember that, unlike TV audiences, listeners zone in to programmes rather than zapping past commercials.*

▶ *As more people work at home, they look for company by using the radio – so the medium becomes ever more important. Plan for emerging markets such as podcasts.*

▶ *Radio is like direct mail that you post in someone's ear and gets delivered to their mind. Target your copy and you'll be on the right wavelength.*

OVER TO YOU

▶ *Write a 30-second radio commercial advertising the power of radio.*

▶ *Adapt a well-known lyric from a pop song to sell a packet of ScotsdaleNorth washing-up powder.*

▶ *Look around your room. Now match six products to six possible locations where people could listen to the radio.*

▶ *Write a five-second sponsored introduction from Directions to a programme about food.*

10

....

Further media to consider

In this chapter you will learn
- *how to write for posters*
- *how to write for transit posters*
- *how to target your poster copy.*

Posters

Keep the message simple. That's the best advice for outdoor poster sites. Unless a poster appears in an area where people are virtually forced to stare at it (e.g. a railway station platform), there is precious little time to get a message across. Instead, think about producing a fast-to-read, easy-to-grasp piece of creativity that relies on blanket exposure rather than intimate targeting. That can be harder than you think. Brevity can lead to banality. Writing four words instead of a long sentence that says the same thing is incredibly difficult. Winston Churchill knew this. It is said that he would spend ten times longer writing a few well-chosen words than preparing a lengthy speech.

Typically, posters are seen by drivers in traffic. As roads become more and more congested, the poster audience becomes greater and, while stuck in traffic, people have longer to read advertising messages. That leads to another benefit of posters: apart from informing, they can turn a drab tarmac environment into a colourful and entertaining landscape.

Poster copy – including copy for in-store posters – needs to be blatantly obvious. There's no point in writing something lengthy (except in situations where the reader has nothing other to do than to read your message). Take outdoor posters. Owing to their physical size and positioning, most are designed to be seen from distances in excess of 50 metres. If a motorist is passing a poster that is three-quarters of a kilometre away whilst driving at 80 km per hour, they will have less than three seconds to take in its message.

Graphics can be lavish but not overcomplicated. Also, there is a safety argument for not overdistracting a driver's attention. For example, a poster featuring a naked woman hitching a ride with the headline:

> Don't goggle at me, watch the road!

… may be an interesting way to promote driving safety, but it may have the reverse effect from what it is trying to communicate!

Three features of an effective poster are:

1 *Intriguing headline.*
2 *Dynamic complementary graphic.*
3 *Strong company branding using logos.*

Often poster copy is too short to sell a detailed commercial message. Commercial posters can remind people about a larger campaign on TV, the web, in the press or on radio. Poster copy can be a shortened adaptation of a TV, radio or press advertisement or creatively different, yet part of a single-minded campaign. Posters can also be used as the sole medium to convey a message direct to the buying centre of a community.

Unlike TV, radio or the press, posters do not rely on editorial content. No one can zap out posters with a TV remote control. No one can skip pages. No one can turn a poster off. Having no editorial background, posters are only as effective as their creative message and location.

Ever since the first poster appeared in 1866, the medium has been an integral part of the environment. People often take posters for granted, so creativity has to work hard to get noticed. However, because posters are part of the everyday environment, when messages are read and appreciated the advertised product or service takes on the kudos of something that is part of everyday life and therefore a community commodity. Here are some creative ideas.

Good posters make people think.

(Burnt poster site – half the board burnt away.)
Headline:

FIRE KILLS.

Good posters often make people laugh.

POSTERS ARE SEXY
(THIS ONE'S TOPLESS)

Good posters get to the point.

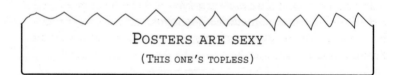
£55 to go in Seine (Fly to paris at crazy prices)

Good posters are unsubtle.

(Picture of car suspended in the air over a road, figures and words painted below it on the tarmac.)
£12,500
On the road price

Good posters make a dull journey stimulating.

Poster 1:
(Picture of housewife at busy check out desk, looking directly at the 'camera', in shock.)

This is a hold-up

Poster 2 – 50 yards down the road:
(Same housewife, smiling as she shops on line at ScotsdaleNorth.com.)

This isn't

Good posters offer a different interpretation.

Poster showing two pictures:
Computer and PenPal
Headline:
  At least one of these Word Processors will never let you down.

TARGETING YOUR MESSAGE WITH POSTERS

Many copywriters assume that posters are purely for the mass markets. This is not always the case. Posters can be targeted by carefully placing them in key locations. For example, to attract business people you could consider placing a poster along a main business traffic route.

(A super-sized poster for ScotsdaleNorth glue – three cars actually stuck to the poster.)
Headline:
Stuck in traffic.

You can also target by area:

(Poster featuring a picture of new ScotsdaleNorth superstore covered by a gigantic curtain.)
Opening soon. Queenstown's biggest ever Superstore

NEXT STOP – START BUYING

Transit posters on buses and trains allow you to write longer and more detailed copy. It doesn't matter if the passenger doesn't read all your message the first time. Like all poster advertising, the medium relies on sustained and broad coverage rather than a one-off impact.

Some of the best transport advertisements take full advantage of the environment in which they appear. Copy can discuss commuting to work by bus or train. The poster can be designed to utilize the shape of, for example, a double-decker bus. Use coach or bus front, back and side poster messages to talk directly to drivers. For example:

> (On the back of a bus, read by motorists.)
> Headline:
> *For the latest traffic news tune in to Traffic FM*

Or:

> *Follow me to the newest ScotsdaleNorth superstore*

Today, many public transport posters are electronic. For example, London Underground stations often feature electronic posters. Write your poster as if writing a banner advertisement. Allow for up to four words per screened message – draw on moving content, such as three-second clips of an advertised product, to grab attention. If writing for posters on escalators, let each poster tell part of a story with a series of no more than four posters completing the message.

Posters are fun to write and create. You can smash holes through them. You can suspend things from them. You can make them move. Some poster contractors offer revolving poster faces that feature slats like blinds which revolve one after another to display different advertisements. The blinds can be controlled to revolve in one direction and then another in a timed sequence. PenPal could feature a series of revolving blinds to give the impression of a hand-written line of ink that grows longer and longer, developing into the headline copy.

You can use posters on buses and coaches to spread the message all around town.

Posters quick tips

- ▶ *Keep copy short.*
- ▶ *Utilize shapes and surroundings.*
- ▶ *Think nationally, write locally.*
- ▶ *Let visuals do half the talking.*
- ▶ *Take longer to keep copy shorter.*
- ▶ *Amuse, attract and arrest.*

OVER TO YOU

▶ *Write an in-store poster for a High Street printer promoting 25% off printing charges.*

▶ *Write a transit poster promoting alternative transport to cars.*

▶ *Explain how you would design a poster for the blind.*

▶ *Today it is commonplace for many posters to be electronic, often featuring video footage. Prepare three-frame storyboards for electronic posters selling:*
  ▷ *freshly baked bread*
  ▷ *24-hour news service*
  ▷ *halal or kosher burger chain.*

11

The Internet

In this chapter you will learn:

- *how to assess your web copy*
- *how to plan your site*
- *how to deal with PDFs*
- *how to plan your home page*
- *writing for social networking sites*
- *how to develop compelling and useful (known as 'sticky') copy*

In the West, when you read, you do so from the top of the page down. Not on the web. In fact, surfers don't actually 'read' in the traditional sense of the word; they scan. Scanning is a quick overview of what is on the screen. Interestingly, tests have shown that this general idea starts from the top middle of the screen. Then a surfer's eye darts about trying to pick up 'scent' words.

Scanning looks like this:

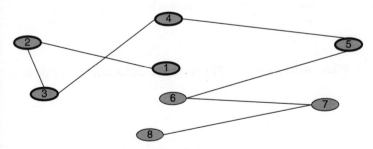

Scent words are keywords (not to be confused with meta-name keywords – see 'Search and they will find' below). Scent words confirm and clarify that the surfer is on the right page. For example, if a surfer wanted to buy a dress, she would look for 'scent' words confirming the dress size, style, colour, price and so on.

Scent words should appear towards the beginning of paragraphs. If not, the surfer would have to hunt for clarification and probably lose interest.

Once a page is 'scanned', it is then 'skimmed' in more detail. Eye-tracking tests show that such skimming results in 'F-reading'. The longer the surfer lingers on a part of a page, the darker the 'F'. This evolved from Jakob Nielsen's eye-tracking study of 2006 and you can see an illustration of this on a number of websites including www.useit.com/ and www.searchenginejournal.com/. Nielsen has been referred to as the 'king of usability' and has published a number of books on the subject.

In psychology there is a term called 'cognitive miserliness'. It refers to an instance when someone doesn't want to dwell over why or how they do something. This typifies a normal surfer. They don't need to be told 'click here' – they can infer the instruction through the power of a reason to click. (I try to avoid the term, 'click here'.)

For example:

Photoshop is my favourite design tool.

As opposed to:

Click here to see why Photoshop is my favourite design tool.

Even syllables on the web are diminutive:

- *Not many* > *few*
- *Not the same* > *different*
- *Not strong enough* > *weak*
- *Did not remember* > *forgot*

Did you know?

During 2009, a record-breaking £1.75bn spent on online advertising made the UK the first major economy to spend more on web ads than TV.

Kiss your copy

One great way of getting to the point with your copy is 'kiss it'. This is when you write straight to the crux of a matter, rather than edge around the sides. For example, 'kiss' the problem in an orphans charity website:

> **Don't you get annoyed when you hear about homeless kids becoming parents rather than playing 'Mummy and Daddies'?**

'Kiss' the possible – encourage your surfers to imagine themselves interacting with your product or service or realizing an ambition – through your proposition:

> **Imagine if every step you took chased away poverty?**

In terms of language and pace, remove as many stumbling blocks or barriers as possible between what you propose a surfer should do and them taking simple steps to achieve goals. This includes reducing the number of steps a surfer has to take before getting to a point of action. This is helped by incorporating embedded commands:

- *I want you to read this website and then you will discover money-saving ideas. (Embedded command)*

- *Reading through this website you'll discover great money-saving ideas. (Embedded command)*
- *Read on and then you will learn how poverty strikes the heart of a community. (Embedded command)*
- *Reading this, you are learning how poverty strikes the heart of a community (This technique is also known as, 'linguistic binding').*

Less is more

Aim to keep your word count between 140–60 per page. (Captions and headlines should be no longer than eight words.) Any longer for your main copy and the surfer will be forced to scroll the page. Scrolling should be reserved for feature writing or for when the surfer has particularly keen interest in the content (such as in a news story). Once the surfer has read the 'nuggets' of a story – perhaps via a series of substantiated bullet points, they can choose to follow it up by exploring related articles on your page. Related articles are normally assigned the left or right of the central bodycopy. This helps keep your central message text section clean and clear – without hypertexts interrupting reading. (Incidentally, if you do have to write hypertexts, only include them towards the end of a paragraph, rather than in the middle – once again drawing the surfer away from your copy.)

Related articles could include:

- *Short cuts – to deeper information with more detail.*
- *Outside official websites, with a disclaimer stating that you do not take responsibility for external content. (Be sure to check that the outside link is 'live'.)*
- *'Low decibel' information of interest to specialists without compromising main readers.*

Did you know?
According to the *Guinness Book of Records*, the longest web scroll (written by Ralf Laue) is 563.62 km (350.2 miles) long yet only 21.698 kb in size.

Keep the length of your sentences below 23 words. Most sentences should be between 14–16 words. Also be purposeful with your pacing. Open with a short sentence. Then try another one. If you're stuck on pacing, go with the comma-separated compound sentence. (Two thoughts in one sentence – restrict yourself to one comma-separated sentence for each page.) It's okay to slip in a passive verb occasionally. After all, this is how people speak. (As with a good book, the surfer virtually 'hears' the words leap off the screen and into their consciousness.)

For most consumer sites, it is best to write in the second as opposed to third person:

Third-person perspective:

Clients can count on us to deliver copywriting tips, hints and techniques that work to increase their sales.

Second person perspective (the 'you' is understood in the first part of the sentence):

Count on us to deliver copywriting tips, hints and techniques that increase sales.

For most people, writing website copy isn't new. You may be updating an existing site. If so, rather than starting from scratch, review your existing copy and decide which parts remain useful and which you can dispose of. Web analytical tools will help you decide which pages are 'hit' and which are regularly 'missed'. Even if existing pages are relatively popular, it is still a good idea to sort out your content into logical sections.

To do this, either carry out an extensive 'content inventory' covering, in bullet form, what is on each page, or a 'content audit' which offers an overview of several page sections at a time. (I tend to only use an inventory for sites under 200 pages.)

During this process, you'll decide if content could be moved or merged with copy in a different section. Ask yourself if the content is:

- *Redundant?*
- *In line with current thinking?*
- *Outdated?*
- *Trivial?*
- *Of historical value?*

Once it is all sorted, start assimilating your content into a logical flowchart. In turn this will start to suggest the overall shape of your updated and improved site.

There's no place like home

Every site starts with a homepage. This should convey what your site is actually about: what it delivers and how it delivers it. This can all be implied through a combination of design and words. (Avoid if possible flash introduction pages – unless for a lifestyle or high fashion product/service.)

As proven with sites like Twitter, featuring only 40 characters per message, attention spans tend to dwindle, so surfers spend less and less time on home pages. In fact, in the case of social networking sites this can be as short as half a blink of the eye (50 milliseconds). During this remarkably slim window of time, the surfer decides if your site is:

- **Fresh.** *Is it emotive? Is the online brand innovative? Brave...*
- **Adaptive.** *Does it respond to the surfers' needs – Is it data-savvy and updated?*
- **Relevant.** *Is it useful and targeted?*
- **Transformative.** *Does it raise expectations – does it do more than just what it says on the 'label'?*
- **Social.** *Is it a social networking site experience? Is it newsy and/or democratic, communal and sharing?*

- ▶ **Immersive.** *Is it multi-sensory – can the surfer lose track of time by becoming totally engaged with the site? (Such as with a mainstream news site.)*
- ▶ **Authentic.** *Does it seem genuine? Does it feel transparent? Is it consistent and humane?*
- ▶ **'Sell' vs 'tell'.** *Particularly with social networking sites, the more your copy sounds commercial, the less credible it appears. So, whenever possible strike out any words which suggest crass insincerity. To tackle this, print out your copy and, armed with a highlighter pen, highlight any phrases that sound artificial and then either rewrite them or scrap them. (As sites like YouTube start featuring sponsored advertising, surfers will increasingly look for sites which offer greater democracy through 'free-search'.)*

Before:

> **As the world's premier provider of email services to the chicken rearing industry, we are proud to offer the most imaginative delivery of highly targeted email messages directed at consumers and workers involved with the proud tradition of plucking and clucking.**

After:

> **To send email about the chicken rearing industry, call us.**

Reduce jargon terms to the absolute minimum and, if your company is using a content management system, be sure to list standard names and terminologies so that everyone calls everything the same.

When writing Frequently Asked Questions, ensure that they appear genuine:

Wrong:

> **Is it true that PenPal is the world's finest pen?**

Right:

Where can I buy PenPal refills?

Testimonials work particularly well on the web. When writing them (with the permission of the person being quoted) be sure that they sound natural and always name the person being quoted.

Jonathan Gabay: 'I think Teach Yourself is brilliant.'

As opposed to:

Author: 'I think Teach Yourself is brilliant.'

With so many companies opting to sell directly from the web, it becomes increasingly difficult to get your web tone of voice to sound genuine. So before writing web sales copy, ask yourself, what do you want your surfers to do:

First, Do ('Response'):

▸ *Click, Read, Disclose, Buy?*
▸ *How will you persuade them ('Offer value')?*

Second, Think ('Rational'):

▸ *What value are you offering them? ('What's in it for me?')*
  ▹ *Why should they believe you? ('Proof & Resolution')*
  ▹ *Why should they trust you? ('Reassurance')*

Third, Feel ('Emotional'):

▸ *About you and your products ('Positioning, Tone of voice, email personality')*
▸ *About themselves ('Positioning, Tone of voice')*

Remember, today's brands have to offer an emotional as well as practical benefit. Make your site a cause not just a series of facts.

To PDF or not to PDF?

Whilst PDFs are fine for certain forms and instruction charts or guides, they shouldn't become a universal panacea for all marketing collateral. In fact, for many, the thought of using their ink to print out your marketing material is at the least, uncomfortable. Help them by hyper-texting contents of long documents, so they only have to print certain pages. Also let them know just how large your PDF file is – including data size and pages.

For non-PDF pages, include options to send content to social networking sites, and offer printer-friendly options.

Did you know?
Ted Nelson invented hypertext in the 1960s. It is a non-sequential matrix of information, creatively linked by allowing the user (or reader) to click with a mouse on a word or phrase.

Search and they will find

According to the CIM (Chartered Institute of Marketing) 41 per cent of search engine users change engines or search term if they don't find what they want on the first page, and 36 per cent of search engine surfers believe that the companies whose websites are returned at the top of search results are the top brands in their field. Search engines like Google are so sophisticated that the 'old school' method of Search Engine Optimization – writing rich keywords in meta-tags (searchable html data) no longer guarantees a high ranking on engines.

All search engines use 'Bots' – software that crawls the web for data. The Bots search for content based on relevance and usefulness.

Initially Bots will look at up to 14 keywords per page of section of a site. These keywords are any sequence of words separated by a comma so *Teach yourself copywriting book, Jonathan Gabay, marketing, copywriting* would be counted as four keywords.

(In Google's case, don't waste keywords with misspelling alternatives as Google can usually detect misspellings for itself.)

Next, the Bots look for meta-descriptions in the html coding:

Jonathan Gabay's Teach Yourself Copywriting offers a great foundation for all would-be copywriting experts.

The more specific your description, the better.

For example, your site is about Siamese cat breeding and boarding. The keyword 'cats' is too broad and competitive. Your targeted market wants to buy (what?) 'cats' or board (where?) in 'London'.

Meta keywords:

Siamese cats summer boarding in London.

You could also brainstorm attractive key phrases. List what your targeted surfer might type into a search engine to find sites similar to yours:

For example:

Siamese cat breeders (your competitive market).
Cat boarding (another competitive market).
Siamese cat boarding.
Siamese cats (very specific)?

Consider writing meta-tags showing alternatives:

Siamese kittens

Another good SEO technique is to repeat the precise phrase. For example, *'Siamese cat boarding'* no more than three times for every 200 words in your actual website copy. This shows search engines that your content is reflecting – rather than replicating – what your meta-tags discuss.

Now the Bots begin searching words within the pages themselves. They are particularly interested in words and phrases within headings including your site header in the URL box – as in www.gabaynet.com. Bots hover over anchor text of hyperlinks (the bodycopy which is hypertext linked). They also examine image descriptions as well as so called 'ALT' text which is the copy that appears when a mouse rolls over an image. (Many people find websites via image searches.)

Google in particular, also looks for:

▶ *Number of references to a key phrase or word on a page. (Frequency should be 2–4 per cent.)*
▶ *Bold mark-up.*
▶ *Proximity of phrase to the start of document and the gap between individual keywords.*
▶ *External links in but also outbound. (You can encourage external links by creating useful so-called 'sticky' content and services. Also, team up with complimentary partner sites, trade associations and suppliers. Wherever possible, build communities for your site using tools like Facebook, YouTube, Vimeo and Twitter.)*

As the web continues to evolve, words will start taking second place to other multi-media. Many journalism moguls have already announced their intention to stop traditional printing in preference to complete online publishing, including publishing newspapers on 'e-paper' that can be populated daily with new interactive content. Film, PowerPoint, photographs and sound files (podcasts) will become increasingly integrated into websites. Web platforms and operating systems will become universally accessible via phones, Netbooks and other Wi-Fi enabled technologies.

So the web writer of the near future will be a communications polymath, equally at home with film editing software as they are with traditional proofreading.

The web quick tips

- *Feature your site IP address (URL) or email address on all company literature.*
- *Use multi-media and social networking sites such as Twitter.*
- *Make sure that all technical hitches are sorted out before publicizing your site. Surfers don't appreciate being treated as guinea pigs.*
- *Make your site as 'sticky' and interesting as possible – discuss latest industry issues, consider making your site an interactive game: Keep your site updated.*
- *Use SEO – Search Engine Optimization.*
- *Keep your copy Clear, Brief and Useful.*
- *Turn an everyday sales site into a site with cause and purpose.*
- *Test your site on sample users – ask what they think? How can the site be improved?*
- *Spell-check your site. Better still, get others to spell-check it.*

I have a spell cite programme
Its part of my win doze
It plainly marks for my revue
Ear ors I did knot no

I've run this poem on it
Its letter purr fact you sea
Sew I don't have too worry
My checker looks after me.

▶ *Involve designers with your copy ideas from the outset.*
▶ *Learn multi-media techniques, including film.*
▶ *Make sure your site is relevant to your business.*
▶ *Substance rules over marketing sizzle – make sure your site features useful information.*
▶ *Always keep your site up-to-date and spell-checked.*
▶ *Don't make your site too complicated to navigate.*

You can learn more about writing copy and designing for the web by visiting www.brandforensics.co.uk

OVER TO YOU

▶ Visit three popular retail websites selling similar clothes (such as a black cocktail dress). In each case, note the different 'scent' words used to attract a surfer's attention to the retailer's fashion.

▶ Which of these two sentences is more effective and why?
  ▷ Click here to buy our books.
  ▷ Buy our books.

▶ List four things your social networking site should suggest at first glance.

▶ Turn this 'tell' sentence into a 'sell' sentence:

   The laptop features an illuminated keyboard that automatically lights up in poor lighting conditions.

▶ Visit two tourism sites. Look at each one's main attractions. Now turn the standard copy into a 'kiss the possible' approach.

▶ What are the three things to consider before writing web sales copy?

▶ List three pros and three cons for featuring PDF documents on sites.

▶ How many words should you typically aim to have on a standard web page?

▶ Generally speaking, when writing for the web, what is more effective: writing in the second person or writing in the third person – and why?

12

Press release copy

In this chapter you will learn:
- *how to structure your news release*
- *how to define the right kind of press release*
- *how to handle bad news.*

> **News is what someone somewhere doesn't want you to print: the rest is advertising.**
>
> William Randolph Hearst

Public relations

Strictly speaking, public relations is outside the remit of many copywriters. However following the recent recession, many organizations ask copywriters to wear more than one hat – so encouraging them to also learn PR skills.

PR is not free advertising. Its value far exceeds that. Good public relations covers everything from staff communications and product launches to handling bad news and a simple sign by a roadside that apologizes for any inconvenience during repair works.

Did you know?

According to the British Institute of Public Relations, 'Public relations practice is the planned and sustained effort to establish and maintain goodwill and mutual understanding between an organization and its publics.'

In your capacity as a PR writer you have to act as the special correspondent to every news medium dealing with your client's interests. As such you must understand how to make an average everyday type of story newsworthy. You must be able to present the facts of your story in a form that does away with advertising hype and concentrates on interesting news angles. You have to think like a newshound – ready to track down all the elements of your story as well as the markets who will be interested in publishing either your version directly or, more likely, their version as explained by you and your press release. Finally, you have to show a sense of responsibility to your client, the media and the truth. Nobody will ask you for a second story if your first one was eventually discovered to be nothing more than a cover-up or a pack of lies.

Get to know your media. As in advertising copywriting, you need to know:

- *which kind of publication or website features which kind of story*
- *which suit your needs*
- *how (in what style) they like a story explained.*

For the purposes of this chapter let's concentrate on how to write a general news release and accompanying support material. This is the most basic form of PR writing and, as it is written from a broadly neutral stance, it offers the greatest attraction to the broadest media sources.

Every news story is divided into three essential components:

1 *the headline*
2 *the lead*
3 *the body.*

Your press release should be tagged as an urgent matter. Consider including a FOR IMMEDIATE RELEASE notice or adding an air of privileged information: EMBARGO UNTIL (date).

Never use the word 'exclusive' unless the story really is exclusive to one publication. To get round this, you can always make your story exclusive to one publication and after that 'special' for another publication. (Specials may be appropriate for local papers who would want a particular regional bias given to the story or trade publications which wish to discuss a specific business angle.)

Always include:

▶ *the date when you sent the press release*
▶ *if very urgent, the time*
▶ *your contact details.*

From a press release angle, think of the headline as a calling card between you and an editor. It announces in one or two sentences what you have to offer. For example:

> ScotsdaleNorthside – Britain's best loved retailer celebrates 100 years of service.

Notice that the majority of words were directed towards the subject features and benefits matter: *best loved ... celebrates ... 100 years of service.*

Once you have cast your bait with a headline, you have to hook an editor's interest with a lead paragraph. Within two sentences, your lead (the whole story) has to be sufficiently interesting and relevant for an editor either to read the rest of your press release or get a staff journalist to make further enquiries.

Leads – the whole story – are fact, rather than prose, led:

> ScotsdaleNorth is celebrating 100 years of serving the UK consumer. As part of the festivities to mark the event, on Friday 8th October at 7 pm, each of its superstores will feature a fireworks display.

From a practical point of view, it is seldom possible to write a different press release for each publication. However, it is a good idea to target the story to a type of medium. In addition to giving you a theme for your story, that gives you assurance that when your lead is read it has a greater chance of working.

Here is the ScotsdaleNorth lead adapted for the popular press:

> On Friday 8th October, the skies will be lit up from John O'Groats to Land's End. It's part of the year-long celebrations to mark the 100th birthday of one of England's best loved retail chains, ScotsdaleNorth.

Every news story is divided into three essential components:

1 *the headline*
2 *the lead*
3 *the body.*

Always include:

▸ *the date when you sent the press release*
▸ *if very urgent, the time*
▸ *your contact details.*

Editors often take mere seconds to decide if the story is of interest or not. They want something that is going to spark their readers' interests.

Once you have written your lead, write your main body section. This should cover the so-called 'Six Journalist Friends' (see page 56): who, what, why, where, when and how.

Consider the main thrust of your press release.

1 *Give further details of what's so different or new about the product or service. Who is likely to want it?*

2   *What are the benefits to the readers, surfers, viewers or listeners?*
3   *How best can it be used – what kind of problems does it address?*
4   *How does it compare to the competition?*
5   *What does it feel like?*
6   *What does it look like?*
7   *How does it perform?*
8   *Who does the editor contact for further information?*

Always include a quote from a named person, preferably a satisfied customer rather than the boss of the company.

Did you know?

Avoid sending a press release that discusses something that has already occurred – editors work in the news business, not the history library. Often the best stories are the human-interest angles.

If writing about a person joining a company, allow a paragraph that provides background detail on the person. For example, that he or she is married, hobbies and so on.

> Ralph Soames (aged 41) is married with three children. A great classical music lover, he plays both the piano and violin.

Next comes a call to action paragraph. This includes mobile phone numbers and email details.

At the end of the main section of your press release, write the word 'ENDS' and perhaps leave space to note the number of words in the body of the release. (If possible all the above should be included on the equivalent of one side of A4 paper.)

Once complete, add two paragraphs, each featuring two sentences providing background information on the company publishing the press release. This section is called 'Notes to Editors' and should be updated at least once a year.

Finally, as you will be sending the release by email, condense the contents to an email-able format:

Subject box (headline): six words

First paragraph: one sentence

Main body section (who, what, why, where, when, how):
one sentence

For personal stories, drop the background information on the personality.

Include a call to action, which leads to either a pdf or .doc of the prepared fuller release. Alternatively, point the surfer to a special Press Office section of a website.

Other types of press release

1 **Announcement release.** *This is concerned with brief details about such subjects as a change of address or a new team member. Trade publications often feature short announcements on who's moving to what company. All that is usually required is a few lines of detail: who's moving from where to what position and with what responsibility.*

2 **Background notes.** *Another kind of press release is a support piece – the background notes release. This is not usually for publication. It provides useful details about technical aspects or historical points related to the main release. Typically, background notes may feature previously published articles, research figures, brochures and company reports. In the case of Ralph Soames, the background notes could include biographical details.*

3 **Technical release.** *This is often longer than the usual one-page, one-side main release. It does all the additional*

technical homework for an editor or journalist so they can write a complete and accurate account of how a particular product or service developed.

4 **TV or radio release.** *Finally, you may be required to write a special press release for TV or radio. An Audio News Release (ANR) would be an mp3 pre-recorded piece featuring personalities' testimonials. A Video News Release (VNR) is a pre-filmed piece which features both testimonials as well as general background footage that saves a television or web broadcaster from sending film crews to a location.*

For both an ANR and VNR remember the points discussed previously in the sections relating to the broadcast media:

▶ *Write as people speak.*
▶ *Sentences need to be crisp.*
▶ *Information needs to be distilled to its simple points.*
▶ *Wherever possible try to include at least one quote that encapsulates the entire message within ten seconds of 'talk time'. (This type of quote is often called a 'sound bite' and is usually an edited highlight from a recording.) For example:*

> Ralph Soames has joined ScotsdaleNorth. 'This is one of the most exciting developments in our on-going communications programme that will take us into the first two decades of the 21st century,' said ScotsdaleNorth's chairman Roger Dale.
>
> Ralph Soames is best known for his innovative marketing on the web. 'I am proud to have been part of the team that established our interactive social networking site. I am sure that ScotsdaleNorth's amazing brand range will soon be the 'tweet' of the nation!'

When bad news is good news

The worst kind of news for a publicist is bad news. For example, a dead cockroach could be discovered in a tin of ScotsdaleNorth baked beans. A senior member of PenPal's management board could be exposed as a crook.

The first thing to accept is that the saying, 'All publicity is good publicity' is a fallacy. Too many people have been driven to desperation by bad publicity for the saying to have any real credence.

There are three ways to deal with bad publicity. Here are the first two:

1 **Deny the allegations.** *This is the most obvious course to take. However, there are times when the facts are weighted too heavily against your client to make any denial plausible. In this case resort to option 2.*
2 **Admit and counter.** *Journalists want a news story. Give it to them. Only as well as one juicy bit of news, offer another, much more tempting morsel. This is a barter method and shows the journalists that you are on their side, helping them to get a good story – not a piece of tittle tattle – and above all to get to the bottom of what happened.*
   So, a dead cockroach is found in a tin of ScotsdaleNorth baked beans. Firstly, you must withdraw all tins from the batch and conduct a full enquiry into the supply chain. This is a potential health hazard. Don't exacerbate issues! Next, if you really believe something is afoot, you can start to work on your story. Who sabotaged the tins? Offer a reward to find the culprit. The public's health is at risk. ScotsdaleNorth will leave no stone unturned to expose the culprits. Go further, announce plans to redesign tins so that they are tamper proof. Invite journalists to see the production line for themselves. Remember, your client has nothing to hide.

*As with all cases of actual wrongdoing, if you must, face
the music and be prepared to admit that a mistake was
made. Then close the matter. People will respect you for it.
Sometimes by prolonging a dispute you will make things
worse. An early settlement can stop a one-off piece of gossip
turning into a prolonged sensational piece of news tittle-tattle.
Avoid direct advertising attacking the parties attacking your
client. If you have to advertise, produce only advertising
that advises on any immediate risks to the consumer and
demonstrates a positive response by your client:*

WE'RE RECALLING OUR BEANS BECAUSE WE ARE RESOLUTE IN OUR PROMISE OF QUALITY

Have you recently purchased a tin of ScotsdaleNorth baked
beans (batch number 12345)? If so, please return it to your
local ScotsdaleNorth store. You will be given a voucher
worth £10.00 that is redeemable against any future
own-brand purchases.

This unfortunate action has to be taken due to the actions of
criminals who are being sought by the police. ScotsdaleNorth
is offering a reward of £50,000. If you have any information
that can lead to the conviction of these people please dial
0800 123 123 or email in confidence
catchthem@scotsdale.com.

If all that fails, the third way is still open to you:

3 Sue. *Wherever possible, avoid this. It is costly, drags things
out and highlights a problem. For instance, even if you have
a good case, libel is difficult to prove. If, on the other hand,
you are 100% confident that an injustice has been done, never
be afraid to resort to law. It is, after all, there to protect your
client's interests.*

If none of the three strategies is an option, hire a professional
publicist. Even a great copywriter like you can only achieve so much!

Deviating for a minute from the business world, a technique called, the 'David and Goliath move' is often used by movie stars who are caught cheating on their partners.

Rather than hiding the fact, spin doctors may throw open the affair to the general public via web and magazine forums:

- ▸ *Would you leave your partner if they had an affair?*
- ▸ *What would you do in my shoes?*

Another avoidance technique for movie star couples who have hit the headlines is to allow a story to have a good run in the press, then get a key person to make a statement in a TV interview. The news of the up-and-coming statement will itself stimulate media interest. During the interview the person who cheated on their partner could apologise for their wrongdoing:

'It was a one-off. I can only hope that they will one day find it in their heart to forgive me.'

Once the interview has been broadcast, the press can again be encouraged to ask their audience to comment.

The next step may be to get the aggrieved party to announce that they are so hurt that now they just want to be left alone to 'figure things out'. About a month later, however, they come out of hiding and announce that love may yet bring them back together again. All this could lead to a tip-off to a press photographer that the couple are getting away from it all by taking a vacation at an exclusive tropical island. A photograph taken with a zoom lens, showing the couple walking hand in hand on a beach, is then published in the papers.

Soon publicity gets underway to launch the latest movie of one of the couple – or, even better, one about adultery in which they have joint starring roles. For guaranteed interest, a movie might star the wrongdoer and the alleged one-time extra-marital partner. Needless to say, whatever is most relevant will be a box-office success!

Press release quick tips

- ▶ *Try to get all your facts onto one side of a sheet of A4 paper.*
- ▶ *For email, condense your main text and include the original release as either a PDF or .doc.*
- ▶ *Show where the news is from.*
- ▶ *Don't use capital letters to write a company name: ScotsdaleNorth, not SCOTSDALENORTH.*
- ▶ *Avoid underlining text – especially in email, unless denoting a hypertext link.*
- ▶ *Show the date of embargo or make your announcement on the day – news is now, not history.*
- ▶ *Time embargoes accurately to match a launch or special event.*
- ▶ *Write your story from the top down. Editors edit from the bottom up.*
- ▶ *Concentrate on facts, not flourishes.*
- ▶ *Show who to contact for further information and where.*
- ▶ *Avoid obvious hidden advertising for products or services.*
- ▶ *Tailor the emphasis and style of a story to suit a media sector.*
- ▶ *Follow up a press release with a phone call. Does the journalist need any further details?*
- ▶ *Read and write your story as you think an editor would wish it to be received by their target audience.*
- ▶ *Double-check spelling.*
- ▶ *Use quotes only if they are relevant to the story.*

OVER TO YOU

▸ *Write seven press release heading variations announcing PenPal's new pen.*

▸ *Write a 200-word background autobiography.*

▸ *Imagine you have been caught cheating on your partner. Devise a 12-point plan that would prove your innocence and have you coming out smelling of roses.*

▸ *What does SOLAADS stand for?*

▸ *Construct an advertisement from ScotsdaleNorth commenting on why a small section of the roof of one of its superstores caved in overnight – narrowly missing a pedestrian.*

▸ *Write three short sentences that will encourage a news editor to read a press release about an industrial nail manufacturer who wants to announce a new length of nail that's being added to the production line.*

I'm a copywriter – still care to join me? Then, believe in yourself, practise your craft.

People will believe in you and you'll go far. Now go out there, have fun, write, sell and meet the deadlines – you will be brilliant – you taught yourself!

If you have any further questions, email me at jj@gabaynet.com or visit www.brandforensics.co.uk

Appendix

Making the jargon make sense

You will need to understand the language of copywriting. Here are some definitions. Terms in bold are themselves defined in a separate entry. See also pages 242–3, where you will find a list of technical jargon used for TV and radio commercials.

A/B split The creative testing of two variations of one element in a direct mail package.

above-the-line Originally referred to a form of agency remuneration; nowadays refers to **advertising** and **marketing** budget spent on TV, radio or published media. This concept has been superseded by through-the-line and integrated marketing, which offers a combination of above-the-line and below-the-line advertising.

account
1 *A client of an advertising agency or promotions/public relations agency.*
2 *A general term used to describe a client's marketing affairs.*

account executive The person, usually at middle management or junior management level, who liaises between the agency and client.

account group Agency team that works on an account.

ACORN A Classification of Residential Neighbourhoods. This is a consumer-targeting system which provides a listed selection of residential property information.

adsterbation Self-gratifying advertising.

advertising A planned and considered method of marketing that informs consumers about something and persuades consumers to do something, through doing so establishing a sales or marketing communication link between a service or product provider, its distributors, users and advocates.

advertising agency A company that produces advertising and organizes advertising campaigns on behalf of clients.

advertising platform The main benefits of facts to be conveyed through a piece of advertising.

advertising rate The fee charged for time or advertising space in the media.

Advertising Standards Authority The body responsible for overseeing public complaints about printed advertising.

advertising wedge A product or service's leading benefit or feature that is highlighted within an advertisement.

advertorial A combination of advertising and editorial style of copy to give the appearance of a pure piece of editorial. Often features the words 'advertising feature'.

advid An advertising video tape often used by job and American college applicants as an electronic CV.

advocacy advertising See issue advertising.

advt Abbreviation for advertisement.

agency commission The fee paid by the media to an agency for placing advertising.

American Marketing Association Founded in 1936, it is recognized as the leading US association of marketing managers and teachers.

animatic A semi-finished TV commercial usually presented in a rough animated format. It is often used for research purposes.

annual publication Publication that is produced once a year.

answer print The final print of a TV commercial for approval before broadcasting.

art buyer A person employed by an advertising agency to commission creative suppliers such as printers and photographers.

art director The person responsible for the visual concept design and execution, including graphical or photographic management, of a creative advertising project. Often advertising agencies team art directors with copywriters, thereby creating macro units of creativity – often supervised by a creative director. Where such team work occurs, generally creative ideas are jointly conceived.

artwork The final creative execution of a piece of advertising material ready for print.

atomistic test The research testing of individual parts of a design or advertisement.

author's alteration A proof-reading correction made by a copywriter.

awareness A measurable capacity for people to recall a specific advertisement either when unprompted ('Can you name a brand of pen?') or prompted ('Have you ever written with a PenPal?').

back-to-back The broadcasting of commercials in a direct sequence.

backgrounders Public relation support material to aid journalists.

bait and switch advertising The now outlawed process of advertising a low-priced item in order to build customer traffic and then switching to selling a similar, higher-priced item.

bangtail An envelope designed with an attached perforated 'tail', used as a coupon or order response device.

banker envelope An envelope with a flap on the longest edge.

bastard size Special size of paper.

beauty shot A close-up shot of a TV or cinema advertised product.

believability The scale by which an advertisement is believed.

below-the-line Advertising and marketing budget spent on promotions, including direct marketing and sales promotions as well as those areas not dealt with in above-the-line advertising.

bill-me-later Payment charged once the goods have been received.

bill-stuffer Please refer to statement stuffer.

billboards American term for poster sites; known in the UK as hoardings.

billing
1 *The fee charged to a client by an agency.*
2 *The net charge made by a media supplier to an agency; the gross charge less the discount given to the agency.*

bi-monthly Publication produced every two months.

blind ad A classified advertisement which does not reveal the identity of a client.

blow-in card A loose reply card inserted into a magazine.

blurb
1 *Basic product or service descriptive copy.*
2 *Short introductory copy on a book jacket that highlights, explains and enthuses about the text within the covers.*

body type The typeface used in the bodycopy.

bodycopy The main text of a piece of copy.

border The perimeter line that distinguishes one advertisement from another on the printed page.

BRAD (British Rates and Data) A monthly reference source of media and advertising cost and circulation data.

brand A name, term, symbol or design (or a combination of them) which is intended to signify the goods or services of one seller or group of sellers and to differentiate them from those of competitors' (as defined by Philip Kotler, the author of *Marketing Management*).

brand association The mental link between a specific product or service and its general category.

brand attitude A consumer's opinion of a product or service.

brand differentiation The ways in which a product or service is perceived to be different from its competitors.

brand image The emotive 'gut feelings' conjured up by advertising or marketing, felt by the consumer towards a product or service.

brand loyalty The ultimate aim of a brand manager – to secure the continued custom and product or service endorsement from a client.

brand switching The act of changing from one brand to another.

BRE (Business Reply Envelope) A pre-addressed envelope from a mailer to be returned by a recipient.

broadsheet Large-sized newspaper, as opposed to a small-sized tabloid.

broadside The traditional name given to paper printed on a single side only.

brochure A printed bound pamphlet (derived from the French word meaning to stitch, brocher).

bromide A photographic print. (The world's first photographically illustrated advertisement was placed by the Harrison Patent Knitting Machine Company of Portland Street, Manchester. It appeared on 11 November 1887 and showed the company's staff near a display stand.)

buck slip A US-dollar-sized piece of paper that announces an offer for prompt reply.

business press Specialist press aimed at the business community.

byline The name of a journalist responsible for a specific article or report.

campaign A planned and co-ordinated sequence of advertising, marketing and promotional activities constructed to achieve a calculated result.

CAP Code of Advertising Practice.

caption Copy that describes a specific illustration or photograph.

centrefold spread Centre spread of a publication, which can be opened flat to show large headlines and pictures.

CERP Centre Européen des Relations Publiques, otherwise known as the European Federation of Public Relations Organizations.

character count The overall number of typespaces in a piece of copy, including spaces between words.

Chartered Institute of Marketing Europe's largest professional body for marketing and sales practitioners.

Cheshire label A name and address label used as an alternative to a window envelope.

circular A widely distributed piece of advertising material.

clean copy An error-free piece of copy.

clean proof An error-free typeset proof.

clip A short piece of film.

club line An unsightly first line of a paragraph at the foot of a page or column, with the rest of the paragraph being printed on the next page or column.

cluster A group of people sharing a common interest or feature.

cluster analysis A statistical method of sorting samples of people into clusters.

cognitive dissonance A consumer's disappointment when there is a vast perceived difference between what is expected from a product and what it actually delivers. It can be avoided by stating clear product and service facts within copy and by featuring money-back promises or guarantees if the consumer is not completely satisfied.

cognitive psychology A general approach to psychology stressing the internal mental processes.

coin rub Please refer to scratch off.

coined word A word created for a specific purpose.

cold lists Lists of prospects which have not been previously contacted by a specific advertiser.

collectable A one-off object or series of objects sold as limited editions using direct marketing techniques.

column inch The unit of measurement for a standard newspaper or magazine column.

column inch rate The cost of a column inch.

concertina fold A paper fold which opens out in the form of the bellows of a concertina.

contact report A written account of a meeting between a creative supplier or agency and their client.

contest A sales promotion method that awards prizes to consumers who perform tasks such as completing a phrase.

continuity writer A person who writes programme publicity and information copy for commercial broadcasters.

control The standard by which quality is gauged. Direct mailers feature a control package that has proved the most effective of at least two mailings. All variations of a creative theme are measured against this control. The term is also applied to the most successful creative interpretation of an advertisement within a campaign.

controlled circulation The free distribution of a publication to targeted addresses.

conversion pack A direct mail piece that is meant to convert an enquiry to a sale.

copy approach The main theme or creative thrust in a piece of copy.

copy chief/head Senior copywriter with management responsibilities.

copy editor The journalist who approves and edits journalistic copy produced by reporters.

copy platform Creative rationale and description based on an agreed advertising strategy.

corporate identity Material representation through the logo, corporate colour scheme, uniform or livery of an organization.

cost per thousand The cost of an advertisement per 1,000 viewers or readers. Also known as CPM (Cost per Mille).

To calculate, divide the cost of the advertisement by the circulation of the publication. In the case of TV or radio you have to take into consideration the time at which the commercial is broadcast.

cost plus An advertising execution produced at production cost + agency expenses.

counter card A point-of-sale notice highlighting a product name and price.

coverage
1 *The geographical reach of a specific medium.*
2 *The declared parameters of a market.*
3 *The percentage of the audience within a market able to see an outdoor poster.*
4 *The total number of people or households, irrespective of location, that buy or receive a publication or see/hear a broadcast.*

CPE Cost per Enquiry. The total cost of a mailing divided by the number of enquiries that it produces.

CPO Cost per Order. The total cost of a mailing divided by the number of orders that it produces.

creative director Employee of an agency who is responsible for the output or creative work and overall supervision and co-ordination of creative staff (or teams).

creative strategy A communications goal based on an intended result, product or service benefits and the data to support the marketing aim.

customer relations Public relations programme aimed at consumers using communication devices such as questionnaires, newsletters and after-sales support services.

cut off See **deadline**.

daily rate The fee for advertising space charged for all editions of newspapers published during the normal working week.

database A computerized pool of information from which selected data can be utilized.

deadline The latest time a completed advertisement or piece of copy can be accepted.

dealer listing A list that is included in a piece of copy, showing regional dealers who market a product or service.

dealer relations PR directed at commercial distributors of products or services.

demarketing The method of discouraging consumers from buying or consuming. For example, for a summer water conservation campaign: 'By all means splash out on the sun oil, but please conserve your water.'

demographics Classification of an audience make-up based on economic and social influences and conditions. Classifications can be segmented by age, sex, income and working status.

desktop publishing Computer-generated advertising and publications including newsletters, leaflets and press advertisements.

de-dupe The method of identifying and eliminating duplicate names from mailing lists. Once completed, the information is referred to as 'de-duped data'. (Please refer also to merge and purge.)

die-cut Paper or cardboard that has been cut to a specific shape.

direct mail The targeted sending of advertising and promotional items direct to likely consumers.

direct mail advertising A term to describe advertising or promotional material sent or distributed via a mailing system.

direct marketing A direct channel of distribution using any form of marketing communication that encourages a response and delivers a measurable result.

dirty copy proof Copy with hand-written comments and amendments. (Opposite: clean proof.)

display face Typeface designed for display-sized advertisements.

DMA Direct Marketing Association. British professional body for direct marketing practitioners.

DMSB Direct Mail Sales Bureau. An organization started by the Post Office to promote the use of direct mail.

donor list List of people who have donated to a charity.

door-to-door The direct marketing distribution of material by hand, usually to residential neighbourhoods.

double-decker An outdoor poster in two separate tiers.

double-duty envelope An envelope designed to be torn yet retain its return envelope features.

dummy A mock-up sample of a communications piece.

dump bin A point-of-sale item which carries products in a bin.

edit suites Audio and video post-production facilities for editing purposes.

EDMA European Direct Marketing Association.

electronic cottage The term given to the home of a freelance copywriter, designer or person who uses computer technology to link their home with their clients.

embargo Request to withhold press information until a specified date and time.

English creep The spread of English as an international language. Over 345 million people use English as their first language and an extra 400 million use it as a second.

envelope stuffer Direct marketing material enclosed in a direct mail piece already containing a business letter, invoice or statement.

exclusive A press release or other kind of information written for one media source.

eye camera A special camera used to measure visual stimulation and record eye movements of research volunteers when reading copy.

face
1 *A specified set of typefaces belonging to a 'family' of typefaces.*
2 *The bare frontage of an outdoor poster.*
3 *A page which when opened naturally faces the reader.*
4 *The opposite page from a piece of copy.*

family life cycle This is in six stages:
1 *Young single people.*
2 *Young couples with no children.*
3 *Young couples with their youngest child under 6.*

4 *Couples with dependent children.*
5 *Older couples with no children at home.*
6 *Older single people.*

....

farm out Subcontract work.

....

feedback Data fed from consumers that helps managers
to assess the overall performance of a product or service
advertising and marketing campaign.

....

filler advertisement An unbooked advertisement used to fill
up blank publishing space.

....

flanker Another term for a line extension brand, referring to a
spin-off companion product to a successful brand name (e.g.
Soft and Gentle Bath Foam could lead to a flanker, Soft and
Gentle Shower Gel).

....

flat animation Two-dimensional animation.

....

flier Simple sheet of advertising material usually found in a
mailing piece.

....

flush and hang Text which features the first line of
copy flush with the left margin and subsequent lines
indented.

....

FMCG Fast Moving Consumer Goods. Products which are
meant to have short retail shelf life and high
stock requirement based on a fast repurchase demand
(e.g. soap, biscuits, butter).

....

fount Alternative word for 'font', meaning a complete set of
type of one style and size.

....

four-colour process Colour printing featuring primary colours
separated by a filter.

frankly I'm puzzled Traditional style of direct marketing copy, which asks why the recipient has not responded to an offer.

free flier An extra insert in a direct mail piece that offers a special gift for prompt reply.

free keeper A low-cost item that the recipient of a mailing piece can keep at no obligation.

free newspapers Typically, weekly local newspapers delivered door-to-door.

free ride A cost effective way to save mailing costs by including a specific offer within a different mailing.

free-standing stuffer A loose insert stuffed into a publication.

free trial See sample.

freelancer A self-employed person who works independently (e.g. freelance copywriter).

freepost A Royal Mail service whereby the mailer finances the cost of postage.

frequency The average number of times that a prospect is exposed to a specific advertisement during a specified period of time.

fuzzword A seemingly defined word that actually confuses a piece of communication – in other words, elegant gobbledegook.

fuzzy sets Psychologist's term for imprecise language that confuses the reader.

galley proof The proofed copy text prior to being formatted into pages.

gatefold
1 *A leaflet folded so that its two edges meet in the centre.*
2 *A multi-part insert or cover of a publication that has to be unfolded in order to be read.*

generic advertising An advertisement or commercial that highlights product or service benefits without mentioning a brand name or local outlets.

generic terms Product descriptions such as 'cornflakes' which describe a product yet are not registered trade names. (One could have ScotsdaleNorth Cornflakes.)

ghost writer A person contracted to write in the name of someone else.

glossy magazine Publication printed on high-quality paper.

Greek Also known as Latin – garbled text on a rough layout that represents the size and position where final copy will eventually sit.

guarantee An advertiser's promise to a consumer.

guardbook Portfolio of a client account's creative work.

gutter Space between columns of text without a vertical dividing rule, or between pairs of pages.

hack A hired writer who is probably willing to write about anything for any reasonable price.

hanging indent First line of paragraph set wider than the subsequent lines.

headline The largest display of text, setting a theme and agenda for the subsequent copy.

heart-stopper A lottery card sales technique whereby a scratched card reveals all but one number in a sequence required to win a prize. This 'just missed' sequence of numbers usually encourages the purchaser to buy another card.

hidden persuaders Relates to advertising techniques first described by Vance Packard in the 1950s. The term is sometimes used to describe the role of PR professionals.

hoardings See billboards.

hotline A specially promoted telephone response line which encourages sales, provides information or acts as a form of customer contact service. (The world's first telephone helpline was introduced by the Samaritans on 2 November 1953.)

house agency An agency owned and/or managed by an advertiser.

house corrections Type errors noted and marked on a first proof before a proof is seen by a client.

huckster A bygone, insolent term for an account executive.

hype Overstated publicity.

hyphenless justification Justification of lines of text which avoids breaking words up over two lines.

iconic medium A medium such as TV or video in which images appear as reality.

idea bank A pool of creative ideas that are logged and referred to when required.

ideogram A graphic device that represents an idea or meaning.

illustrated letter A letter that incorporates some kind of illustration or graphic.

imagery Figurative language; the illustration and emphasis of an idea by parallels and analogies of different kinds to make it more concrete and objective.

impact The tangible effect that advertising has on an audience.

impressions The total number of exposures to a specific advertisement during a specified period of time.

in-ad coupon A coupon featured within a press advertisement.

in-flight magazine Magazine published by an airline and placed in the back of seats in an aircraft.

in-pack coupon A coupon that can be redeemed at an outlet.

in-pack premium A premium item offered free with a product.

in the can Completed radio, video or filmed commercial.

Independent Television Commission Deals with complaints about advertising on TV.

independents Privately owned and managed media companies or publicity and advertising agencies.

inquiry response mailing A mass-targeted mailing meant to generate enquiries rather than orders.

insertion An individual advertisement or commercial.

Institute of Direct Marketing Trade organization and educational body for direct marketing users, agencies and suppliers.

Institute of Public Relations British professional body for PR practitioners.

International Public Relations Association Senior professional body for PR practitioners around the world.

island position Advertisement surrounded by editorial.

issue advertising Sometimes called advocacy advertising. Used by an organization to discuss its views on topical issues.

jingle track Musical score for a commercial.

job sheet Standard agency administration form describing the expenditure on and progress of a client project.

joint promotion
1 *A promotion promoting two companies; one features a product or service that supports another's product or service.*
2 *One company endorses another.*

junk mail Unsolicited, poorly targeted mail.

key account
1 *Important client of an agency.*
2 *Important retailer or distributor for a client.*

key code Form of letter or numerical coding to measure effectiveness of a campaign.

landscape See **portrait**.

launch The introduction of a new service or product to a market.

layout Sketch or blueprint that shows the intended order of contents and visual styling of an advertisement mail piece, poster and so on.

lead Opening section of copy.

lead time The time gap between the creative concept and the final result.

LHE Left-hand edge.

LHS Left-hand side.

lifetime value The entire term value of a consumer to an organization. Typically the cost of acquiring a consumer is high. The longer the consumer remains loyal, the less the investment costs and so the greater the overall lifetime value.

lift letter A second letter within a direct mail piece designed to 'lift' response. (See also **publisher's letter**.)

list ad An advertisement listing more than one item (e.g. a series of records).

list broker An agent who sells databases of sales prospects.

list cleaning Removal of inaccurate data from a database.

list manager An agent for database lists.

list segment Section of list chosen against specific criteria such as sex and job title.

literal Error made by a typesetter.

live copy Copy read 'live' on air.

live names A term that describes active customers contacted through direct mail techniques.

live tag 'Live' message read on air to provide additional local information relating to a pre-recorded national commercial.

livery Corporate design and styling on all forms of transportation.

logo An abbreviation of 'logotype'. A particular shape, design or trademark that distinguishes an organization. Also known as a 'signature', 'sig' or 'sig cut'.

loose insert Please refer to free-standing stuffer.

lottery A sales promotion prize contest based on chance.

lower case Small letters of the alphabet.

Madison Avenue Generic term referring to the US advertising industry.

mail list seed A 'planted' named recipient of a mailing list (a process known as 'salting'). Seeds are typically used to monitor the effectiveness and accuracy of a direct mail piece.

mail merge Computer program that combines a database with copy for a mailing. (See also **merge and purge**.)

mailing list profile The characteristics by demographics of a mailing list.

mailing list sample An indiscriminate selection of names to test the response to a mailing list.

mailing list test A random pick of names to test the effectiveness of a mailing list.

Mailsort Term for pre-sorted discounted Royal Mail mailings.

mandatory copy Legally required copy.

market atomization Term used when each consumer is treated as a unique market segment.

market profile A term to describe the psychographic, demographic and geographical characteristics of prospects.

marketing The management process responsible for identifying, anticipating and accomplishing customer requirements profitably.

marketing department An organizational department responsible for marketing either for profit or non-profit (in the case of a voluntary organization). Areas of marketing responsibility may include or be a combination of direct marketing, sales promotion, advertising, sales, market research, product development and planning and administration.

marketing director Employee responsible for co-ordination and approval of marketing programmes.

marketing mix The combination of promotion, price, product and distribution that creates the foundations of an organization's marketing agenda.

mass media TV, press and radio which reach a large proportion of the public.

media A collective term for cinema, press, radio and TV – also known as mass media.

media buyer An advertising agency employee who co-ordinates and negotiates media schedules.

media kit A sales folder containing information about a specific media publication, programme or resource.

media plan A proposal that details media budgets and recommended channels for an advertising campaign.

media speak Journalistic fad which is a corruption of the English language.

merge and purge Assimilation of different databases which also removes duplicated or unwanted information. (See also **de-dupe** and **mail merge**.)

mf. More follows. Marked at the bottom right of a press release when there is a continuation.

MGM Member-get-Member (or Recommend-a-Friend or Word-of-Mouth advertising). When a current customer recommends a product or service to a new prospect.

mini catalogue A shortened version of a larger catalogue, often featuring special seasonal offers.

mnemonic Symbol or acronym to aid memory.

mock-up A near-finished representation of a final creative execution.

mood music Musical track which helps establish a desired atmosphere.

morgue Ready written obituaries for VIPs.

multi-mailer One mailing containing several loose single promotional sheets.

music bed Musical background track.

musical logo A melodic corporate signature.

NABS National Advertising Benevolent Society. Highly respected British charitable organization for professionals working in the media.

news hole The amount of news space in a publication after advertisements have been placed.

newsletter Organizational journalistic-style publication that contains information of interest to members and associates of the organization. They provide a sense of belonging as well as an outlet for planned dissemination of management plans and member or employee developments. (The world's first recorded house journal was the *British Mercury* in 1710 – it was delivered three times a week to the homes of any of the insurance company's policyholders who subscribed.)

novelty format An unusually sized or shaped mailing piece.

nth name A direct marketing database technique that divides the total number of names in a list by a required number of 'test' names to produce a sample. For example, 10,000 'test' names chosen from a 100,000 overall total of names would result in every 10th name being selected for 'testing'.

offer The terms and conditions under which a direct mail item or service is promoted.

on-camera narration Narration delivered on screen by a presenter.

on-pack coupon A coupon attached to the outside of a package.

on-pack premium A free gift attached to the outside of a package.

one-stage/step A promotion in which a sales cycle is completed in one step without any need for further follow-up by letter or telephone. (The prospect reads an advertisement and, on its strength, places an order for a product or service.)

open end
1 *A recorded commercial with allocated space for a tag.*
2 *A programme produced with time for commercials.*
3 *A programme with no set time to end.*

open-rate The most expensive chargeable media rate.

opinion research Research based on opinions rather than facts.

order card A response card to complete and return by mail.

order form A response form to complete and return by mail.

orphan A stand-alone line of copy left at the foot of a page.

package insert A promotional item inserted in a package.

package test The evaluation of mailing elements individually or in their entirety.

page proof The printer's proof of a completed page.

paid circulation A publication that is distributed to people who have paid a subscription.

pamphlet A leaflet that contains eight or more pages.

Pantone Colour-matching system.

passive media Media that require the viewer or listener to do nothing more than watch or listen.

paste-up A camera-ready layout.

peak time Period which attracts the largest TV or radio audience figures.

peel-off label A self-adhesive label that can be attached to an order form.

penetration Another term for reach.

personalization The inclusion of a recipient's personal address details within a mail piece. (Research proves that personalization always increases response.)

piggyback A secondary offer included within a mail piece.

pitch A new business presentation.

planning The activity of predicting future events and using those assumptions to develop strategies that will help achieve the ultimate goal.

poco Brief for 'politically correct', sometimes used by feminists to refer to non-sexist language.

portfolio A case or folder of work.

portrait Upright page (opposite: landscape).

positioning A strategy that 'positions' a product or idea according to how a consumer perceives that product or service relative to competitive offerings from providers of similar goods or services.

. . . .

PPI Printed Postage Impression. The pre-printed Royal Mail licensed mark which typically appears on a direct mail envelope.

. . . .

PRadvertising Cross between advertising and public relations.

. . . .

premium
1 *A free item or an item offered as an inducement to test, trial and eventually purchase a product or service.*
2 *An extra charge for a special advertising position within a publication or as part of a broadcast.*

. . . .

presentation Formal presentation of creative and strategic concepts and proposals.

. . . .

press clipping A published article of interest archived for future reference.

. . . .

press officer PR professional who specializes in press relations. (Ivy Ledbetter Lee, a former New York financial journalist, was the first public relations consultant. He opened for business in 1903 and his clients included a circus, bankers and politicians. The first PR company in Britain, Editorial Services Ltd, opened for business in 1924. The first public relations officer in Britain worked for Southern Railway and was appointed in 1925.)

. . . .

press pack A portfolio of information relating to a specific press release or announcement.

. . . .

price-off A cut price strategy to encourage trial or increased usage of a product or service.

. . . .

production department An advertising department that co-ordinates and supervises all aspects of technical creative production.

programming schedule A notification of programme times and dates which aids a media buyer when selecting TV or radio commercial time.

promotion A concerted marketing method to increase sales of a product or service, usually through using a sales promotion technique.

prospect A consumer who is likely to become a customer.

psychographics Classification of prospects according to lifestyle and personality traits.

publication date The date a publication becomes available to the public.

publicity still A photograph used for publicity purposes.

publisher's letter A lift letter from a publisher.

pull Printer's proof.

pull quotes The enlargement of the text of key quotations to give added emphasis.

pull strategy A method that invests in large advertising and marketing budgets to stimulate consumer demand and in turn encourages intermediaries to handle and promote a product or service.

push strategy A method to encourage consumer demand and stimulate intermediaries to stock a product.

Q&A Question and Answer. In print this usually takes the form of a panel of questions and answers which relate to technical aspects of a product or service. Q&A panels typically appear towards the back of a product or service brochure.

qualitative research Research designed to measure attitudes and perceptions based on kind or condition rather than on amount or degree.

quantitative research Research-based sample quantities based on amount or degree rather than kind or condition. According to AGB research in England, the key quantitative questions are:
- ▶ *Who are you?*
- ▶ *What do you buy?*
- ▶ *Where do you buy?*
- ▶ *How much?*
- ▶ *At what price?*
- ▶ *When?*
- ▶ *What else could you have purchased?*
- ▶ *Where else could you have purchased it?*

quarterly Publication published in a three-monthly cycle.

questionnaire A form featuring a sequence of closed or open questions to be completed and returned by a targeted respondent.

rate card A form detailing specified media advertising costs and support information.

reach The overall total percentage of targeted prospects in a specific area exposed to a specific advertisement during a specified period. (Also known as **penetration**.)

reader ad A copy-only advertisement that appears to be genuine news or editorial. (See also **advertorial**.)

reader profile A demographic classification of readers.

reader response The response of readers to an article or piece of advertising.

readership The total number of people reached by a publication.

redemption
1 *The percentage of coupons or trading stamps that are cashed in.*
2 *The general cashing or trading in of coupons or trading stamps.*

repeat mailing A mailed follow-up sent to the same list of names as a first mailing.

repositioning A planned marketing attempt to reposition a product or service within a market by changing features, price or distribution – or a combination of all three.

research director Agency employee responsible for the purchase and analysis of information that influences a marketing strategy.

response A planned reaction to a planned arousal.

response device Any piece of communication which accommodates a response.

response list List of individuals who have responded to a direct mail campaign.

retainer A fee that secures the ongoing negotiated exclusive rights to call from time to time upon a person's professional services, such as copywriting.

rhetoric The written and spoken language of persuasion. Also sometimes refers to a pompous style of language.

roll fold A way of folding paper – usually a leaflet – whereby each printed section is rolled around the next at the paper's edge fold.

rough A brush-stroke layout indicating a general creative concept.

round robin Traditional name for direct mail letter.

run of book/paper Advertising space and location determined by a publisher rather than an advertiser.

run on To continue copy on the same line rather than go to a new line.

rushes Rough, unedited print of daily film footage.

sales promotion 'The range of techniques used to attain sales/ marketing objectives in a cost effective manner by adding value to a product or service either to intermediaries or end users, normally but not exclusively within a defined time period' (Institute of Sales Promotions, definition).

sample
1 *A group of individuals representative of a percentage of the population.*
2 *A complimentary portion or test quantity of a marketed product (also known as a trial offer).*
3 *A quantity of data picked from a total direct mail database.*

scratch-and-sniff A method of incorporating scent onto paper. When scratched, an impregnated scent panel is activated.

scratch off A direct mail device (also known as coin rub) whereby a coin is used to scratch a coated paper to reveal a special message.

selective demand advertising Advertising aimed to create awareness and provide information about a particular brand.

self-liquidator
1 *A gift or premium which is financed by its offered purchase.*
2 *A sales promotion display provided to a retailer for a fee to the supplier or manufacturer.*

sharpening A cognitive process in which the information retained becomes more vivid and important than the event itself.

shelf life
1 *The amount of time that a product can remain on a retail shelf.*
2 *The longevity of a product or service based on its popularity and demand.*

shelf strip A point-of-sale printed strip attached to the facing edge of a shelf.

shirt-board advertising Advertising printed on the cardboard used to support laundered shirts. Popular in the United States.

sleeper An unpublished 'seed' name. Please refer to **mail list seed**.

spokesperson A person who endorses an advertised product or service.

sponsored programme
1 *A TV or radio programme that is partly financed by a named advertiser.*
2 *Any event may be financially subsidized for marketing or advertising purposes.*

statement stuffer A small printed advertisement inserted in an envelope containing a bill. (Also known as **bill-stuffer**.)

stock Music, art, graphics or photographs available from specialist libraries.

style book Manual of approved corporate styling for ad design.

suit Generic term referring to a non-creative employee of an advertising agency.

suspects A consumer who may or may not become a customer.

sustaining advertising Advertising that maintains consumer demand rather than increasing it.

sweeps The months of November, February and May, set by a US TV rating service to establish the ranking of TV network shows. This sets the level of advertising rates for local stations.

sweepstakes A below-the-line technique in which prizes are offered to participants on a random chance, no skills basis. An assumption is made that the technique will eventually encourage the consumer to buy a product (no immediate purchase required). A sweepstake condition requires that a sweepstake or prize draw is run according to a set of published rules.

take one
1 *Leaflets or pamphlets freely distributed via a sales promotional desk top or mounted dispenser.*
2 *In the United States, an attachment to a transit advertising vehicle card. The take one is a coupon or information request sheet. It often incorporates an envelope or is part of a pad.*

talking heads A TV production featuring extreme head-and-shoulder close-ups of subjects discussing a specific item or area of interest.

talking shelf strips A point-of-sale printed strip or item attached to or near the facing edge of a shelf which contains a movement sensitive electronic device. As the consumer passes, the device triggers a pre-recorded sound track which discusses the product. (Belgian advertisers have found that such devices may increase sales by 500%.)

target audience The ideal prospective audience which would be interested in a specific product or service.

tear sheet A page torn from a publication sent to an advertiser as proof of publication.

teaser campaign A series of brief announcement advertisements which stimulate curiosity.

telemarketing Market prospecting, selling, servicing and informing via the telephone.

television director/producer A person employed to manage and co-ordinate the production of TV commercials.

test marketing See zone plan.

thank you letter A direct mail copy technique in which a customer is thanked for making a purchase or enquiry.

threshold effect The stage at which the effectiveness of an advertising campaign can be seen to be working.

thumbnail A miniature, rough layout.

tie-in promotion A promotion which markets more than one product or brand.

time-sheet A standard form to record the amount of time spent working on a client project.

tip in A loosely placed publication insert. See also **free-standing stuffer**.

tip-on A coupon reply card or sample glued by its edge for easy removal from a printed piece of advertising.

tombstone Originally a Wall Street financial advertisement used in the USA for, among other things, announcing new stock issues. So called because the copy only provides the bare facts – the bare bones.

tone of voice General attitude, expression or approach given to a message.

traffic building An advertising communication that can include sales promotion or direct marketing, designed to encourage retail store traffic.

traffic department The department within an advertising agency which co-ordinates the work flow of projects between departments.

treatment The overall styling or approach to a piece of advertising.

trial close A copy technique whereby the reader is asked for an order at an early stage of a direct mail letter. The copy then directs the reader to the coupon. This technique can be repeated several times during one direct mail letter.

trial offer A special marketing offer, meant to encourage future consumer purchase, made within a particular period of time. See also **sample**.

TV shopping Also known as shop-at-home. TV programmes or channels that are likened to shopping catalogues. (This area is also embraced by the Internet.)

Two-stage/step A promotion in which a sales cycle is completed in two steps with a fo'low-up by letter or telephone. (The prospect reads an advertisement and, on its strength, applies for further details of a product or service.) See also **one-stage/step**.

ultra Short for the 'ultra-consumer', who insists on purchasing the very best – regardless of personal income.

usage pull The power of advertising to encourage individuals to purchase an advertised service or product.

USP Unique Sells (or Selling) Proposition. The outstanding benefit or family of features which distinguish a product or service from the competition.

voice Breadth of media coverage.

Voice Over The voice of an unseen narrator or presenter.

voucher copy A copy of an entire publication sent to an advertiser as proof of publication and position as agreed.

white mail Letters sent to mail order firms which result in more paper work (e.g. complaints and enquiries).

white space Unprinted space which gives greater emphasis to printed advertising.

window envelope An opening or 'window' die-cut into a direct mail envelope which shows part of the contents of the mailing inside. The cut is usually covered by glassine, a type of transparent paper.

word spacing The space between words in a line of justified type.

wraparound A cover/holder which carries a mail order catalogue and supporting material such as sales letters and order forms.

X-factor The undefinable aspect of a person or a company that can't be copied but brings success.

yes/no envelope A response direct mail envelope which encourages readers to reply to an offer, irrespective of whether or not they intend to make a purchase.

yes/no stamp Similar to the yes/no envelope response enhancement device. Instead, a YES and a NO stamp are attached to a response device. This encourages customer involvement and gives a sense that the mailing is an 'active' item.

Z fold A method of folding paper such as a sales letter into three equal parts. The middle third forms the diagonal column of the letter Z.

zip envelope A direct mail envelope which is opened by pulling a tab.

zone plan A strategy to test a new product or service using advertising in a highly targeted small geographical area. Also known as 'test marketing'.

Taking it further

Further reading

Gabay, J. Jonathan, *Soul Traders*, Marshall Cavendish, 2009

Gabay, J. Jonathan, *Gabay's Copywriting Compendium*, Hodder, 2010

Gabay, J. Jonathan, *Make a Difference with Your Marketing*, Hodder Education, 2010

Further learning

<u>www.gabaynet.com</u>

Index

Reference should also be made to the Appendix (pages 295–331)